THE STORY OF
ARCHAEOLOGY

THE STORY OF
ARCHAEOLOGY

THE 100 GREAT DISCOVERIES
EDITOR: PAUL G. BAHN

Weidenfeld & Nicolson
London

Compilation © 1996 Paul Bahn

First published in Great Britain in 1996 by
George Weidenfeld & Nicolson Ltd
The Orion Publishing Group
5 Upper St Martin's Lane
London WC2H 9EA

British Library Cataloguing-in-Publication Data
A Catalogue for this book is available from the British
Library

Picture researcher: Joanne King
Design by Bradbury and Williams
Designer: Bob Burroughs
Maps by ML Design
Printed in Italy

TITLE PAGE: Sculpture from the Temple of the Feathered
Serpent, Teotihuacán. Photographer: Richard Atkinson.

LIST OF CONTRIBUTORS

DR PAUL BAHN, General editor and contributor, Hull, England (Early periods, Western Europe)

DR GINA BARNES, Professor of Japanese, Department of East Asian Studies, University of Durham, England (Far East, Southeast Asia)

DR CAROLINE BIRD, School of Archaeology, La Trobe University, Melbourne, Victoria, Australia (Australia and the Pacific)

DR PETER BOGUCKI, School of Engineering and Applied Science, Princeton University, USA (Later periods, Central and Eastern Europe and ex-USSR)

DR PHILIP DUKE, Department of Anthropology, Fort Lewis College, Durango, Colorado, USA (North America)

DR CHRISTOPHER EDENS, Peabody Museum, Harvard University, Cambridge, Massachusetts, USA (Near East, Central Asia, India)

DR DAVID GILL, Department of Classics and Ancient History, University College, Swansea, Wales (Classical archaeology)

DR JOHN HOFFECKER, Argonne National Laboratory, Argonne, Illinois, USA (Early periods, Central and Eastern Europe and ex-USSR)

DR CHRISTOPHER MEE, School of Archaeology, Classics and Oriental Studies, University of Liverpool, England (Greece and the Aegean)

DR KATHARINA SCHREIBER, Department of Anthropology, University of California, Santa Barbara, USA (South America)

DR STEVEN SNAPE, School of Archaeology, Classics and Oriental Studies, University of Liverpool, England (Egypt and the Levant)

DR ANDREA STONE, Department of Art History, University of Wisconsin, Milwaukee, USA (Mesoamerica)

DR SARAH TARLOW, Department of Archaeology, University of Wales, Lampeter, Wales (Later periods, Western Europe)

DR ANNE THACKERAY, Department of Archaeology, University of the Witwatersrand, South Africa (Africa)

Contents

PREFACE

Archaeology is worlds away from Indiana Jones. It is not just about treasure, not just about rich burials – but it is no less exciting for all that. Once upon a time, decades ago and more, it was indeed a subject focused on the spectacular discovery and the exotic find, but over the years, as it became a serious discipline, with aspirations to being scientific, archaeology become increasingly concerned with the more mundane aspects of the past, with the traces of the lives of ordinary people, rather than of kings and emperors. It concentrated not on finding things but on finding *out* things, on seeking to explain when and where and how and why things happened and changed in the past. In recent years archaeology has turned a great deal of its attention to theoretical musings, to examining its most basic assumptions. Are there any 'facts'? Can one say anything meaningful and objective about the past when studying (highly incomplete) evidence in the present? Most recently, archaeologists have come to realize that they are not alone in having an interest in the material traces of the past, and that indigenous groups (in North America, Australia or New Zealand, for example) or religious groups (most notably in Israel) may have serious and vociferous objections that can affect or even curtail activities such as excavation or museum curation that used to be undertaken without the slightest consultation with, or permission from, local groups.

And yet . . . archaeology remains (indeed is increasingly becoming) dependent on public interest for its very survival in these financially stringent times, and it is extremely difficult – if not impossible – to present the public with an account of archaeology that will hold their interest also while explaining the everyday tedium of most fieldwork and analysis, let alone the navel-gazing and self-doubts of the theoreticians. Occupants of ivory towers may sneer and patronize, but in these days of multichannel television, CD-ROMs, and so on, the attention span of most adults and especially that of children is shrinking, so it is only the dramatic and spectacular, the romantic and fantastic that will attract them and incite them to delve a little further into the world of archaeology.

It is therefore inevitable that any book that sets out to present the 'Story of Archaeology' through only one hundred discoveries will be forced to concentrate on the 'headline grabbers', on archaeology's 'greatest hits', on the finds that caused a major stir – the kind of material one would expect to find in *National Geographic* or in television documentaries. As with the worlds of modelling or movie-making, it is self-evident that 99% of archaeology is humdrum, plodding, tedious toil, with little glamour – reading, excavating, surveying, recording, analyzing, classifying, interpreting – but, as the late Glyn Daniel remarked, one of archaeology's most important roles is that it is a source of great pleasure, and this pleasure, at least in public eyes, generally comes in the form of the spectacular or beautiful discoveries.

That being so, we quickly realized that one hundred topics are remarkably few for the vast subject of world archaeology, and tough decisions were made by all the contributors as to what was of world-class importance in their region or period. Naturally, one hundred spreads could easily be conjured up for any part of the archaeological record – such as Egypt, for example, the Classical World or the Maya. We set out to be rational rather than politically correct in the allocation of space, and inevitably there are apparent geographical and chronological imbalances: after all, serious archaeology only began quite recently in Australasia and much of Africa, whereas through historical accident Europe has been the scene of intensive work for far longer. Conversely, the Palaeolithic period – despite constituting 99% of the archaeological record – was assigned less than 20% of the book, while comparatively short-lived cultures or periods received more space than their timespan alone would allow.

We also had to decide from the outset what we meant by 'archaeological discoveries'. The term could not encompass advances in scientific techniques, such as radiocarbon dating, pollen analysis or aerial photography, since these were developments by scientists in other fields which merely proved applicable (and invaluable) to archaeology. The same applies to methods of detecting what lies beneath the soil, tracing the sources of raw materials, or X-raying or scanning bodies. Many major sites such as Stonehenge, Tikal or Angkor could not be included since they were never really 'discovered' but were always a known part of the landscape. We admit, however, that our criteria for inclusion have not been entirely consistent since most rock art (other than that inside lost caves) must also have been known to local inhabitants and was likewise 'discovered' only by western scholarship. Few things in the realms of medieval or industrial archaeology could be classed as true 'discoveries' either.

Despite the inevitable quota of tombs and impressive objects, we have tried to convey some idea of the amazing range of material that archaeologists study – houses, mines, cargoes, documents – though here too we are far from exhaustive.

A further motivation for producing a book of this kind is to be found in the recent re-emergence of the Von Dänikenesque (*Chariots of the Gods?*) 'God is a Spaceman' message. We had hoped that books promoting the theory that anything impressive or bizarre in the archaeological record must be attributable to extraterrestrial visitors were a freak phenomenon of the 1970s, and that, having sold in tens of millions, they had faded away. Now, however, the success of the film *Stargate* (a science-fiction fantasy suggesting that ancient Egyptian civilization was produced by an extraterrestrial) and the unexpected appearance in the 1995 bestseller lists of *Fingerprints of the Gods* (a book arguing that the monuments of the ancient world were built 15,000 years ago by a race of super-beings whose lost civilization now lies in ruins beneath Antarctica) shows that the monster was merely dormant; it can easily awake and devour an army of gullible readers. So we hope a book that sets out the 'real past', the astonishing variety of human achievements, the end-products of our ancestors' sweat and ingenuity, will not only help explain what archaeologists do and why (albeit in a very incomplete account of that) but also go a little way towards counteracting this resurrected obsession with ascribing our heritage to fantasy super-heroes.

The past *is* human, and only archaeology can uncover and elucidate its wonders. It is still a very young discipline, though, and since the contents of this book constitute the tiniest fraction of what has been recovered and learned in a couple of centuries, imagine what the ever-growing and improving battery of archaeological and scientific techniques will reveal about our past during the next century.

The future, therefore, looks exciting. The real joy of archaeology is that it is constantly changing through an endless stream of new discoveries, any one of which can radically alter our picture of the past: it may be a fragment of a fossil human, an earlier date for a phenomenon (such as cremation or pottery) or for an event (like the arrival of humans in the New World or Australia), or something completely unexpected such as the Chauvet Cave or the Iceman – finds that immediately became major news stories all over the world.

Archaeology has never been more popular (an ironic fact when it has all but disappeared from television schedules), and indeed archaeological tourism is of enormous importance in many countries, most notably Egypt, Peru and China. Yet its very popularity carries the tremendous risk of people loving it to death, by visiting fragile sites and monuments in excessive numbers. In the next few years, a massive worldwide effort will be needed to conserve what we have already recovered. One of the trickiest conundrums in archaeology is how to weigh the protection of world heritage (from vandalism, pollution or simple wear and tear) against the public's right to visit and appreciate the remains of humanity's past. There are sites – such as many decorated caves – which it is physically impossible for the public to enter, and the next few years will see increasing opportunities for visits to such sites through exact facsimiles and virtual-reality simulations. The new technology will therefore not only enable archaeologists to make further progress in reconstructing the past, but also help in relieving tourist pressure on the more fragile remains of that past and hence contribute to its conservation for future generations. ■

PAUL G. BAHN

THE DISCOVERY OF HUMAN ANTIQUITY

One of the most fundamental developments in archaeology's history was the gradual realization, and eventual acceptance in the mid-nineteenth century, that humans had a very long history, extending back long before the biblical Flood.

Although the idea that humankind was tens of thousands of years old had existed among the Greeks, Egyptians, Assyrians and Babylonians, as well as in ancient Mesoamerica, in the scholarship of medieval Europe the only framework for human affairs and the origins of the world lay in written documents, and especially in the Bible. The claim made in 1650 by James Ussher, Archbishop of Armagh, that the world was created at noon on 23 October in 4004 BC has often been the subject of ridicule in modern times. However, such attempts to develop a chronology for all human history were a major focus of seventeenth-century scholarship, and Ussher was by no means the first to put forward such a date: the Jewish calendar still places the creation of the earth at 3761 BC, while the Venerable Bede, the eighth-century English theologian, had estimated 3952 BC. It was a feature of the age to regard the Bible as God's infallible word. Moreover, these scholars were living in a pre-scientific age, before techniques had been developed enabling a chronology to be built on the basis of natural science rather than hallowed text.

Flint tools from the Palaeo-lithic (Old Stone Age) were turn-ing up sporadically, but their importance was not yet recognized: for example, in c.1690 a big point of black flint was found in a gravel pit in Grays Inn Lane near London by John Conyers. We now know that it was a handaxe (several hundred thousand years old), associated with 'elephant' (perhaps mammoth) bones. At the time, though, it was assumed to be a weapon used by a Briton to kill an elephant brought over by the Romans in the reign of Claudius. The conception of early periods could not go beyond written memory: megalithic monuments, for example, were attributed to the Celts or pre-Roman Gauls, or other local peoples.

Archaeology was soon to benefit from the observations of Niels (Nicolaus) Stensen, a Danish scholar known as Steno, who in 1669 drew the first geological profile, establishing the principle of sedimentation and stratigraphic superimposition and noting that later layers lie on top of older ones. The first archaeological applications of this principle occurred in western Europe when in 1797 John Frere, a gentleman farmer and later a member of parliament, found worked stone artifacts including Lower Palaeolithic handaxes in a brick quarry at Hoxne, Suffolk. They lay at a depth of 4 m (13 ft) in an undisturbed deposit that also contained the bones of large extinct mammals. Frere's great insight was that he not only recognized them as artifacts but attributed the find to a very distant period. He presented the discovery to the Society of Antiquaries in London, and it was published in their journal *Archaeologia*, but like the 'Ancient British' handaxe found by Conyers in 1690 his finds remained unknown outside England, and were ignored by the British for decades.

In 1771 Johann Friedrich Esper, a Bavarian pastor, found human bones associated with the remains of cave bear and other extinct animals in Gaillenreuth Cave near Bayreuth in the German Jura. He described the finds in 1774, and asked whether they belonged to a Druid or an antediluvian or a mortal man of a more recent period. His conclusion, however, was that the human bones were intrusive to the deposits containing the fossil animal re-

One of the handaxes found by John Frere in 1797 in a quarry at Hoxne, Suffolk, which suggested that humans had lived in the remote past.

T.R. Underwood, del. 1797.

Flint Weapon found at Hoxne in Suffolk.
Archaelgia Vol. XIII. p.204.

ABOVE: Excavations in rockshelters such as this one at Les Eyzies in the Dordogne provided vital information about the early prehistory of Europe.

BELOW: This engraving of a mammoth on a piece of mammoth ivory helped prove the co-existence of humans and extinct animals.

mains. Nevertheless, scholars were clearly beginning to challenge the view given in Genesis of the earth's formation. In France, Georges Cuvier, father of comparative anatomy, perceived differences between fossil animals and their modern equivalents, the differences increasing with the age of the layers. This perception eventually culminated in the notion of evolution. However, *human* history was unaffected by these developments in the natural sciences. The discovery of 'fossil man' was needed to change the situation, and Cuvier doubted that a fossil man had co-existed with vanished species found in 'antediluvian' deposits. He went by the Bible, believing Man appeared *after* the animals, and this seemed to correspond to all geological findings so far. Unlike his pupils and disciples, however, he did not deny the *possibility* that fossil man had existed; he merely denied that any had ever been found.

These first inklings in the late eighteenth century became a certainty in the nineteenth. One of the pioneering researchers responsible for this development was Paul Tournal, a pharmacist from Narbonne in southern France, who dug in the cave of Bize (Aude) in 1826 and found human remains associated with bones of extinct animals and stone tools. By 1834 he had become more confident of his findings, having noticed on bones of 'lost species' marks of cutting tools that must have been made by people. Researchers in other countries in the 1820s, such as Austrian geologist Ami Boué and English chaplain John MacEnery had also found flint tools mixed with the bones of extinct fauna.

In this period, geologists — most famously, Charles Lyell — proposed the concept of 'Uniformitarianism', the idea that all past

geological processes were the same as those of the present, spanning a huge period, so there was no need to believe in supernatural catastrophes like the Flood to explain the fossil and stratigraphic record. The new Fluvial and Glacial theories (i.e., that slow processes of sedimentation by rivers and erosion by glaciers explained the features of the earth) led many people to change their minds about the contemporaneity of humans and fossil animals, and had a huge influence on British biologists like Charles Darwin, Alfred Wallace and Thomas Huxley and the development of the concept of evolution. Similarly, biologists turned from an understanding constrained by a biblical seven-day creation to the vista of an immensely long past. It then became crucial to establish that crude stone tools could be identified as the work of humans.

The followers of Cuvier continued to deny that people had lived at the same time as extinct animals. Geological proofs from excavations in caves, like those of Tournal or MacEnery, were rejected because their deposits were often complex and their stratigraphy disturbed. What was needed was an indisputable association of humans and extinct fauna in the open air − like that of Frere, already forgotten − and the man who was most responsible for this breakthrough was Jacques Boucher de Perthes (1788–1868), a French amateur archaeologist, customs officer and polymath.

The conclusive evidence was found in open-air sites around Abbeville in Picardy, northern France. In 1842 Boucher de Perthes discovered a flaked stone tool associated with a mammoth jaw, and followed this with many similar finds. He illustrated his books on these discoveries with drawings of sections through his sites, describing the position and contents of each layer like a geologist, to demonstrate the truth of his arguments. In 1858 and 1859 the area was visited by several eminent British geologists (including Lyell) and archaeologists who confirmed the truth of Boucher de Perthes's claims. So by 1859, the year when Darwin published *On the Origin of Species*, a long-standing but still doubtful idea was transformed into a widespread consensus among scholars.

The final convincing pieces of evidence for human antiquity appeared in 1864. Edouard Lartet, a French lawyer turned palaeontologist, had begun excavations in 1863 in some of the innumerable rockshelters around Les Eyzies, in the Dordogne region of France, which had been inhabited in the last Ice Age and which were to loom large in the early prehistory of Europe. He was aided and financed by his friend, the English banker, ethnologist and philanthropist Henry Christy. The Marquis Paul de Vibraye, an agronomist, also started digging at Les Eyzies in 1863 in search of proof of the contemporaneity of people and extinct fauna. He and Lartet simultaneously produced evidence of human antiquity: de Vibraye found the 'Vénus impudique' ('shameless Venus'), a figure of a slim, naked female from Laugerie-Basse, carved in mammoth ivory, while Lartet and Christy, in May 1864, discovered at La Madeleine an engraving of a mammoth on a piece of mammoth ivory, which proved people had indeed lived in the remote past, alongside vanished creatures. ■

AFRICA

THE TAUNG CHILD: THE FIRST AUSTRALOPITHECINE

In 1925 the world was surprised by an announcement made by Raymond Arthur Dart, a young Australian-born anatomist then newly appointed Professor of Anatomy at the University of the Witwatersrand in Johannesburg, South Africa, that he had discovered a fossil that he claimed represented a form intermediate between apes and humans. Charles Darwin had predicted in his 1871 publication *The Descent of Man* that 'It is . . . probable that Africa was formerly inhabited by extinct apes closely allied to the gorilla and chimpanzee . . . and, as these two species are now man's nearest allies, it is somewhat more probable that our early progenitors lived on the African continent than elsewhere.' However, Darwin's idea that evidence for human origins would be found in Africa was dismissed in the late nineteenth and early twentieth centuries, because spectacular finds of early human fossils were being made in Indonesia and

Australopithecines were small-brained ape-like creatures who lived from before four million to just after one million years ago, and who took the first step on the road to humanity by walking on two legs. The first australopithecine fossil to ever be recognized was the face and brain cast of a young child found at the Buxton Limeworks quarry near the village of Taung in South Africa in 1924.

China at that time (see p. 162).

The fossil that shifted the focus in the search for early human remains to Africa was delivered to Dart's doorstep in late 1924 amidst a jumble of material in two wooden boxes that lime-miners had blasted out of a quarry near Taung (Tswana meaning: 'the place of the lion'), on the western fringes of the Kalahari Desert in north-central South Africa. Despite being clad in his finest attire – as he was busy dressing for a wedding – Dart could not resist opening the dusty boxes immediately. In the second one he found a limestone block containing a fossil skull, face and lower jaw of a young child (now thought to be equivalent to a modern six-year-old, or perhaps younger), that fitted another block containing a cast or mould of the inside of the brain. This had formed from sand which filled the inside of the skull after death and had later hardened.

Dart recalled instantly realizing that 'Here, I was certain, was

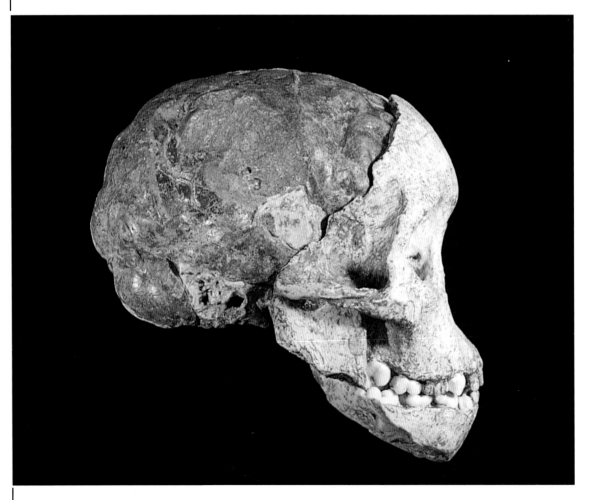

The skull and brain cast of the first australopithecine to be discovered, the 'Taung child' (*Australopithecus africanus*), found in South Africa in 1924, and described by Dart in 1925. Animal bones found at the same site suggest it is about 2 million years old. The position of the hole at the base of the skull (the foramen magnum) shows that this young child (equivalent to a modern 6-year-old or perhaps younger) walked on two legs. Although its face and brain are ape-like, its jaws and teeth are small – like those of humans. Dart's claim that it represented a form intermediate between apes and humans won general acceptance only decades later.

one of the most significant finds ever made in the history of anthropology.' After painstakingly chiselling away for weeks, Dart managed to free the skull from its rock casing on 23 December, in time to celebrate Christmas with his new-found 'Taung baby'.

His description of the Taung fossil was published in the 7 February 1925 issue of the journal *Nature*. Although he named the fossil '*Australopithecus africanus*' (literally, 'the southern ape of Africa'), thereby coining the common name 'australopithecine' that is used today for the earliest known members of the human family, Dart considered that it was intermediate between apes and humans. Tremendous publicity ensued and popular newspapers carried headlines announcing 'Missing Link no longer missing', but the reaction from the scientific community was mixed.

The scholarly opinion prevailing in 1925 was that the so-called 'missing link' between apes and humans would have a large brain and ape-like jaws and teeth, based on bones of a supposed early human found at Piltdown in England between 1912 and 1915 (and shown to be a hoax only in

The Swartkrans Fossil Site

Swartkrans is an ancient cave filling I km (0.6 mile) from Sterkfontein in South Africa. It is a rich source of fossils of heavily built australopithecines and early humans, as well as a remarkable archive of the animal life and differing environments of the South African high veld over the last 1.8 million years.

Burnt bones from Swartkrans which are over 1 million years old may be early evidence for the use of fire. Chemical studies of the bones by C.K. 'Bob' Brain of the Transvaal Museum and Andrew Sillen of the University of Cape Town indicate that they were burnt in a camp-fire rather than a veld-fire. No fireplaces have been found and it is not known whether the fire, if indeed used by early humans, was started by them or gathered from natural fire caused by lightning, or whether the fire was used for cooking, warmth or

to frighten away predators.

Many of the australopithecine bones found at Swartkrans were probably killed by large cats such as leopards and sabre-tooth cats, and probably also hyenas. This part of the skull of a young australopithecine has holes that fit the canine teeth of a leopard found in the same layer. Some australopithecines were probably

dragged into trees, which typically grow at cave entrances, by leopards, to protect their prey from hopeful hyena scavengers. The bones would then have dropped into the cave.

Also found at Swartkrans were early stone tools, as well as pieces of bone and horn that were polished from use, probably as utensils for digging up roots and tubers.

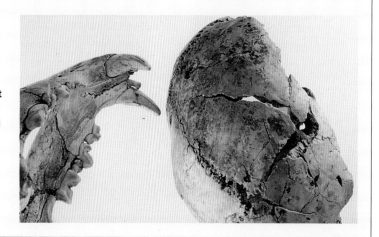

1953), but the Taung fossil had a small ape-like brain and human-looking jaws and teeth. To Dart's immense disappointment, the 'Taung trial' raged for decades in scientific journals, at a time when the trial of John Scopes (the Scopes 'monkey trial') for teaching evolution at a school in Dayton, Tennessee, was being reported in newspapers.

One of the problems that delayed the acceptance of the Taung fossil as a human ancestor was that it belonged to a child, from which it was difficult to be sure of the features it would have had as an adult. Twelve years were to pass before the first adult australopithecine was discovered. This was obtained in 1938 by one of Dart's few supporters, Robert Broom, at Sterkfontein, near Krugersdorp, now in Gauteng Province, South Africa. Subsequent finds of australopithecine fossils were made by Broom at Kromdraai (1.6 km [1 mile] from Sterkfontein) in 1938, by Broom and John Robinson at Swartkrans (1 km [0.6 mile] from Sterkfontein) from 1948, and by the Kitching brothers and Alun Hughes at Makapansgat in the Northern Province of South Africa from 1947.

Continuing work at these and the more recently discovered South African australopithecine sites of Gladysvale, Drimolen and the Cooper's site complex (not far from Sterkfontein) has led to the discovery of more than 1000 bones of early human ancestors in South Africa. These finds show that at least two different kinds of australopithecines, one lightly built (*Australopithecus africanus*) and the other more heavily built (*Australopithecus* or *Paranthropus robustus*), as well as various kinds of early humans, lived in southern Africa between about three and one million years ago. ∎

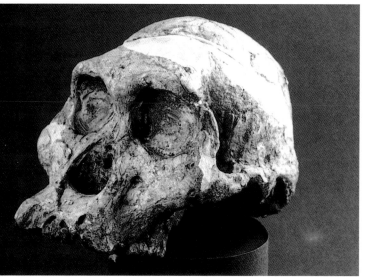

One of the most perfectly preserved and well-known skulls of a lightly built australopithecine, *Australopithecus africanus*, nicknamed Mrs Ples (after being given the scientific name *Plesianthropus transvaalensis* [the almost man of the Transvaal]), was found at Sterkfontein, South Africa, by Robert Broom and John Robinson in April 1947. Only the teeth are missing. Recent study, however, suggests that the fossil is male.

AUSTRALOPITHECINES FROM

EAST AFRICA

A Nutcracker Man

The morning of 17 July 1959 dawned without any hint that it was to herald a new era in human origins studies. As they had done for nearly thirty years whenever time and research funds permitted, Louis Leakey and his wife Mary were looking for early stone tools and human fossils at Olduvai Gorge, a ravine 40 km (25 miles) long and up to 100m (330 ft) deep on the plains of northern Tanzania. Louis Leakey was a Kenyan-born son of an English missionary. Having studied African prehistory at the University of Cambridge he decided to pursue a career hunting for

Australopithecus or *Paranthropus boisei*, more familiarly known as 'Zinj' or 'The Nutcracker Man' (because of its huge cheek teeth).

In 1959, exactly one hundred years after the publication of Charles Darwin's *On the Origin of Species*, the first East African australopithecine fossil was discovered at Olduvai Gorge in Tanzania by Mary Leakey. East Africa has since become established as a key area for human origins studies, on which much of our current knowledge is based, including the discovery that the ability to walk on two legs preceded the development of larger brains and stone toolmaking by over a million years.

early human fossils in East Africa, despite reproving comments from the academic establishment, who thought him a fool to do this in Africa rather than in Asia, which had been placed in the human origins spotlight by spectacular discoveries in the late nineteenth and early twentieth centuries. Although the Leakeys had found many thousands of animal bones and hundreds of early stone tools at Olduvai, bones of early human ancestors remained elusive until the fateful day in 1959.

On that morning, while Louis remained in camp with influenza, Mary set off alone to explore the gorge with her Dalmatian dogs, Sally and Victoria. At a site called FLK (Frida Leakey Korongo (gully), named after Louis Leakey's first wife), Mary spied pieces of skull and teeth eroding from the side of the gorge,

apparently exposed by rains earlier that year. She rushed back to the camp to tell Louis, who, illness forgotten, leaped out of bed and down to the site. As the Leakeys had promised friends that they could film one of their excavations from the start as soon as they found a site that looked interesting, they covered the bones and waited impatiently for the camera crew to arrive. After carefully recovering more than 400 fragments of bone, Mary could reconstruct the skull of a heavily built adult australopithecine, which Louis named *Zinjanthropus boisei* (the genus name means 'East Africa man' and the species name was in honour of Charles Boise, who funded the research). Today, it is termed *Australopithecus* or *Paranthropus boisei*, or, more familiarly, 'Zinj', 'Dear Boy' or 'The Nutcracker Man' (because of its huge cheek teeth). The then newly developed potassium-argon dating technique indicated it was an unexpected and astonishing 1.79

million years old. Louis Leakey is said to have been disappointed that the fossil that had been hiding from him and Mary for nearly thirty years was an australopithecine rather than an early human or *Homo*, though these feelings turned to joy when the first *Homo* fossil at Olduvai was found in 1961.

The impact of Zinj changed the course of human origins studies. By sheer good luck, his excavation was recorded on film for the world to see. Zinj made good television, and the excitement this created among the general public as well as among scientists led to funding for human origins research in East Africa on an unprecedented scale and to the discovery of thousands of fossils and an explosion of information that has accorded East Africa the status of capital of human origins material today. In her autobiography *Disclosing the Past*, Mary Leakey allows that 'it is in no way fanciful to assert that the start of it all was my happening to notice that fragment of skull on a morning in July 1959 when, but for a promise to friends who wanted to make a film, I should instead have been starting a small trial dig at a quite different site.'

Lucy

Just as Zinj profoundly changed the Leakeys' lives, so another East African australopithecine was, some years later, to revolutionize the existence of a young American, Donald 'Don' C. Johanson, then Curator of Physical Anthropology at the Cleveland Museum of Natural History and now Director of the Institute of Human Origins in Berkeley, California.

On 30 November 1974, Johanson and Tom Gray, then a graduate student, were searching for human ancestor fossils in the Hadar region, a barren inferno of a wasteland in the centre of the Afar Desert in northeastern Ethiopia, where they had found an australopithecine knee joint the previous year. Just as they were

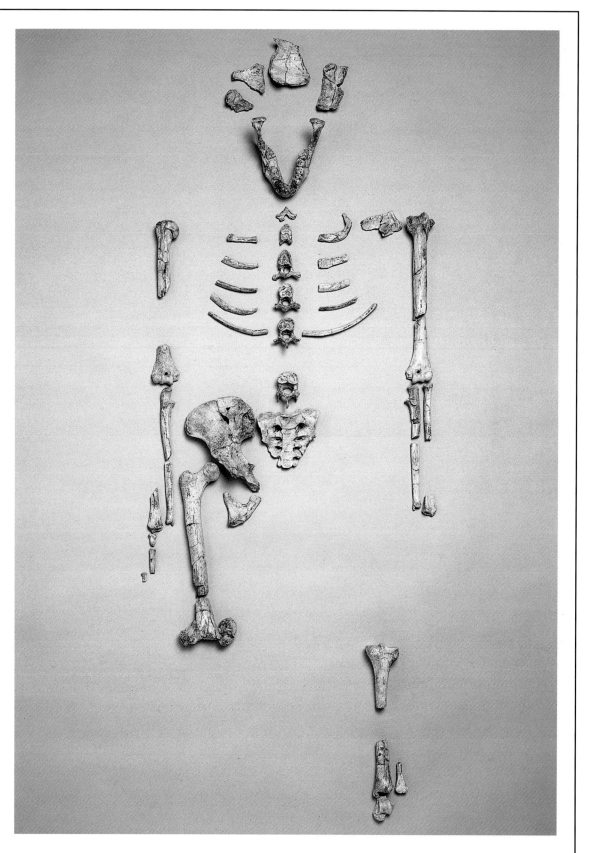

Lucy, our most famous relative, is one of the most complete specimens of an australopithecine ever found. About 40% of her skeleton is preserved, showing her to have been about 1.1 m (3 ft 7 in) tall (about the height of a modern 6-year-old), in her late teens or early twenties (her molar wisdom tooth had erupted), and probably female (on the basis of the shape of the hip bone and the birth canal through it).

The Laetoli footprints are so similar to those of modern people that it is almost eerie to realize that they were made nearly 3.7 million years ago by the kind of australopithecines whose bones have been found at Laetoli and Hadar, and who were the only creatures known from this time who could have made them. The pattern of weight distribution is almost identical to that of a modern person walking barefoot on a wet sandy beach. The big toe lies alongside the other toes and is not splayed from them or considerably longer as in apes.

about to head back to camp, Johanson noticed a piece of arm bone lying on a rocky slope. After intensive excavation, Johanson and his team recovered several hundred pieces of bone making up about 40% of the skeleton of a 1.1 m (3 ft 7 in) tall upright-walking female australopithecine. She was given the scientific name *Australopithecus afarensis*, but is known to the world as Lucy, after the Beatles song *Lucy in the Sky with Diamonds*, which was played at full volume on the field camp tape player on the night of her discovery. Johanson recalls: 'We were sky-high, you must remember, from finding her.'

Human ancestor remains usually consist of tiny scraps of bone, so the discovery of Lucy's partial skeleton was one of the most remarkable such finds ever. Associated with a potassium-argon date of around 3.2 million years ago, she was also the oldest known hominid, that is a member of the biological grouping or family that includes people, at that time.

In 1975, also at Hadar, Johanson and his colleagues found a collection of bones of at least thirteen individuals, male and female, adults and children, a couple of thousand years older than Lucy. These were nicknamed 'The First Family', although it is not certain how the bones came to be found together.

Before the 1970s, it was thought that walking on two legs developed at about the same time as larger brains and stone tools. However, the Hadar australopithecines showed that creatures which had small ape-like brains were already walking on two legs before 3.5 million years ago, at least one million years before the first stone tools known. These have also been found in Ethiopia, in the Middle Awash River Valley, where they are dated to about 2.5 million years ago.

The 'Black Skull', discovered in sediment to the west of Lake Turkana in Kenya, is that of a heavily built australopithecine and is dated to about 2.6 million years ago.

Laetoli: a jewel among the bones

Information about the appearance and behaviour of human ancestors and early humans usually has to be inferred indirectly from bare bones. Among the rare exceptions are trails of footprints made in damp volcanic ash, which later hardened, by australopithecines walking across the landscape at Laetoli, in northern Tanzania.

On 15 September 1976, a group of young scientists visiting Mary Leakey's excavation at Laetoli were amusing themselves by throwing dried elephant dung at each other, when one of them, Andrew Hill, fell and found himself lying face down on a hardened surface on which he could see curious indentations. These turned out to be fossil animal tracks made in damp volcanic ash more than three million years ago.

Even more exciting was the 1978 discovery of two trails of fossil australopithecine footprints made nearly 3.7 million years ago. At least two individuals, the larger one about 1.4 m (4 ft 7 in) tall and the smaller one about 1.36 m (4 ft 5 in) tall, walked alongside each other. In places it seems that a third set of footprints is superimposed on the ones of the larger individual, as if another individual had deliberately stepped in the prints of the larger

one, as modern children playing on the beach are wont to do.

The pattern of weight distribution, as well as the position and relative size of the toes, indicate a two-legged striding walk like ours, rather than the rolling gait of apes like chimpanzees who rarely walk upright. The Laetoli footprints show indubitably that walking on two legs was well established before 3.6 million years ago, and that this, rather than larger brains or the manufacture of stone tools, constitutes the first step on the road to humanity.

Ardipithecus ramidus: the root of us all?

In 1994, some 4.4-million-year-old fragments of fossil skull and teeth of seventeen individuals were reported from Aramis, in the Afar region of Ethiopia. The American and Ethiopian discoverers claim that they represent the oldest and closest known fossil link between humans and great apes. The fragments are very similar to those of great apes, but a few features, especially of the teeth, identify them as representative of the human family. They have been given a new name: *Ardipithecus* ('ardi' means ground or 'floor' in the Afar langauge) *ramidus* (from 'root' in Afar). A jaw and partial skeleton were found in late 1994, which may reveal whether this creature walked on four legs or – like the recently reported large *Australopithecus anamensis* bones from Kenya of four million years ago – upright on two. ∎

OLDUVAI GORGE: GRAND CANYON OF PREHISTORY

The gorge was discovered by chance in 1911 by a German entomologist, Dr Kattwinkel, who was collecting butterflies on the Serengeti Plains of the then German East Africa. Kattwinkel's collection of fossil animal bones elicited great interest when displayed in Berlin and motivated a fossil hunting expedition by a German geologist, Hans Reck, in 1913. Inspired by Reck's specimens, Louis Leakey, a Cambridge-trained prehistorian and Kenyan-born son of English missionary parents, began organizing expeditions to Olduvai in 1931. He was later accompanied on these by his archaeologist second wife Mary.

Despite having little time and money, the Leakeys persistently made the long and difficult journey from their home in Nairobi in Kenya to search the gorge for early human fossils. Years turned into decades, with little to show for their efforts, apart from a collection of crudely worked stone tools – called Oldowan tools in honour of the gorge – which were the oldest known at the time (since the 1970s, 2.5-million-year-old stone tools have been found in Ethiopia).

Their luck changed with Mary's discovery of the australopithecine known as 'Zinj' in 1959 (see p. 16). Although such

Olduvai Gorge is probably the best-known and longest archive of the remains of past humans, their activities and environments in the world. It is a spectacular canyon, 40 km (25 miles) long and up to 100 m (330 ft) deep, carved by an occasionally flowing river into the Serengeti Plains of northern Tanzania to expose a layer-cake of archaeologically rich sediments going back nearly two million years.

creatures are thought to have been an evolutionary dead-end branch of the human family, Zinj awakened a flood of funding, especially from the National Geographic Society, for human origins research in East Africa. Among the fruits of these activities was the discovery in 1961 of the first remains known to science of the earliest member of our genus, *Homo*.

On 4 April 1964, Louis Leakey, Phillip Tobias of the University of the Witwatersrand in South Africa and John Napier of London University announced that these remains represented a hitherto unknown kind of human, which lived about 1.7 million years ago, and had a brain marginally bigger than its australopithecine contemporaries. As suggested by Raymond Dart (the discoverer of the first australopithecine, see p. 14), they called it *Homo habilis*, or 'handy man', as Louis Leakey believed he had at last found the maker of the Oldowan tools. As with Zinj, a delighted Leakey gave subsequent *Homo habilis* fossils found at Olduvai nicknames such as 'Cinderella', 'George' and 'Twiggy', whose skull was squashed flat, named after the popular flat-chested British model. However, only a handful of fossils from East and South Africa are currently ascribed to *Homo habilis*, and the debate over whether this creature really belongs to our genus lingers on.

1470: a brief reign as the world's oldest man

The meagre collection of *Homo habilis* fossils available in the 1960s delayed general acceptance of these remains as the earliest representatives of our genus. Many scientists felt that they were not sufficiently different from australopithecines. The fossil that for a time seemed to corroborate Louis Leakey's claim was found by Bernard Ngeneo, a member of Leakey's son Richard's team, working on the Koobi Fora Peninsula on the eastern side of Lake Turkana (formerly Lake Rudolf) in northern Kenya. The fossil was given the catalogue number KNM-ER-1470 (Kenya National Museums East Rudolf No. 1470), and became known to the world simply as '1470'.

Of particular interest was its relatively large brain, more than 100 ml (3½ oz) greater in capacity than estimates for *Homo habilis*. It was thought initially to be nearly three million years old and thus earned the title of 'the world's oldest man'. Revised dating to 1.9 million years ago has, however, stripped the fossil of its claim to fame. Moreover, apart from brain size, other features of 1470 more closely resemble those of australopithecines. It has most recently been assigned to a new species, *Homo rudolfensis*.

A strapping lad from Nariokotome

Before *Homo habilis* was described in 1964, the earliest known

Olduvai Gorge on the Serengeti Plains, Tanzania, where the 1.7-million-year-old remains of *Homo habilis*, a previously unknown human species, were found in 1961.

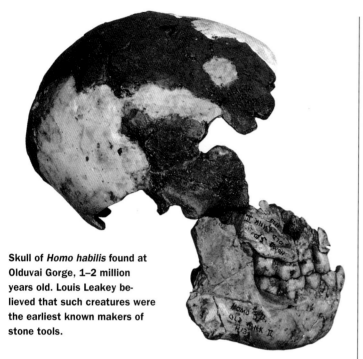

Skull of *Homo habilis* found at Olduvai Gorge, 1–2 million years old. Louis Leakey believed that such creatures were the earliest known makers of stone tools.

member of our genus was *Homo erectus*, discovered in Asia in the late nineteenth century (see p. 162). Even after the discovery of australopithecines in Africa from 1925, and the recognition of Africa as the continent with the earliest humans, Asia continued to be regarded as the place where true people that were beginning to look like us evolved, as no comparable *Homo erectus* fossils were found in Africa until the 1970s.

Among the most remarkable of these finds was the 1984 discovery by the renowned Kenyan fossil hunter Kamoya Kimeu of a young male who died 1.6 million years ago at about nine years old (equivalent to a modern twelve- or thirteen-year-old), in a marsh at Nariokotome on the western shores of Lake Turkana in northern Kenya. His body had been so rapidly covered with mud that no scavengers had had the chance to rip it apart or gnaw the bones, resulting in the preservation of a remarkably complete skeleton (only the feet are missing). He would probably have grown to a height of over 1.8 m (6 ft) in adulthood, and his body proportions are remarkably like those of modern people, except for some differences in the spine, hips and legs. In contrast to *Homo habilis*, who was 200,000 years older, and who would have been considerably shorter than the average modern European or North American, the Turkana boy showed that by 1.6 million years ago people with bodily features and proportions just like ours were walking about in Africa. The period between two and 1.5 million years ago, rather than a more recent period, is therefore now seen as a time when crucial anatomical changes that led to modern people occurred.

The first technology

Many animals use and even make tools, but the hallmark of modern humanity is the complexity of our technology. Wild chimpanzees make tools for immediate use, such as stripping leaves off twigs to make sticks for extracting termites from their nests. Early humans and also, in all likelihood, australopithecines (who could have grasped like humans) probably used such tools before they regularly made ones of stone. Experiments indicate that nearly

two-million-year-old polished bones and horns from Swartkrans in South Africa were quite possibly used to dig up roots and tubers.

Among the most intriguing finds from Olduvai Gorge and, indeed, what lured Louis Leakey to the site, are large collections of early stone tools dating from 1.9 million years ago. Called Oldowan, this first technology has since been recognized in 2.5-million-year-old layers in the Middle Awash River Valley at Hadar in Ethiopia.

The Oldowan tool-kit consisted of small sharp-edged flakes chipped off alternate edges of a cobble (or 'core'), sometimes known as a 'chopper'. Many choppers also show signs of use and were probably opportunistic tools, but the main purpose seems to have been the making of small sharp flakes for cutting and scraping purposes. Damage on early stone tools seen under a microscope indicates that they were used on many different materials, including meat, bone, skin, wood and plants. Experiments with modern copies of early stone tools show that they can easily slice through even thick elephant hide. Early stone tool-kits did not include hunting weapons like spears and arrows. Damage on animal bones found with early stone tools suggests that meat was generally scavenged from animal kills rather than hunted.

Handaxes and a 'chopper', (left to right) 1.7 million, 1 million and 350,000 years old. Although large collections of handaxes have been found, their exact use remains uncertain.

By about 1.5 million years ago, *Homo erectus* and later early *Homo sapiens* people began to produce more complex tools, usually called Acheulean, after St Acheul in France, where they were first recognized in the 1830s. They included stone tools shaped on both sides, called bifaces, which were held in the hand. Pointed, pear-shaped bifaces with a cutting edge around all or most of the circumference are known as handaxes, while examples with a broad axe-like cutting edge are called cleavers.

Acheulean technology endured until nearly 100,000 years ago, making it the longest-lasting technology the world has seen. Extraordinary quantities of Acheulean tools have been found at some sites. At Olorgesailie, in central Kenya, 800,000-year-old handaxes, cleavers and other Acheulean stone tools litter the ground. ■

OUT OF AFRICA, ALWAYS SOMETHING NEW

(*Ex Africa, semper aliquid novi*:
Pliny the Elder, *c.* AD 23–79)

Until the 1970s, it was thought that physically modern *Homo sapiens* appeared in Europe and Africa at about the same time, only some 35,000 years ago. Then new dating techniques and new fossils indicated that modern, or at least 'near-modern', people were present in Africa and the Near East (see p. 138) from 100,000 years ago. Africa may well prove to be the cradle of modern humanity, just as it is of the first of our kind.

The excavations at the spectacular series of caves at Klasies River Mouth on the southern coast of South Africa, by Ronald Singer and John Wymer in 1966–8 and since 1984 by H. J. Deacon of the University of Stellenbosch in South Africa, have produced some of the earliest-known remains of modern or at least 'near-modern' humans. They almost certainly date to over 100,000 years ago and possibly to 120,000 years ago, and are associated with Middle Stone Age stone tools. They include a fragment of a modern-looking face and an almost complete lower jaw, as well as other fragments, which suggest that modern people were evolving in Africa at a time when Eurasia was occupied by non-modern archaic people.

Interestingly, however, although the Klasies people may have resembled modern people physically, they did not behave like recent Stone Age people. They seem to have been ineffective hunters, who had little success with hunting large fierce animals like buffalo and bushpig, and preferred more docile ones like eland. Their technology generally lacked innovation, while art, symbols and burial of the dead hardly existed, if at all, in their times. More ominously, nevertheless, it has been suggested that the scratched, charred and fragmented condition of some of the human bones may have been the consequence of cannibalism. It is possible that the development of the fully modern ability to use culture as a means to forge an existence under particular prevailing social and environmental conditions required further anatomical changes, particularly in the brain, although this is difficult to establish from fossil bones.

Modern-looking, but tantalizing, human remains also associated with Middle Stone Age stone tools have been recovered from Border Cave in South Africa, an inaccessible cavern high on a cliff face on the border between Swaziland and South Africa. A

partial adult skull cap and lower jaw were recovered under uncontrolled conditions during the removal of cave fill for fertilizer extraction during the 1940s. An infant skeleton was found during systematic excavations in 1941, a nearly complete lower jaw during excavations in 1974, and various fragments from collapsed areas in recent years. These remains could well be of the order of 100,000 years old, but the bones are generally better preserved than the animal bones with which they are supposedly associated, and their age remains debated because they were not recovered under modern excavation standards. It is possible that they come from later graves dug into the older underlying Middle Stone Age layers in the cave. The infant burial is the only grave claimed for the Middle Stone Age in South Africa. It contains a mollusc shell with a hole in it (for possible use as a pendant), which must have originated at the coast at least 80 km (50 miles) away.

Much argument about a woman

The fossil evidence for an African origin of modern people enjoyed a brief boost from genetic studies during the late 1980s. Research based on mitochondrial DNA (genetic material inherited only from the mother) was interpreted to indicate that all modern people in the world were the descendants of a single woman (inevitably dubbed 'Eve'), who lived in an African 'Garden of Eden' some 200,000–150,000 years ago. These studies were, however, shown to be statistically flawed in 1992. Nevertheless, the so-called 'Out of Africa' explanation for the origin of modern people still enjoys support from the fossil record and other genetic studies currently under way although it has been strongly challenged by proponents of the idea that modern people arose gradually in many parts of the world, not just in Africa – the so-called 'multiregional hypothesis'. ■

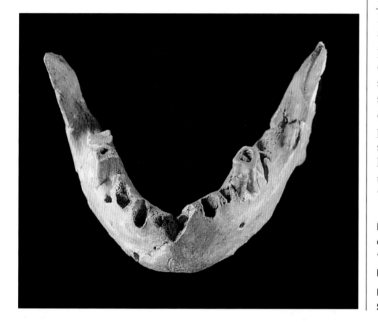

LEFT: A modern-looking jaw bone of the order of 100,000 years old, from excavations at Klasies River Mouth suggests that modern or at least 'near-modern' people were evolving in Africa at a time when non-modern people occupied areas in Eurasia.

BELOW: This partial adult skull of a modern individual from Border Cave in South Africa may be around 100,000 years old, but its dating is uncertain.

LEFT: Layers at Klasies River Mouth. The extraordinary 20 m (66 ft) high pile of archaeological material at the Klasies River Mouth caves in South Africa, stacked like clearly distinguishable cake layers, indicates that modern or 'near-modern' people lived there by 100,000 years ago or earlier. Quantities of limpet and mussel shells in many layers indicate that these people were among the first to exploit shellfish systematically, although they did not have such equipment as fish hooks or nets for catching fish or flying seabirds. Like earlier people and recent hunter-gatherers, most of their food probably came from plants and small animals. They were wary hunters who had more success hunting docile animals like eland, rather than fierce ones like buffalo or bushpig.

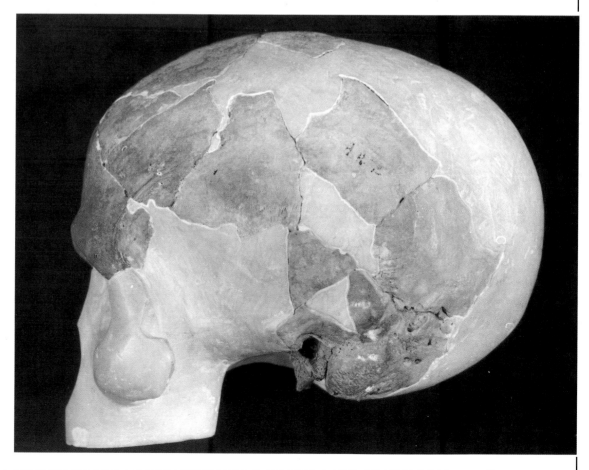

SOUTHERN AFRICAN ROCK ART: 'IMAGES OF POWER'

Many thousands of paintings are found in rockshelters main-ly in mountainous areas, while thousands of engravings are found on boulders on the inte-rior plateau regions of southern Africa. There are also examples of small painted stones found in archaeological layers in caves, and rare painted engravings.

Only in recent years has southern African rock art been recognized as one of the supreme achievements of humankind, dating back nearly 30,000 years. Although first regarded as a quaint record of daily life, some researchers have since the 1970s argued that it is a religious art, and that some of it records the experiences of the shamans (medicine men and women) who used it as a source and demonstration of power to heal sickness, bring rain and attract game.

Rock paintings can be monochrome (one colour), bichrome, polychrome or shaded polychrome. Engravings can be scraped, incised lines, or pecked out. Common depictions include wild animals (especially antelope such as the eland), domestic animals (such as sheep and cattle after 2000 years ago and horses from the nineteenth century onwards), scenes with human figures, combi-nations of animal and human figures (called therianthropes), handprints, designs such as dots, grids, zigzags and patterns, and historical scenes including ox wagons and soldiers on horseback. Most of the art is thought to have been done by Bushmen (also called San), the indigenous hunter-gatherer people of southern Africa. Some of the art in the Western Cape Province of South Africa may have been done by Khoikhoin herders, but this

answer is difficult to establish with certainty.

The oldest dated examples of southern African rock art are seven broken painted slabs from the Apollo 11 Cave in southern Namibia. The site was named by the excavator, Eric Wendt, in honour of the 1969 moon land-ing, to which he listened on his transistor radio while working there. Incredibly, two of the slabs, found in separate excavation seasons in 1969 and 1972 respec-tively, fitted together. Charcoal from the same layers as the slabs was radiocarbon dated to between 27,000 and 19,000 years ago, thus assigning the paintings to the end of the Middle Stone Age or the beginning of the Later Stone Age. This is the same order of age as the earliest dated rock art in Europe (see p. 61). The paintings found by Wendt are of a feline-looking animal with human-like rear legs, two examples of a white animal with black stripes, an outline of a rhino in black, the body of an antelope covered by a red line, and black lines with a red patch.

Southern African rock engravings also have considerable antiq-uity as dated examples from Wonderwerk Cave in the Northern Cape Province of South Africa are more than 10,000 years old.

The most recent art can be dated by what it depicts, such as domestic animals (intro-duced only in the last 2000 years) and paintings of British soldiers in uniform (the 1860s).

Bushmen believed that shamans could activate super-natural power and make contact with the spirit world by going into a dream-like state called trance. At a ritual dance around a camp-fire, clapping, music, dancing and singing, as well as rapid breathing and great con-centration enabled shamans to enter trance. As they did so, the shaman often bent forwards, sweated, trembled, and bled from the nose, actions that seem to be depicted in the rock art. The shamans were said to 'die' metaphorically when go-ing into trance, because a dying antelope behaves similarly. Some researchers believe that

certain paintings clearly correlate a dying antelope with a 'dying' shaman. It was thought that the eland, the largest and spiritually most powerful antelope, released its power at death and that this could be used by the shaman to perform tasks such as curing sickness, bringing rain, or ensuring hunting success.

A shaman entering trance experiences a number of stages of hallucination which are apparently recorded in the rock art. At first, patterns of light forming shapes like grids, zigzags, chevrons, spirals and dots are seen. These images are produced by the nervous system and are seen by people all over the world who enter trance, and even by some people who suffer from migraine headaches. During the second stage, people try to make sense of the shapes they see in terms of things that are important to them. For the Bushmen in many parts of southern Africa, few things were more important than animals, among which the eland was most important of all. In the final and deepest stage, people see themselves as part of their hallucinations. Bushman shamans, feeling that they had turned into animals, may later have painted this experience in the form of part-human, part-animal figures.

Saharan Rock Art

Although the greatest strides in interpreting African rock art have been made in southern Africa, there is a great wealth of both Stone Age and Iron Age rock art throughout the continent. Some of the most arresting examples come from massifs in the central and western Sahara, such as Adrar des Iforas, Air, Hoggar, Tassili-n-Ajjer and Tibesti. In the Sahara, it is thought that the earliest art comprises engravings of wild animals dating to before 8000 years ago. This period is thought to be followed by paintings of human figures, ranging in size from small to gigantic, often with round, featureless heads, dating to perhaps 8000–7000 years ago. The following period is believed to date to between perhaps 7500 and 3200 years ago, and consists of many polychrome paintings and engravings of domesticated cattle. Subsequent periods show horses, camels and horse-drawn chariots (see illustration from the Acacus region, Algeria, below). ■

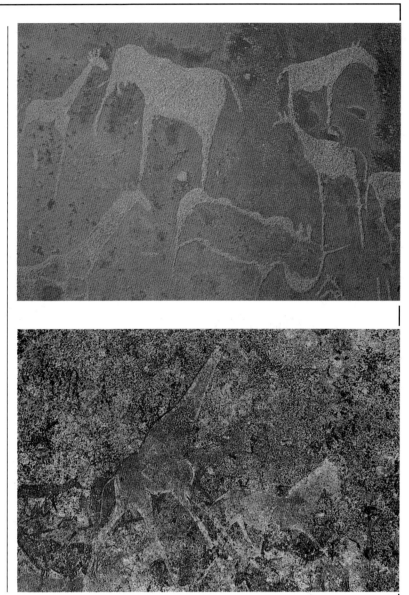

TOP: Engraving from Twyfelfontein, Damaraland, Namibia, a valley containing clusters of boulders engraved with some 2500 depictions, mostly of human footprints, animal spoor and animals, particularly giraffe. This part of the so-called 'Carstens panel', which includes about 70 individual engravings, is a typical example.

ABOVE: Giraffe and zebra from Nswatugi Cave in the Matopos Hills of Zimbabwe. Wild animals had spiritual significance and are common depictions in southern African rock paintings.

OPPOSITE: Later Stone Age rock painting from Tanzania interpreted as a recording of a shamanistic trance dance, an example of the great wealth of rock art that exists throughout Africa.

ABYDOS

Individuals of relatively modest means set up small mudbrick shrines containing limestone stelae (upright slabs or pillars) which bore images and identifying texts of themselves, their families and their friends. These little chapels

By the New Kingdom (*c.* 1550–1069 BC) the site of Abydos had become famous as the burial place of the god Osiris, the Egyptian god of the dead. Many Egyptians therefore, including kings, wished either to be buried or to be represented at Abydos, thus making it the most important cemetery site unconnected with a royal capital.

creation of Egyptian creation myths, rising from the waters of chaos and symbolizing rebirth.

Petrie's achievements at Abydos are best exemplified by his previous work on a much earlier part of the site. The procession of Osiris mentioned above led

seem to have covered the slope of the plateau called the 'North Cemetery' which overlooked the Temple of Osiris and the route of the procession of the Mysteries of Osiris, which was rather like a passion play. Early in the nineteenth century the Abydos cemeteries became the target for plunderers seeking a rich hoard of easily handled and readily saleable stelae.

More spectacular were the royal versions of these private cenotaphs. The cenotaph temple of King Seti I (1306–1290 BC) is the largest and the most extensively decorated, with painted relief carving of the finest quality, and was intended to stress the relationship between Seti and the god Osiris. But the temple itself is

from the temple to what is now a low mound in the desert called the 'Umm el-Qa'ab', 'the Mother of Pots'. Many of these pots, now mostly broken sherds, are the remains of vessels left as offerings at the supposed tomb of Osiris, the divine, but dead, king of Egypt. In fact the Umm el-Qa'ab is an actual burial site, but that of real kings, those who ruled at the very beginning of Egyptian history. In 1895–6 the French scholar Emile-Clément Amélineau went through this cemetery in a destructive excavation which was partly recovered by re-excavation and recording by Petrie in 1900–1. Petrie realized the importance of the site as the royal cemetery of all the kings of the first dynasty, and two of the sec-

ABOVE: Mudbrick offering-chapel containing a limestone stela, commemorating a family of the Middle Kingdom. From the excavations of John Garstang at Abydos, 1906-9.

RIGHT: King Seti I, father of Ramesses II, worshipping the God Osiris on a wall from his cenotaph temple at Abydos.

only one half of Seti's monumental arrangements at Abydos. In 1901–2 the British archaeologist Sir Flinders Petrie, when digging behind the Seti temple, discovered a unique structure – a building constructed below ground level that was based on the plan of a typical New Kingdom royal tomb from the Valley of the Kings, but whose central hall, with its massive granite pillars supporting the granite roof, consisted of an 'island' surrounded by a channel which was partly filled with water. This (probably) unique structure may have been intended to represent the original island of ond. The upper parts of these tombs had long been lost, but were probably squat, rectangular, mudbrick structures called 'mastabas' (from the Arabic for bench). The tombs themselves are rather modest, brick-lined pits, with later examples divided into a series of rooms, and flanked by rows of subsidiary burials of courtiers; whether these royal servants were all buried at the same time as their royal master (i.e. were 'encouraged' or wished to die with him) remains an open question. However, enough remains of the funerary furniture from these repeatedly pillaged tombs to assign them to kings (and possibly one queen, Mer-Neith) of the earliest period of Egyptian history, and to their predecessors, the local rulers of the late predynastic period, buried nearby. ∎

Miniature ivory statue of an early Egyptian king, wearing the special 'Jubilee robe', from Abydos.

Hierakonpolis Main Deposit

Like Abydos, the southern Egyptian site of Hierakonpolis has provided evidence of the early history of Egypt. It seems to have been an important political centre at about the time of the unification of Egypt (*c*.3050 BC). The site was excavated between 1897 and 1899 by J. E. Quibell and F. W. Green, who discovered an early mudbrick temple enclosure. Within this temple they discovered a group of votive objects which, having once been presented to the temple, were now considered surplus to requirements and buried within the temple precincts. This included the so-called 'Main Deposit' which contained some of the most important objects for the archaeology, history and art of the unification period. They include the ceremonial mace-head of King 'Scorpion' and, most famously, the ceremonial slate palette of King Narmer, considered by some to show the unification itself as the southern king Narmer defeats his northern enemies to become the first king of Egypt.

The ceremonial palette of King Narmer depicts the monarch slaying his enemies at the beginning of Egyptian history.

THE PYRAMIDS AT GIZA

The pyramid itself is only one part of an elaborate collection of buildings which made up the king's mortuary complex, including structures used during the funeral and temples necessary for the continuing provision of offerings for the dead king. The burial of nobles and members of the royal family around the pyramid was also an important aspect of the total pyramid package, and it is in the subsidiary burials of both people and objects that surround the Great Pyramid (belonging to Khufu, or Cheops) that we find the evidence which demonstrates that the Giza plateau is far from being exhausted as

Since their construction, the pyramids at Giza, built by kings of the Fourth Dynasty (2575–2465 BC), have dominated the skyline to the west of Cairo. They constitute the world's most impressive examples of the ingenuity and determination of pre-modern peoples to produce works which can still inspire us with awe. Their very obviousness caused them to be robbed in antiquity yet, grudgingly, they have yielded to archaeologists some of their secrets.

a site for archaeological investigation.

The largest single surviving object associated with the burial of the king was discovered in May 1954 by the Egyptian archaeologist Kamal el-Mallakh. While carrying out clearing work on the south side of the Great Pyramid, el-Mallakh's workmen came across a rectangular pit covered by forty-one limestone blocks, some weighing more than 15,240 kg (15 tons). The pit would prove to be 31 m (102 ft) long by 5 m (16 ft 5 in) deep, but more remarkable still were its contents: a dismantled full-size boat, mostly of cedar, lying in more than 1000 pieces. Once assembled, after painstaking restoration work, the boat was found to be 43 m (141 ft) long, and seemed to have been used at least once – perhaps to convey the funeral cortège of the king by river or canal to the pyramid complex for burial. It may also be that this boat (like those which once filled the three now-empty pits around the pyramid and, presumably, the one still lying in the last

The three pyramids of the Giza group. From right to left, Khufu (Cheops), Khaefre (Chephren) and Menkaure (Mycerinus) with the three queens' pyramids.

The funerary boat of King Cheops. It may have also been used in his lifetime for ceremonial journeys during religious festivals.

BELOW: Greywacke statue of King Menkaure (Mycerinus) from the Valley Temple of his pyramid complex at Giza. To the king's right is the goddess Hathor, to his left a goddess representing the seventh nome (administrative district) of Upper Egypt.

unopened pit) was intended for use in the afterlife, perhaps to allow the king to cross the sky every day with Re, the sun-god.

Although Khufu's pyramid has been thoroughly robbed, like the pyramids of his father, King Snefru, that of his mother has survived. In 1925 the American Egyptologist George Reisner, working around the base of the Great Pyramid, accidentally discovered a vertical shaft 30 m (98 ft) deep, at the bottom of which was a burial chamber containing the funerary equipment of Queen Hetepheres. In fact the alabaster sarcophagus was empty, a fact which led Reisner to speculate that the original resting place of Hetepheres (perhaps close to Snefru's own) had been robbed during Khufu's lifetime, and that this later tomb represented a reburial of Hetepheres' funerary paraphernalia, the body of Hetepheres herself being a rather obvious missing item.

The two smaller pyramids at Giza have also yielded a valuable harvest of archaeological information and objects of great aesthetic merit, largely from the Valley Buildings of Khaefre (Chephren), which were built of massive blocks of red granite and of Menkaure (Mycerinus), hastily completed in mudbrick after the king's death. Khaefre's Valley Building was discovered in 1853 by the French Egyptologist Auguste Mariette. It included a pit containing a life-size diorite statue of the king, one of several which once stood in the T-shaped hall of the Valley Building, the object of cult ceremonies. This find was surpassed by Reisner who, while working in Menkaure's much less impressive Valley Building, came across a group of statues which showed the king alone, with Queen Khamerernebty, and with various deities. The Khaefre and Menkaure sculptures are among the finest masterpieces of Egyptian art from the Old Kingdom (c. 2649–2152 BC). ■

AMARNA

The archaeological site known today as el-Amarna (or Tell el-Amarna) is the only Egyptian city for which we have any detail regarding its internal plan. By great fortune it is also a capital city, containing unique buildings and objects which are among the most famous from the ancient world.

There is little to be seen today of the ancient city of Akhetaten, which was founded by King Akhenaten soon after his accession in 1353 BC. Akhenaten (the prince formerly known as Amenhotep IV) had replaced the primacy of the god Amen as patron of the Egyptian empire with that of the Aten (the deified sun-disc) and had abandoned the capital city of Thebes – and particularly its great temple of Amen at Karnak – with its close associations with Amen, for a completely new capital city on a virgin site in Middle Egypt to be called Akhetaten, 'Horizon of the Aten'. The city was planned with everything the capital of the most powerful kingdom in the ancient world at the time would need: a central 'downtown' containing the main royal palace, administrative buildings and the great temple of the Aten. To the south and north of this central area were suburbs containing the houses of Amarnans of modest means, close to the villas of rich noblemen and the palaces of royalty. Although these were revealed only by a century of continuing archaeological work, the site was known to early travellers and antiquarians because of the fourteen rock-cut stelae (upright slabs or pillars) in the cliffs around the city, marking its boundaries and, to the east of the city, the tomb-chapels of the great and the good of Amarna, in-

cluding the intended tomb of Akhenaten himself. On the walls of these tombs the strangely deformed images of the king and his family puzzled visitors, who had been accustomed to seeing images of Egyptian kings as youthful and physically perfect individuals.

In 1887 a peasant woman was digging in the centre of what was the ancient city, apparently for *sebbakh* – degenerated mudbrick often used as natural fertilizer. In doing so she stumbled upon a cache of some 300 clay tablets inscribed with the wedge-shaped cuneiform script: she had discovered the 'House of Correspondence of Pharaoh', effectively the diplomatic archives of the state records office. The tablets, now known as the 'Amarna Letters', were written in Akkadian, the diplomatic language of the ancient Near East in the Late Bronze Age. The letters revealed Egypt's relationship both with her vassals in the Levant and with other kingdoms in

ABOVE: An 'Amarna Letter'. These small clay tablets, written in Akkadian using cuneiform script, document the relations between the King of Egypt, his vassals, and other great powers in the Near East.

LEFT: Stone stelae recovered from private houses at Amarna, perhaps as objects of reverence, show the royal family sitting underneath the Aten. Depictions of the royal couple and their children in such informal poses are unique to the Amarna period.

RIGHT: The painted limestone bust of Queen Nefertiti. Excavated at Amarna in 1912, it was probably the work of the master sculptor Thutmose, and is one of the masterpieces of Egyptian sculpture.

the Near East which considered themselves her equals. In 1891–2 Flinders Petrie began working in the central city, uncovering remains of the Great Temple of the Aten, the Great Royal Palace, the King's House, the Record Office (including more Amarna Letters) and a number of houses belonging to private individuals. The public buildings in the city were constructed quickly using unusually small stone blocks, so-called *talatat*, which were later reused in buildings across the Nile at Hermopolis Magna after Akhetaten was abandoned following the death of Akhenaten. Archaeological work in the city itself has continued sporadically until the present day, carried out largely by the Egypt Exploration Society, particularly during the period 1921–6. Some of the most famous single objects from Amarna, however, come from the work of Ludwig Borchardt. Digging chiefly in large private houses in the south of the city from 1908 to 1914, he excavated in the house of the royal sculptor Thutmose, where he discovered unfinished and trial pieces, most famously the painted limestone head of Queen Nefertiti.

It is chiefly by examining evidence from el-Amarna itself that archaeologists have tried to reconstruct the tangled history and personal relationships of the Amarna period, including the puzzle of the parentage of Tutankhamen (see p. 32) who, as Tutankhaten, spent his early life, and the beginning of his short reign, at Akhetaten. ∎

The production of elaborate glass vessels in Egypt is a striking development of the New Kingdom. This polychrome fish from Amarna is a particularly fine example.

TUTANKHAMEN

In 1907 a fortuitous partnership began between Howard Carter, English archaeologist and former Inspector of the Egyptian Antiquities Service, and Lord Carnarvon, English aristocrat and amateur Egyptologist. Carter's interest in Egyptology was professional – he had begun working in Egypt as an epigraphic artist with the Egypt Exploration Fund – while Carnarvon's had come about as a result of being forced to winter in Egypt because of ill health. Carter was employed by Carnarvon to provide much-needed expertise for his excavations on the west bank at Thebes. Until the First World War the pair were rather successful in discovering a series of tombs belonging to noblemen buried close to the Theban mountain, but in 1917 Carter was able to start work on what was apparently always his main aim, excavating in the Valley of the Kings itself in order to locate the lost tomb of King Tutankhamen, a monarch who ruled for less than a decade, dying before his nineteenth birthday, in about 1323 BC, in the aftermath of the Amarna period (see p. 30).

By 1921-2 Carnarvon's enthusiasm for chasing what seemed to be a chimera had reached a low ebb, and he decided that work in the Valley should cease. However, he was persuaded by Carter to finance just one more season of work in a small triangle of ground in the Valley, just in front of the tomb of Ramesses VI, which Carter believed was the only possible place remaining where the tomb of the boy-king could be located. The next sea-

In 1922, in Egypt's Valley of the Kings, the most spectacular archaeological find of this century – perhaps the most spectacular there will ever be – was discovered when Howard Carter and Lord Carnarvon opened the tomb of the Pharaoh Tutankhamen.

son of work began on 1 November 1922; three days later, workmen discovered a series of rock-cut steps leading to a plastered doorway covered with the seals of necropolis officials. With what must have been an agony of self-control, Carter ceased work on the tomb until Carnarvon's arrival at Luxor on 23 November.

A re-examination of the doorway revealed that the seals named the tomb's owner – Tutankhamen – and although the re-sealing

ABOVE: The annexe of the tomb. Two gilded statues guard the entrance to the burial chamber.

LEFT: The burial chamber of Tutankhamen, modest in size, today contains the sarcophagus and body of the king.

OPPOSITE: The gilded shrine surrounding the king's canopic chest. The goddesses Isis and Selket spread their arms in protection of the king's internal organs.

of the tomb in ancient times suggested that it had been tampered with shortly after its original sealing, the fact that it was re-sealed in good order raised expectations of a largely undisturbed burial within. The doorway led to a short descending corridor filled with rubble, at the end of which was another sealed doorway in which Carter made an observation hole. The scene which greeted Carter and Carnarvon was much like a sumptuous oriental junk shop; the room they were looking into, the Annexe, was filled in a haphazard fashion with a mass of items of gilded furniture: beds, chests and stools, with two life-size gilded statues of the king flanking the entrance to the burial chamber itself. When this doorway was removed in its turn, Carter was to find another surprise confronting him – almost filling the burial chamber was a huge gilded shrine, the outermost of four which closely nested within each other around the sarcophagus. It was when the granite lid of the sarcophagus was finally lifted, on 12 February 1924, that Carter knew that he had discovered the intact burial of the king. The sarcophagus itself was filled with another Russian-doll arrangement where an outer anthropoid coffin of cypress wood covered in gold foil stared sightlessly out.

Depictions of Tutankhamen enjoying leisure activities with Queen Ankhesenamen are a popular theme on objects from the tomb, like this inlaid casket.

OPPOSITE: **The gold mask of Tutankhamen, probably the most famous face of the ancient world.**

BELOW: **Although now missing its feathers, the scene of Tutankhamen hunting ostrich on this fan perhaps shows the source of those feathers.**

The clearance of the other objects from the tomb meant that the lid of this coffin was lifted only in February 1925, using the silver handles fitted to lower the lid into place over three thousand years before, to reveal the second coffin, again of gilded wood and with details in faience, obsidian and lapis-lazuli. The third and innermost coffin was more magnificent still, over 1.8 m (6 ft) long and of solid gold, 25–30 mm (1–1.2 in) thick, and weighing 110.4 kg (243 lb). But when the lid of this coffin was lifted to reveal the body of the king himself, the tomb had one further surprise for its discoverers: the king's mummy was fitted with the most famous object from the tomb, a magnificent mask covering the head and shoulders of the royal body of solid gold, lapis-lazuli and blue glass.

Ironically, Carnarvon himself was never to gaze on the face of Tutankhamen or know the contents of the sarcophagus; on 5 April 1923 he died in Cairo of pneumonia following an infected mosquito bite, a fate which was seized on by the superstitious as 'proof' that the tomb was cursed. Carter's own curse was rather different, for he found the practicalities of dealing with this great discovery – cataloguing and conserving the objects, dealing with officials and the press – increasingly irksome. He completed clearing the tomb of its objects in 1928, and for the next four years oversaw the conservation of this material and partially published his findings. But the tomb itself is so rich in many ways that it is still today a subject of scholarly study as well as of unparalleled public interest. ■

DEIR EL-MEDINA

The village itself, consisting of approximately seventy well-preserved houses in terraced streets, surrounded by an enclosure wall, is sited in an unlikely location. Away from the River Nile, all necessities of life, including water, would have had to be carried to the village to sustain its population. Yet it continued in existence for almost 500 years of constant occupation. It is the unique nature of this village which ensured both its survival (it was abandoned and quickly covered with wind-blown sand as soon as its function ceased) and its particular interest to archaeologists, for in 1929 the Czech Egyptologist Jaroslav Cerny conclusively proved, after working on the mass of written documents to come from the site, that Deir el-Medina housed the workmen who worked on suc-

Tucked away in a fold of the barren and inhospitable Theban mountain, close to the Valley of the Kings, is the village which housed what is now arguably the best-known community from the ancient Near East.

cessive royal tombs in the Valley of the Kings during the New Kingdom (*c.* 1550–1069 BC). It is likely that the village was founded by Tuthmosis I early in the Eighteenth Dynasty (*c.* 1550–1307 BC), and its occupants worked on the royal sepulchre for most of the kings of that and the next two dynasties.

The first systematic attempt to explore Deir el-Medina began in 1905 when an expedition from Turin Museum, directed by Ernesto Schiaparelli, began to look at the site from which much of Turin's collection had already come: Deir el-Medina had been a major source of the stelae (upright slabs or pillars, often inscribed) and small antiquities which found their way onto the antiquities market in the nineteenth century, and Turin had received its share from the King of Sardinia's acquisition of the collection of Egyptian antiquities made by Bernardino Drovetti, French Consul in Egypt. The most exciting result of Schiaparelli's excavations, which continued until 1909, was the discovery of the intact tomb of the foreman Kha. The cemetery of Deir el-Medina is situated on a low hill immediately overlooking the village. The tombs are modest in size, as one would expect from the status of their occupants, but include splendid examples of painted decoration as the workmen and artists, who practised their skills in the royal tomb, provided for their own eternity by do-it-yourself tomb construction on their days off.

The most important excavator to work at Deir el-Medina was Bernard Bruyère (1879–1971), whose excavations in the period 1922–51 revealed much about the community by concentrating on the village itself rather than on its cemetery and the contents of the tombs. His work was significant in its exploration of the physical remains of one of the few towns or villages which has survived substantially intact from Ancient Egypt. His most important single discovery, however, was a large rubbish pit, which contained thousands of *ostraka* – chips of limestone or pottery

Deir el-Medina – Stela of Neferhotep.

An attendance register for workers on the royal tomb in the Valley of the Kings.

used as cheap and readily available writing material – which contain the sort of day-to-day jottings by villagers which illustrate the ordinary functioning of a real community, made possible by the unusually high level of literacy among the population of the village. It is this combination of the survival of the village itself, the tombs of its inhabitants, and documentation referring to ordinary activities of everyday life, which makes Deir el-Medina a unique site at which to study the *modus vivendi* of non-royal and non-noble Egyptians. ∎

Painted scene from the tomb of the royal tomb-builders,
a case of ancient do-it-yourself.

TANIS

Tanis was most likely founded by, and the capital city of, kings of the Twenty-first and Twenty-second Dynasties (*c.* 1069–712 BC) who ruled parts of northern Egypt after the collapse of the New Kingdom. To embellish their new capital, the Tanitic kings brought to their city ancient statues and dismantled buildings, especially temples, from earlier cities – most notably from Pi-Ramesses (a mere 20 km [12.5 miles] upriver), the capital city established in the eastern Delta by Ramesses II (1290–1224 BC) of the Nineteenth Dynasty whose temples, statues and obelisks were transported wholesale to Tanis.

Tanis was an early target for archaeologists in Egypt. The name of this city was already well known from the Bible (as Zoan, e.g. Numbers 13:22) and the enormous town-mound (or *Tell*) at San el-Hagar made the site very noticeable; in fact the connection between the two had been made as early as 1722. Between 1860 and 1864 the French archaeologist Auguste Mariette dug in the great temple enclosure (visible on the ground through remains of massive mudbrick walls) and recovered an important series of statues, particularly those of earlier periods of Egyptian history. The

About 130 km (80 miles) to the northeast of Cairo, in the Delta of the Nile, lies San el-Hagar, the site of the ancient city of Tanis, certainly the largest and probably the most important of the archaeological sites of the Delta. It surpasses the Valley of the Kings itself in the number of intact royal burials found there.

English Egyptologist Flinders Petrie worked there in 1884, making a detailed plan of the temple area, but it was only with the work of the French archaeologist Pierre Montet that Tanis achieved world-wide fame as one of the great discoveries of Egyptology.

By the time of the Third Intermediate Period (Dynasties 21–25, *c.* 1069–664 BC) royal burial in pyramids (Old and Middle Kingdom) and in hidden rock tombs (especially in the Valley of the Kings at Thebes) had been abandoned as efficient means of protecting the royal burial. Instead, and particularly in the Delta (where the lack of solid geology for massive foundations or underground tunnels made both these methods impractical anyway), royal tombs were built within the protective enclosure walls of the main temples of the capital city. This seems to have been the method chosen by local hereditary rulers and their families at Sais, Mendes, Bubastis, Leontopolis and Tanis.

In February 1939, after working at Tanis for ten years, Montet was excavating within the temple enclosure when workmen discovered an underground chamber blocked by a stone entrance. It was a tomb of four decorated limestone chambers, containing the

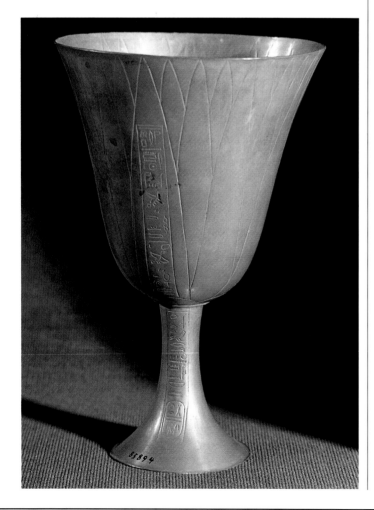

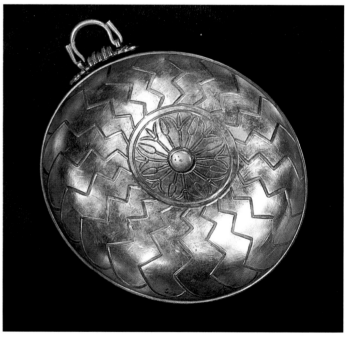

ABOVE: Silver bowl with gold handle and incised lotus-pool decoration. From the tomb of Psusennes, possibly the king's wine cup.

LEFT: Gold lotus-shaped chalice inscribed with the names of the Theban High Priest Pinudjem and Princess Henut-Tawy, who may have sent it as a gift to King Psusennes.

sarcophagi of Osorkon III and Prince Hornakht, and the remains of burials of Takelot II and Osorkon I. Immediately to the north of this burial suite was another tomb, this time of five rooms which was to prove to belong primarily to Psusennes I. In the antechamber, lying on a stone base, was a silver falcon-headed coffin belonging to Shoshenq II. Work in this tomb was continued only at the beginning of the next season, a period overshadowed by the outbreak of the Second World War. Nevertheless, Montet continued his work at the site, opening the plundered tomb of Shoshenq III, located to the northwest of that of Psusennes. Within Psusennes' tomb Montet realized that the western wall of the antechamber concealed two entrances – these proved to be the burial chambers of Psusennes himself and, to the south, that of Amenemope. The burial of Psusennes I can only be compared with that of Tutankhamen as an intact and opulent interment of an Egyptian king. The chamber was opened by moving the granite door-block on its original bronze rollers to reveal a long narrow room, big enough to contain a pink granite coffin with the figure of Psusennes sculpted as the god Osiris on its lid and, at the foot of the sarcophagus, canopic jars containing the king's internal organs and vessels of gold and silver. Within the outer sarcophagus was a mummiform sarcophagus of black granite, and within that a coffin of silver and – as in the case of Tutankhamen (see p. 35) – a gold face mask. The body of the king was further protected by amuletic jewellery of precious metals and semiprecious stones.

Gold mask from the body of King Psusennes. Less elaborate than that of Tutankhamen, the mask bears inlay to emphasize the eyes and chin-strap for the false beard.

Amenemope's vault yielded a similar, though less rich hoard; it is possible that this chamber was originally intended for Queen Mutnodjmet, but was pressed into service for Psusennes' successor rather than using the tomb originally prepared for him. This tomb yielded its final surprise in 1946 when the French team realized, while drawing their plans, that there was an unexplained void within the structure. Further investigation revealed yet another burial chamber, that of General Wendjebaendjed, a contemporary of Psusennes. Although the royal tombs at Tanis now seem to have revealed most of their secrets, the rest of the site is so vast that archaeologists have, quite literally, only scratched its surface. ■

THE ROSETTA STONE

After conquering Egypt, Napoleon's forces began to prepare the defence of the country in readiness for the expected response from the British, particularly the Royal Navy which, under Nelson, was an active thorn in the side of the French in the Mediterranean. The strengthening of the defences of ports on the Mediterranean coast was an obvious first step, and one of the ports to be treated in this way was that of Rashid (Rosetta is its Europeanized form), on the main western branch of the Nile running through the Delta to the sea. During the construction of Fort St Julien at Rosetta a French officer overseeing the work, Bouchard, noticed that the workmen had uncovered a slab of black basalt covered with inscribed texts. This was in itself not very surprising: like many important Delta cities, Rosetta stood on the ruins of an ancient city, and the finding of antiquities during casual building works, or deliberate antique-hunting expeditions was quite usual. But the basalt slab was uncommon in that it was inscribed with text in three different languages one of which, Greek, could be read. In fact each of the three texts bore the same inscription and so it can immediately be seen that the Rosetta Stone, as it came to be known, was in effect a crib to the decipherment of the other two scripts, Egyptian Hieroglyphic and the cursive Demotic.

The defeat of the French Navy by Nelson at Aboukir Bay, and the subsequent surrender of the French garrison of Alexandria,

After centuries of being effectively lost to the world, Ancient Egypt experienced a revival of interest as a result, curiously enough, of the activities of Napoleon Bonaparte. The invasion of Egypt in 1798 by the French emperor-to-be provided the curtain-raiser to Egypt for the West, and accidentally also provided the key to understanding Ancient Egypt through its own writing system, the hieroglyphic text.

made the British masters of Egypt. The Rosetta Stone, like many of the antiquities collected by the savants attached to Napoleon's expedition, became a prize of war. The booty was dispatched to Britain, arriving in Portsmouth in February 1802, before being transported to the British Museum where it is still proudly displayed today.

But the real importance of the Rosetta Stone is not its discovery but its crucial role in the decipherment of the mysterious hieroglyphic script which covered the tombs and temples of Egypt. Attempts to 'read' hieroglyphs were not new; 'scholars' such as Athanasius Kircher (1602–80) had looked at the script, with its characters of little people, animals, birds and objects from the material world, and decided that it was a symbolic language designed to convey the strange esoteric knowledge of the ancients. In this there is a very small grain of truth. There are two basic types of hieroglyphic sign: phonetic signs and ideograms. Phonetic signs express sounds and, much like individual letters of our alphabet, when arranged in various combinations they express a series of noises forming a word. The most common hieroglyphics are either simple signs making up a form of Egyptian 'alphabet' where the sign broadly equates with a single sound or letter, or other signs which may be biliteral (expressing the sound made by two letters) or triliteral (the sound made by three letters). Ideograms, by contrast, express not sound but meaning; they are most often used as determinatives - that is to say, they appear at the end of a word, which is spelled out phonetically, in order to emphasize what the word is about. For instance, the hieroglyphic sign representing an eye appears at the end of words connected with seeing, the hieroglyphic sign for two legs walking appears at the end of many Egyptian words connected with movement, while Egyptian words for non-concrete concepts (such as *mn*, 'to be enduring') often have a papyrus-roll book as their determinative.

European scholars, particularly Akerblad and Young, made initial progress, recognizing that the oval rings (cartouches) in Egyptian inscriptions, including the Rosetta Stone, contained royal names. But it was the work of the young French prodigy Jean François Champollion (1790–1832) which largely cracked the hieroglyphic code. The royal names Ptolemy and

Egyptian monuments are often usefully self-dated; this inscription refers to 'year 1, third month of summer, day 6' of an unnamed king.

The Rosetta Stone with its text in 3 scripts, the keystone to the decipherment of the ancient Egyptian language.

A cartouche containing one of the most commonly seen royal names, that of King Ramesses II of the Nineteenth Dynasty.

Cleopatra appeared on the Rosetta Stone in their cartouches, as Champollion knew from the Greek text; he was therefore able to go through each cartouche-encircled name, sign by sign, giving it an alphabetic value. This provided an initial list of signs of known values which he could then apply to other royal names and thus, by deduction, work out the values of new signs as he came upon them. Once the phonetic values of the signs were recognized, Champollion and his successors were able to work towards a true translation of Egyptian texts, often comparing the unknown language of the ancient Egyptians with its modern descendant, Coptic, which Champollion knew. It is therefore as much through the texts they have left as through their monuments that we can gain an insight into the civilization of the Ancient Egyptians. ■

ROMANS IN NORTH AFRICA

In the province of Tripolitania, the city of Lepcis (or Leptis) Magna contains a well-preserved theatre dating to AD 1–2, given by a local member of the élite, Annobal Rufus.

Some of the best-preserved of all Roman buildings have survived in North Africa, partly due to the fact that the cities there had not been plundered for building materials to the same degree as is found in other parts of the classical world.

Not only is his name Punic, but the dedicatory inscription is in fact bilingual in Latin and Punic. Another important building from this Augustan period was the market, built in 8 BC. It was enhanced between AD 31 and 37 by the creation of surrounding porticoes, and included two octagonal pavilions within the open courtyard. Some of the most intact buildings are the 'Hunting Baths', where there is still much of the original vaulting over the different rooms of the complex. They appear to date from the late second or early third century.

The emperor Septimius Severus (193–211) was born in the city, which consequently benefited from his patronage in the form of a range of monumental buildings. In addition to a new forum and

basilica, a triumphal arch was erected in his honour, perhaps on the occasion of Septimius' visit to the city in 207. In a series of reliefs the emperor was shown in a chariot alongside his two sons, Caracalla and Geta. Analysis of marble from the city, carried out to trace its source-quarries, has shown how imperial patronage allowed the city to draw on the resources of the wider empire to bedeck itself. In particular, marble from Asia Minor may have been accompanied by sculptors to work on the projects.

The hinterland of the city has also revealed important evidence for the intensive cultivation of olives, whose oil was used for food, lighting and as a cleansing agent. This is also reflected in the

These baths, dating to the late second century AD, are named after murals inside showing a leopard hunt. Sand has protected the concrete roof.

The reconstructed stage building at the theatre at Sabratha.

substantial fine of 3 million Roman pounds of oil which was imposed on the community by Julius Caesar. Large processing 'factories' containing several olive presses have been found. Production on this scale is not likely to have been for the city, and it seems that the owners of the estate were exporting the oil for consumption in cities such as Rome. The wealth derived from this commerce was ploughed back into the city by local patrons.

Lepcis was not the only city to have been preserved in this fashion. On the Libyan coast, excavations at Sabratha – first by the Italians and then after the Second World War by the British archaeologist Dame Kathleen Kenyon – revealed evidence for the earliest Punic settlement as well as the later Roman city. Particularly notable buildings include the first century AD forum and the late second century AD theatre. The increasing use of marble for new buildings, as well as the refurbishment of the old, reflects the way in which the community's prosperity was increasing.

North Africa was also garrisoned, and several large military forts have been explored. In Numidia the colony of Timgad was set up by the Third Legion, which was stationed at nearby Lambaesis. This was a carefully planned city based on a strict grid plan. Under the reign of Septimius Severus a monumental triumphal arch was erected in the city on the road from Lambaesis. The legionary fortress itself has yielded one of the most important documents for the Roman army – the base of a monumental column recording the visit of the emperor Hadrian in AD 128. It consists of an address to the troops, including a comment to the cavalrymen of the Sixth Commagenian Cohort: 'Because of your zeal you kept us wide awake by doing enthusiastically what had to be done.' ∎

The theatre at Sabratha, dating to the late second century AD, was one of the largest in Roman Africa.

NIGERIAN ART: A 'FABERGÉ-LIKE VIRTUOSITY'

The art dates from the mid-first millennium BC to the end of the first and early second millennia AD, a period which saw the transformation of West African societies from Stone Age hunter-gatherers to highly structured iron-using states with power and wealth in the hands of god-like kings. Much more archaeological information needs to be collected before this process and the remarkable artworks and craftsmanship that accompanied it can be understood.

In the late nineteenth century, the museums and art markets of the world were flooded with a vast quantity of extraordinary 'bronze' castings and ivory carvings that had been seized by the Royal Navy as reparations during the Benin Punitive Expedition of 1897 in West Africa. The subsequent plundering of Nigeria's remarkable art heritage resulted in there being little, if any, documentation on the exact sources and contexts of most pieces.

The earliest known terracotta (fired clay which is still porous) human head was found in river gravels during tin-mining operations on the Jos Plateau in central Nigeria in 1928. It was later assigned to the first identifiable iron-using society in West Africa, that of the Nok culture, which is associated with sites having radiocarbon dates between the sixth and second centuries BC, and which is considered to have continued into the first half of the first millennium AD.

Nok terracottas include animals as well as humans, and some are life-size. Characteristics of the human heads include elaborate hairstyles, showing eyes as triangular areas delineated by grooves with a circular hole for the pupil, and clearly negroid features. Physical features and deformities were reproduced with care. Some figures provide information about the Nok culture by carrying tools like hafted axes, or sitting on stools, or wearing beads. It is possible that the heads were part of complete figures, for fragments of limbs and torsos have also been found. It has been suggested that the Nok terracottas are altar figures associated with an agricultural fertility cult.

A remarkable record of the changes in economic and political organization that had occurred by the end of the first millennium AD in the forests of southern Nigeria was unearthed at Igbo Ukwu by the British archaeologist Thurstan Shaw. A cache of bronzes had been found at this site in 1938, but it was Shaw's 1959–60 excavation that led to the discovery of one of the most extraordinary archaeological sites in the world, and evidence that by the ninth century AD wealth was concentrated in the hands of a minority who held religious and probably also political power.

The Igbo Ukwu site was a grave of an important individual, who was seated on a stool placed with three ivory tusks in a deep wood-lined and roofed burial chamber. An upper chamber contained the remains of at least five attendants. Grave goods included a bronze staff and whisk, a copper chest ornament, a crown and over 100,000 glass and carnelian beads, probably originally from India. Two further caches of artifacts were discovered nearby.

The bronze objects, cast by the *cire perdue* or 'lost wax' process, and the finely smithed and chased copper objects, attest to the existence of exceptionally accomplished West African craft specialists. Although the exact source of the copper and tin used at Igbo Ukwu is unknown, the techniques used to work them as well as their chemical composition indicate that they were not of Arab or European origin.

Among the most significant discoveries at early second-millennium AD sites in southern Nigeria are those at Ife. These include a remarkable collection of near life-size terracotta or 'bronze' (actually brass) heads in a naturalistic style. It is thought they were created for various ritual occasions, as they seem to have been kept on altars or shrines in houses. The Ife style is thought by some to be derived, probably indirectly, from the centuries earlier Nok culture.

Cire perdue bronzes of near life-size human heads, plaques, and other figures were produced on a large scale at the southern Nigerian city of Benin from the fifteenth to nineteenth centuries AD, for the ruler, known as the Oba. Suggested stylistic connections with Ife are disputed. ■

A terracotta head from Nok.

Lydenburg Heads

The oldest surviving Iron Age art in southern Africa is a collection of fired clay heads dating to about AD 500, found in 1962 by Dr K. L. von Bezing at Lydenburg in the Eastern Transvaal Province of South Africa, when he was a teenager. Some years later, when Von Bezing went to the University of Cape Town to study medicine, he mentioned his finds to an archaeology student at a meeting of the student Archaeological Field Club. The student in turn reported it to her lecturer, and systematic descriptions of the material and site were undertaken. When assembled and reconstructed, von Bezing's collection of sherds comprised two large sculpted and decorated pottery heads and five smaller ones. They are thought to have been used in rituals, possibly initiation rites, after which they seem to have been deliberately smashed and the pieces discarded into deep pits. Fragments from similar sculptures have been found on other South African Iron Age sites, suggesting that the use of such heads was a widespread practice at the time.

ABOVE: An early-sixteenth-century ivory ornamental mask that formed part of the regalia of an *Oba* (king) of Benin.

LEFT: A head made by the lost wax process of bronze casting, possibly thirteenth century AD. It is thought to be a portrait of an *Oni* (ruler) of Ife.

THE GREATEST ZIMBABWE OF THEM ALL

Zimbabwe is the term used by Shona-speaking Zimbabweans for the court or house of a chief, traditionally comprising a series of stone-walled enclosures built on a hill. Over 150 zimbabwes are known, mostly from the central plateau of Zimbabwe, of which Great Zimbabwe is the largest and most impressive.

The first occupation of the site was by Early Iron Age people, who did not build in stone, between about AD 500 and 900. After about AD 900, Shona people arrived and construction in stone began. Between about AD 1270 and 1450, Great Zimbabwe was the capital of a large southern African Shona empire that stretched from the Zambezi River to the Northern Province of South Africa and eastern Botswana, and was home to some 18,000 people.

At this time, it consisted of three parts: stone-walled enclosures

Perhaps no other archaeological site in the world has so inspired the spread of myths, mystery, romance and patriotic fervour as Great Zimbabwe – a Late Iron Age town in the southern African country of Zimbabwe (which took its name from the archaeological site on achieving independence from Great Britain in 1980).

on and around a bare granite hill, including the residence of the king, members of his family, and officials, as well as places of religious importance; in the valley below, a central area comprising the royal wives' complex, grain bins, and the Great Enclosure (also known as the Elliptical Building); and the surrounding town where the commoners lived. In contrast with most other contemporary southern African societies, the social organization of the Great Zimbabwe people was based on a distinction between commoners and rulers.

The Great Enclosure, the largest and most impressive structure at Great Zimbabwe, has most recently been interpreted as a pre-marriage school. It was built in several stages and its massive outer walls, on one stretch topped by a double chevron design (considered to be a symbol for 'young man' status), are estimated to contain 900,000 stone blocks.

Inside features of the Great Enclosure include a giant conical tower, a solid structure thought to represent a grain bin, which was a symbol for one of the most important functions of the king.

Kings accumulated much wealth and prestige by controlling trade in gold and ivory with the East African coast, as well as a local network of trade in tin, iron bells, copper, salt, soapstone, cattle and grain.

The 18,000 people living at Great Zimbabwe must have placed a huge strain on local resources such as firewood and fertile soil. By AD 1450 it was abandoned, probably for social and environmental reasons, and the capital shifted to Khami in western Zimbabwe. Records of Portuguese missionaries and traders as well as Shona oral tradition show that the Zimbabwe culture persisted in some areas and zimbabwes continued to be built until the nineteenth century, though none as grandiose as Great Zimbabwe.

The first foreigner known to have visited Great Zimbabwe and who revealed the ruins to the western world was an adventurous young German geologist, Carl Mauch. He set off in May 1871 to find 'the most valuable and important and hitherto most mysterious part of Africa', inspired by old Portuguese tales of King Solomon's Ophir recounted by the Rev. A. Merensky, a German missionary in South Africa. After reaching the ruins on 5 September 1871, Mauch set about exploring them during three visits over the next nine months. His romantic account in 1872 of the overgrown but impressive architecture of the ruins and his resurrection of the centuries-old story that they were built by the Queen of Sheba led to immediate popular interest.

Among those whose imaginations were fired by Mauch's account was Cecil John Rhodes, an English-born South African politician and financier, who had ambitions to expand British authority in southern Africa. He was convinced the ruins were a long-lost Phoenician city which stood as a monument to civilization in 'darkest Africa', and which symbolized the need for an external superior colonizing power to uplift 'backward' Africans.

Rhodes' British South Africa Company occupied the region in which Great Zimbabwe is situated in 1890. With the help of the British Association for the Advancement of Science and the Royal Geographic Society, the company sponsored the first investigation of Great Zimbabwe by J. Theodore Bent. Despite his description of the finds as 'native', Bent decided that the ruins had not been built by any known African people.

In 1902–4, Richard Nicklin Hall, a journalist who represented Rhodes' business interests, vandalized the site while ostensibly preparing it for tourist visits. As a result, the British Association for the Advancement of Science sponsored two further expeditions. The first of these, by David Randall MacIver, a trained archaeologist, in 1906, did not produce conclusive evidence. It was not until the second expedition, led by the archaeologist Gertrude Caton Thompson in 1929, that the recovery of datable artifacts in unquestionable contexts established beyond doubt the African origin and medieval date of the ruins.

Despite this and subsequent confirmatory evidence gathered by further scientific investigations over the following decades, however, Great Zimbabwe has never been of purely academic interest, but remains explicitly political. On the one hand, it continues to be burdened with exotic interpretations, fuelled by colonialist and settler beliefs that Africans were incapable of great architectural and cultural achievements. On the other hand, Africans claim the ruins as a reminder of past glories and a symbol of freedom from colonial rule. Some Africans now reject any interpretation of the site that has not been made by black Zimbabweans. Probably no other archaeological site has elicited such divergent and emotional responses as this dramatic ruin.

The Hill of the Jackals

The first site to show many of the characteristics of the Great Zimbabwe tradition was Mapungubwe ('the hill of the jackals'), a flat-topped hill that rises suddenly from the surrounding valley in the Northern Province of South Africa, close to the borders of Zimbabwe and Botswana. It is a natural fortress with almost vertical sides that can be approached only through a single narrow cleft, and was occupied between about AD 1220 and 1270.

In the 1930s, the presence of stone walling, pottery, iron tools, copper wire, glass beads, goldwork and skeletons alerted local farmers to its existence. Subsequent research showed that, like Great Zimbabwe, it had an élite hilltop area where rich burials were found, and further extensive settlement in the valley below, where deep archaeological layers show that houses were built and rebuilt over decades. The impressive goldwork from the graves on the hilltop includes a model of a rhinoceros, as well as carved wooden items covered with sheets of gold held in place by gold tacks.

Mapungubwe seems to have been the capital of a Shona state which controlled trade, initially in ivory and later in gold, with Islamic city states on the East African coast, in exchange for items such as glass beads and Chinese ceramics. It represents a period during which a highly stratified society with ruling chiefs enjoying great wealth and status developed, unlike the simple social structure of its contemporary Iron Age communities in southern Africa. ∎

EUROPE

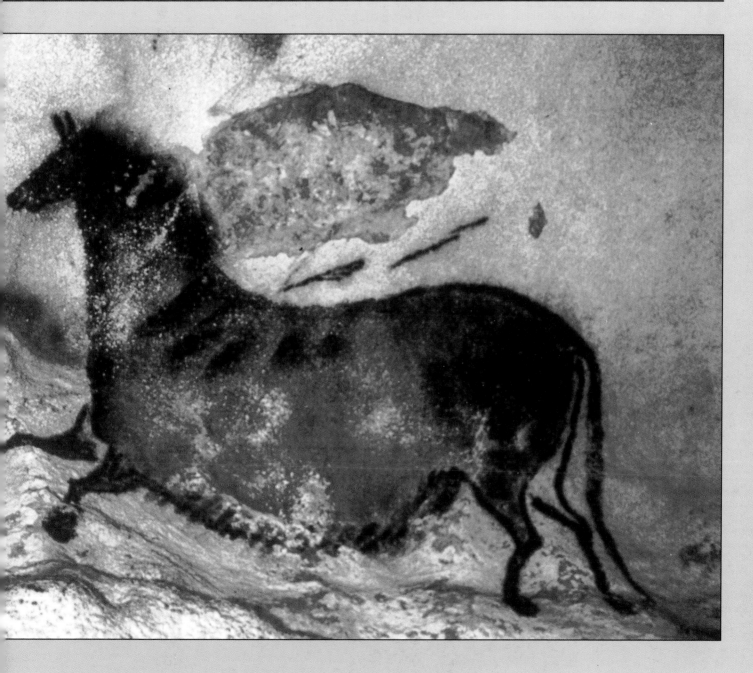

EARLY HUMANS IN WESTERN EUROPE

There were sporadic finds of what were probably Ice Age human remains with stone tools and/or extinct animals in the eighteenth and early nineteenth centuries, but the human bones were never adequately studied or reported. The first real breakthrough occurred in Belgium where, in 1833, Philippe-Charles Schmerling, a Dutch doctor of Austrian origin, published his work in caves around Liège, where he had discovered humans with archaic traits (probably Neandertal burials) in deep layers, associated with tools and remains of extinct fauna. He was the first scholar to discover, save and investigate the potential age of such bones. In 1848 a fairly complete skull – also now known to be a Neandertal – was found in Forbes' Quarry, Gibraltar, but remained forgotten till it was 'rediscovered' in a cupboard in 1862. By that time 'Neandertal Man' had made his appearance. In August 1856 limestone quarrying of a cave in the Neander Valley (the apt name, Greek for 'New Man', came from a hymn-writer called Neumann) near Düsseldorf, Germany, led to the discovery of a skull cap and some other fragments. The skull cap had very prominent ridges above the eyes. A local schoolmaster, Carl Fuhlrott, realized this was not a modern human, and sent a cast to Hermann Schaaffhausen, an anatomist at Bonn University. They argued in a publication that the bones represented a form of human now 'not known to exist' that preceded the Celts. Sceptical academics, however, dismissed the find variously as a Celt, an

In tandem with the discovery of human antiquity (see p. 10), which took place primarily in western Europe, there came the realization that these early humans differed physically from ourselves – a notion that was hard to swallow until the evidence became overwhelming.

ancient Dutchman, a hermit, a wild cannibal, a hydrocephalic idiot, and an 1814 Cossack. The world was not yet ready to accept the physical appearance of fossil humans.

It was somewhat happier with the accidental discovery by railway quarrying at Les Eyzies, Dordogne, in 1868, of the more modern-looking skeletons of three men, a woman and a child, buried in the late Ice Age layers of the Cro-Magnon rockshelter, a site that would give its name to modern humans as a whole.

The next major find – made long after the antiquity of humans had been established and widely accepted – was that of the full Neandertal skeleton at the French site of La-Chapelle-aux-Saints, unearthed in 1908 by three clerics who sent it to anatomist Marcellin Boule for study. Boule, who did not believe Neandertals could be ancestral to modern humans, suggested the features of this old man's deforming osteoarthritis were characteristic of the group, and this distorted view was firmly established for decades. The earliest reconstruction drawing, produced under Boule's guidance, depicted the Neandertal as brutish, shaggy and extremely primitive, with virtually no culture. However other drawings, reflecting the opinions of those with more enlightened views of Neandertals, depicted them as very human-looking, quite cultured, and not shaggy at all, albeit stockier and more robust than modern humans.

The dominance of Belgium, France and Germany in the discoveries of fossil humans in Europe – reinforced by the 1908 find

The skull cap of a Neandertal, found by quarrymen in the Neander Valley near Düsseldorf, Germany, in 1856.

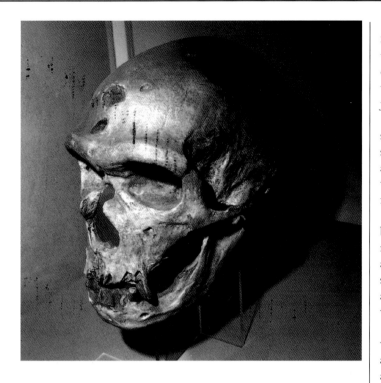

The skull of the skeleton of an arthritic old Neandertal man, found at La Chapelle-aux-Saints, Corrèze, France, in 1908.

Even more remarkable is the site of Atapuerca in northern Spain, which has recently produced over 1600 bones from at least thirty-two and perhaps even fifty individuals: these are also apparently transitional between *Homo erectus* and Neandertals, and date to at least 200,000 years ago. Their accumulated bones are all jumbled together in a 12 m (40 ft) shaft, the *Sima de los Huesos* (Pit of Bones). Most are adolescents and young adults of both sexes. It is thought they may have been thrown into the shaft over several generations in a form of mortuary ritual which, like Neandertal burials, may point to rudimentary religious beliefs. This was not an occupation site, and the bodies were not accumulated in the shaft by carnivores.

The Atapuerca bones represent about 90% of all pre-Neandertal bones ever found in Europe. They were of robust build, with males reaching up to 2 m (6 ft 6 in) in height and weighing an average 65 kg (143 lb). The remains include three very well-preserved skulls with large brow-ridges and projecting faces. One has a brain capacity of 1390 cc (85 in³) – bigger than *Homo erectus* and within the range of modern humans.

A few hundred metres away, in a site called Gran Dolina, excavators in 1994 and 1995 found some very primitive human teeth and skull/jaw fragments from two individuals aged about fifteen and three or four years. They are thought to be between 800,000 and one million years old, which would make them the oldest human remains known in Europe at present. ■

of the extremely archaic Mauer (or Heidelberg) jaw in Germany, possibly 500,000 years old – led to the Piltdown hoax in 1912–15 when a perfect 'missing link' – later found to be a combination of a modern human skull and an ape jaw that had its teeth filed to appear human – emerged from a Sussex gravel pit. Trumpeted as the 'earliest Englishman', Piltdown man was only proved a fake by chemical analysis in 1953.

Authentic finds continued to turn up too – notably, in the 1930s, a whole series of Neandertal burials at the site of La Ferrassie, Dordogne, one of them beneath a stone slab decorated with cupmarks. A Neandertal skull found in the Italian cave of Monte Circeo in 1939 was for decades erroneously interpreted as evidence for cannibalism, whereas it now seems that the cave was a hyena den, and the animals had gnawed the skull.

The fate of Neandertals in western Europe – whether they were somehow wiped out by disease or competition with moderns, or interbred with modern humans – has been made more problematic through recent finds of Neandertals in Spain dating to less than 30,000 years ago (by which time modern humans had been present for millennia), and by the remains at Saint-Césaire, France, of a definite Neandertal associated with a fairly modern tool-kit, which dates to 36,300 years ago.

A spectacular find was made very recently in the cave of Altamura, Puglia (southeast Italy). A complete human skeleton has been discovered deep inside, where it was enveloped by cauliflower-like stalagmite formations, some growing on and around it. Thought to be the oldest intact human skeleton in Europe, it lies on its back; and the features of its skull have led specialists to estimate that it is an archaic *Homo sapiens*, transitional between *Homo erectus* (known in Europe at least 500,000 years ago) and Neandertals (who appeared between 200,000 and 130,000 years ago) – an age of 400,000 years has been tentatively suggested.

The skull of the skeleton from the rockshelter of Saint-Césaire, Charente-Maritime (France); dating to 36,300 years ago, it is one of the last Neandertals in Europe, though even more recent specimens are known from Zafarraya in southern Spain.

ICE AGE SETTLEMENT OF THE NORTH

Although the first humans evolved in Africa (see pp. 14–23), early humans in the form of *Homo erectus* spread eastward into the tropical regions of Asia roughly two million years ago. By at least a million years ago, people had also moved into the temperate zone of Eurasia. At 'Ubeidiya in Israel, people camped along the shore of a lake, leaving the remains of stone chopping tools and crude handaxes. Recently, a *Homo erectus* jaw was discovered, along with simple stone tools, at Dmanisi on the southern slope of the Caucasus Mountains in the Republic of Georgia. Both of these sites may date as far back as 1.5 million years ago. It is widely believed that an increased emphasis on meat in the diet – obtained through hunting and scavenging – permitted this dispersal across the lower latitudes of Eurasia.

Sites have also been reported from Europe that date back to a million years or more, but they remain controversial. These sites typically contain fractured pebbles and rocks interpreted as crude chopping and scraping tools, and are often associated with the re-

One of the most dramatic and controversial topics in archaeology is the early settlement of northern areas. The earliest sites in Europe and southern Siberia now appear to be at least several hundred thousand years old, but the debate continues over claims of even older traces of human settlement, raising the question not only of when people first invaded these northern landscapes, but of how they managed to cope with these comparatively hostile environments and how their adaptations may have influenced the course of human evolution.

mains of various extinct animals. The best-known site is the cave of Le Vallonnet on the southern coast of France. More convincing evidence has been unearthed at several somewhat younger localities, including the open-air site of Prezletice near Prague and the newly reported cave of Treugol'naya in the northern Caucasus. Perhaps the most startling recent discovery is the Diring site, located along the banks of the Lena River in Siberia at a latitude of 61° North, and thought by some to date to a million years. Diring provides an excellent illustration of the debate that invariably surrounds a new find of this sort. Although most archaeologists have accepted the stone artifacts as genuine products of human manufacture, the dating of the site remains hotly disputed, and many believe that it is much younger.

Regardless of the outcome of the Diring controversy it is apparent that, by at least 700,000 years ago, people had colonized the cooler temperate landscapes above latitude 45° North. It is not yet clear whether these first northern settlers were representatives of *Homo erectus*, or very primitive early forms of our own larger-brained species, *Homo sapiens*, but the oldest known human fossil in Europe – a jaw discovered in a quarry at Mauer near Heidelberg in 1907 – appears to belong to the latter. How did people adapt to these new landscapes that are likely to have challenged their existing way of life in terms of cooler temperatures, increased seasonal fluctuations, and reduced wealth of plant foods? Much of the adjustment may have been technological, involving the control and use of fire and improve-

LEFT: Treugol'naya cave, northern Caucasus, Russia, where evidence of early humans in Europe was found.

ments in clothing. What role did these new adaptations play in the evolutionary transition to _Homo sapiens_? Too much uncertainty continues to surround the dating of human fossil remains from this time period to answer this question at present.

If some of the more temperate regions of Europe were settled over half a million years ago, many parts of northern Eurasia remained unoccupied for another several hundred thousand years. Not until after 150,000 years ago is there convincing evidence for human colonization of the central Russian Plain at sites such as Khotylevo on the Desna River, and of southern Siberia at several caves located in the Altai region. The people who invaded these regions were the contemporaries, and perhaps the relatives, of the European Neandertals; although their fossil remains are scarce, their tools are common and very similar to those of the Neandertals. As before, the reasons for this new expansion are obscure. The environments of central Russia and southern Siberia were much harsher than those of temperate Europe, even during the warmest intervals of the Ice Age. In fact, with the onset of the last major cold period of the Ice Age roughly 70,000 years ago, many of these newly colonized regions may have been abandoned. Eventually, they were reoccupied by modern human populations. Some archaeologists believe that modern humans had developed a significant organizational advantage over their Neandertal predecessors as an adaptation to the scarcer and less predictable food resources of the harshest glacial landscapes in Europe.

Despite their ability to cope with glacial environments, humans did not advance into the modern arctic zone until the close of the Ice Age between 12,000 and 10,000 years ago. Russian archaeologists working in northeastern Siberia some years ago discovered a camp site dating to this period on a small river near the Arctic Ocean at latitude 71° North. This site, which is known as Berelekh, is the northernmost Ice Age occupation in the world. It was the successful colonization of such regions that opened the door to the New World by permitting a human population to spread across the land bridge between northeastern Asia and Alaska that was formed by the lowered sea-levels of the glacial period. ∎

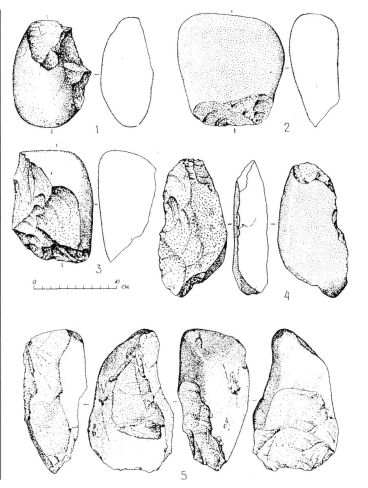

MAMMOTH-BONE HOUSES
OF EASTERN EUROPE

The remains of several mammoth-bone houses may have been encountered as early as the turn of the century at Kiev in the Ukraine. However, not expecting the presence of 'ruins' among Ice Age deposits, the excavators apparently failed to appreciate the significance of the mass of large bones found at this site. In the years following the Bolshevik Revolution, archaeologists working in Russia and the Ukraine adopted a Marxist theoretical approach to their research, and placed strong emphasis on the social and economic character of the prehistoric record. This new outlook seems to have stimulated recognition of previously overlooked aspects of that record, including the remains of various types of dwelling structures in Stone Age sites. The first such dwelling was reported in 1927 from an Ice Age camp site along the Don River in Russia by the young Soviet archaeologist, Sergei Zamyatnin. It now appears likely to have been a mammoth-bone house, although most of the mammoth bones were apparently washed away after its Stone Age occupants had abandoned the site. In the years following the Second World War, archaeologists working in Eastern Europe discovered mammoth-bone houses at a number of sites in Russia, the Ukraine, Belarus and Poland. Radiocarbon dating of the houses revealed that they had been built during the last major cold period of the Ice Age – between 25,000 and 14,000 years ago – when eastern Europe was a largely treeless arctic steppe.

Besides the cave art of Europe, the most spectacular archaeological discoveries of the Ice Age are undoubtedly the remains of houses constructed from the bones and tusks of the woolly mammoth. They represent the most ancient human architecture known on earth – some of them are at least 20,000 years old.

The most carefully studied mammoth-bone houses are those at the site of Mezhirich, located along the banks of a small river near the city of Kiev. The houses at Mezhirich are es-

A pit with mammoth tusks at Kostenki on the Don River in Russia.

pecially well preserved and apparently typical of mammoth-bone structures on the east European Plain. Excavation of the site, which began in 1966 under the leadership of the late Ukrainian archaeologist and palaeontologist Ivan Pidoplichko, has continued to the present decade. At least four collapsed structures have been discovered to date. They are composed of several hundred bones and tusks arranged in a rough circle, between 6 and 10 m (20 and 33 ft) in diameter. A hearth typically lies near the centre of the former dwelling, and stone tools and other debris are scattered within and outside the structure. Large pits filled with stone tools, bone fragments and ash have been found near the houses.

Considerable effort must have been required to assemble these structures. Even in a dry state, large mammoth bones weigh hundreds of pounds. It has been suggested that the bones and tusks were recovered from hunting episodes in which entire herds of adult mammoth and their young were slaughtered. A more likely explanation is that they were gathered from natural accumulations of bones, perhaps at the mouths of streams and gullies near the sites. The primary purpose of the mammoth-bone dwellings, which were presumably covered with animal skins, was probably shelter from extreme cold and high winds. Some archaeologists, impressed with the size and appearance of the structures, have argued that they also possess religious or social significance. They have been described as the earliest examples of 'monumental architecture' and as evidence of increased social complexity and status differentiation during the final phase of the Ice Age. ∎

A reconstruction of a mammoth-bone house at Mezhirich in the Ukraine.

PALAEOLITHIC PORTABLE ART

The first pieces of portable art from the last Ice Age were found in 1833 at Veyrier, Haute Savoie. They comprised a decorated harpoon and a crude engraving, possibly of a bird. In 1852 an engraving of hinds on a reindeer bone from Chaffaud, Vienne, was catalogued as 'Celtic' in a museum – the oldest period that could then be envisaged – until it was recognized as Palaeolithic (i.e., of the Old Stone Age) by Edouard Lartet (see p. 11) a few years later.

In 1860 Lartet dug in the cave of Massat in the French Pyrenees, and found Ice Age tools and fauna together with a bone with a bear's head engraved on it. It was the first piece of Palaeolithic art ever found by someone with a knowledge of stratigraphy and human antiquity. The subsequent excavations in the Dordogne region resulted not only in the discovery of the La Madeleine mammoth engraving (see p. 11) and Vibraye's 'Venus', but also in a wealth of other art objects: decorated tools, carvings, engravings on stone and bone. These finds triggered an uncon-

The discovery of Ice Age portable art in Europe – dating from over 30,000 to 10,000 years ago – coincided with the period when the antiquity of humans was being established and accepted (see p. 10). It revealed to the world for the first time the astonishing sophistication and the mastery of a wide range of techniques displayed by what were then considered the 'first artists'.

trolled, random 'gold rush' as people began to pillage rock-shelters with pickaxes in search of stone and bone tools and, especially portable Ice Age art. There was no conception yet of noting the position or context of finds, and fine objects, dug up like potatoes, were of supreme importance. Ignorance and greed on the part of the untrained labourers employed on most sites led to a great deal of theft and fakery – a few famous specimens of Ice Age art 'found' at this time may well be fakes. In 1867 Paris's 'Universal Exhibition' displayed Palaeolithic portable art to the world for the first time.

The first similar discovery in central Europe occurred in 1874 when a young teacher, Konrad Merk, found the famous engraving of a reindeer in the Swiss cave of Kesslerloch bei Thayngen. Great collections were amassed in western Europe, most notably by the French pioneer Edouard Piette, a magistrate and geologist whose series of major excavations in the Pyrenees (at Brassempouy, Le Mas d'Azil, etc.) produced an unrivalled assemblage of Palaeolithic

An antler carving, 10.5 cm (4 in) long, from the rock-shelter of La Madeleine, Dordogne, France, depicts a bison turning to lick a wound or parasites on its flank, and displays the Ice Age artists' acute observations of the natural world.

RIGHT: One of the 400 engraved schist plaques from the open-air site of Gönnersdorf, Germany, dating to 12,600 years ago. These figures are interpreted as highly stylized female forms with prominent buttocks.

BELOW: An antler spearthrower from Bruniquel, Tarn-et-Garonne, southwest France; such objects had animals carved in the round at the hook-end, where the roughly triangular area of available antler dictated the posture and size of the figure – here a leaping horse.

portable art which he donated to the Musée des Antiquités Nationales, despite being financially ruined by his researches. It was also Piette who initiated a young priest, Henri Breuil (see p. 59), into the study of Palaeolithic art by employing him to draw his art objects.

Unlike cave art (see p. 58), portable art did not appear mysterious in any way, so it was generally explained as simple decoration, although in 1887 French prehistorian Gustave Chauvet suggested it had a magical motivation, whereby an injury to the image would also be inflicted on the real animal.

Important finds of Palaeolithic portable art continue to be made to this day. Among the most notable examples are 'super sites' like the caves of Isturitz and Le Mas d'Azil, in the French Pyrenees, with hundreds of fine specimens in each; the Pyrenean cave of Enlène, which has yielded over 1100 engraved plaques of stone, as well as many bone and antler carvings; the Spanish cave of Parpalló, with over 5000 engraved and/or painted stone plaques; a group of caves in southwest Germany which have produced a highly sophisticated series of ivory carvings of animals and humans dating to before 30,000 years ago; the German open-air camp of Gönnersdorf, with 400 engraved plaques, including a remarkable collection of what appear to be highly stylized women. Most spectacular of all, perhaps, are the engraved stone slabs from the French rockshelter of La Marche, which feature some wonderful depictions of a wide variety of animals, but are particularly noteworthy for their 115 caricature-like portraits of humans, dating to 14,280 years ago. ■

PALAEOLITHIC CAVE ART

Don Marcelino Sanz de Sautuola (1831–88) was a gentleman landowner in Santander Province, northern Spain, who had become a well-known collector of antiquities. In 1878 he visited the Paris Universal Exhibition, and was deeply impressed by the Palaeolithic portable art on show there (see p. 56). In 1879 he returned to the cave of Altamira where, a few years earlier, he had noticed black painted signs on a wall. In November, while he was digging in the cave floor, searching for prehistoric tools and portable art, his little daughter Maria was playing in the cavern. Suddenly she spotted the cluster of great polychrome bison paintings on the ceiling.

Her father, at first incredulous, became more interested when he found that the figures seemed to be done with a fatty paste, and noticed the close similarity in style between these huge figures and the small portable depictions he had seen in Paris. He

Although by no means the world's oldest art, or the only Ice Age art in the world, the decorated caves of Europe have long held a special place in archaeology, largely because of the early date at which their existence and antiquity were established and because of the spectacular nature of much of their imagery.

therefore deduced that the cave art was of similar age, but his attempts to present his views and his discovery to the academic establishment met with widespread rejection and accusations of naivety or fraud: at the 1880 International Congress of Anthropology and Prehistoric Archaeology in Lisbon, his claims were dismissed contemptuously by Emile Cartailhac, a leading French prehistorian who had been forewarned by the virulently anti-clerical prehistorian Gabriel de Mortillet that some anti-evolutionist Spanish Jesuits were going to try to make prehistorians look silly. (De Sautuola died prematurely in 1888, a sad and disillusioned man.)

Figures had also been noticed on the walls of some French caves in the 1860s and 1870s, but their dates, and therefore their

One of the remarkable polychrome bison painted on the low ceiling of the cave of Altamira, northern Spain, and dating to about 12,000 BC.

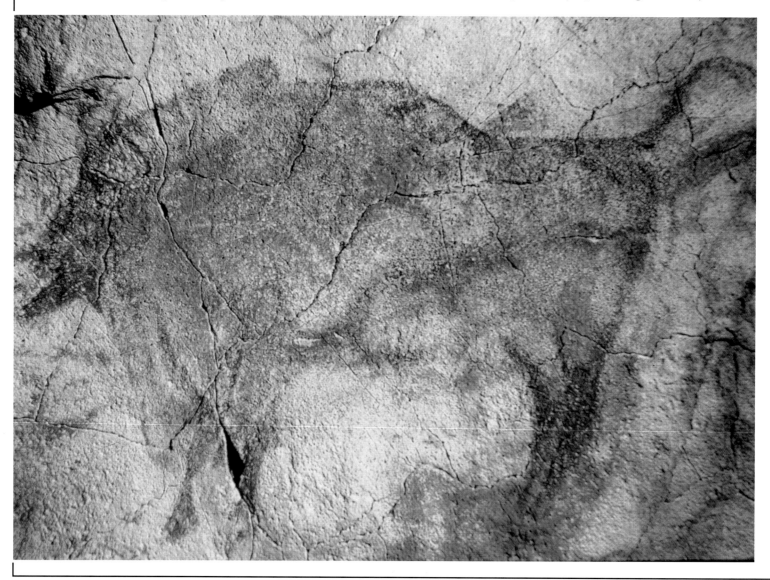

The so-called 'Chinese horses' of Lascaux Cave, Dordogne, France. Discovered in 1940, it is one of the richest of all Ice Age decorated caves, with about 600 paintings and nearly 1,500 engravings. (Note how perspective is suggested by the far-side limbs being left unconnected to the body.)

significance, remained unknown. The breakthrough came in 1895 at the cave of La Mouthe, Dordogne, where the removal of sediments containing Palaeolithic material exposed an unknown gallery with figures engraved on its walls: these were clearly very ancient. Discoveries followed in other French caves, culminating in those of Les Combarelles and Font de Gaume in 1901. By 1902 the 'prehistoric establishment' had officially accepted the existence and authenticity of Palaeolithic cave art; Cartailhac published his famous article, 'Mea culpa d'un sceptique', in which he openly (though somewhat grudgingly) admitted his earlier mistake; and de Sautuola was vindicated. A new 'gold rush' like that for portable art was now triggered, and a great number of decorated caves were discovered in the early twentieth century.

Henri Breuil's talent for drawing Piette's finds (see p. 57) eventually brought him to the attention of Cartailhac, with whom he began to study the newly discovered cave art of La Mouthe, Altamira, etc. By his own reckoning, Breuil spent over 700 days underground, copying cave drawings. Until the end of his long life he dominated not only the field of Palaeolithic art but the whole study of prehistory.

Whereas Palaeolithic portable art was generally explained as simple decoration, it was the acceptance of cave art at the turn of the century, together with emerging ethnographic accounts from Australia that in 1903 led Salomon Reinach, director of the Musée des Antiquités Nationales, to replace the 'art for art's sake' theory with the concept of hunting magic (see p. 57) which, through Breuil's influence, was to dominate for decades, until replaced by French ethnologist André Leroi-Gourhan's theories (now largely abandoned in their turn) of sexual symbolism and of caves decorated according to a standardized blueprint.

Once the authenticity of the cave art had been proved, discoveries snowballed of caves and rockshelters containing engravings, paintings, bas-relief sculpture or even work in clay. In southern France there was a whole series of decorated caves of huge importance – for example, Niaux (1906); Le Tuc d'Audoubert (1912) with its clay bison; Les Trois Frères (1914); Pech Merle (1922), with its famous panel of 'spotted' horses; and Montespan (1923) with its clay statues including a large, sphinx-like bear.

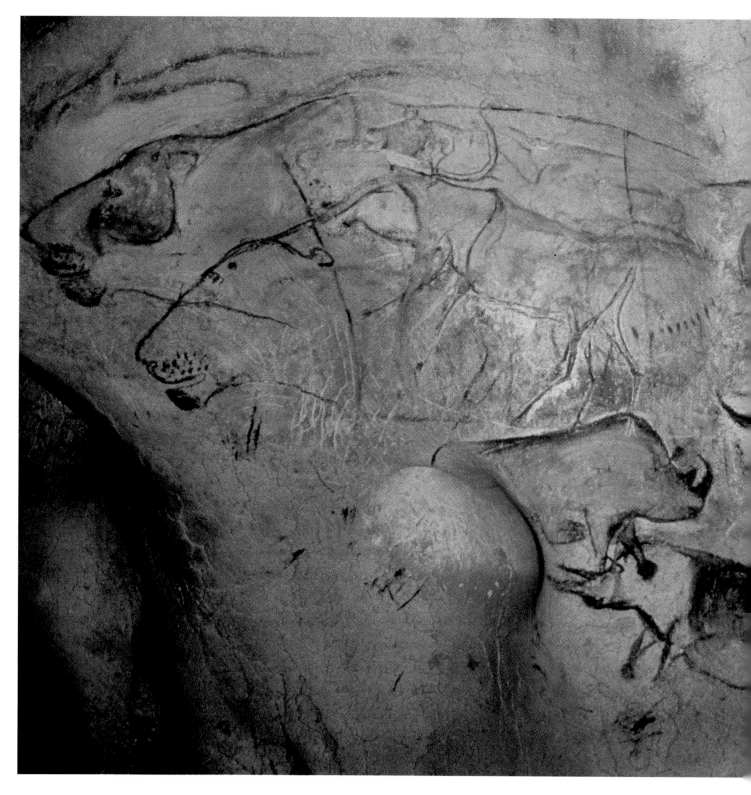

Likewise in northern Spain, Hermilio Alcalde del Rio, a professor from a vocational school who had worked with Cartailhac and Breuil at Altamira, discovered art in a whole series of caves, such as El Castillo, Covalanas and Pindal.

The best known find of all was the cave of Lascaux, still the most spectacular and magnificent gallery of Ice Age art ever discovered. Located near Montignac in Dordogne, it was found in 1940, in wartime, by four teenage boys exploring a hole they had discovered in some woods. Once deep inside, they lit a lamp and began to notice colour on the walls: what they had stumbled upon was an incredible collection of 600 paintings and nearly 1500 engravings, preserved in astonishing clarity. The art is generally seen as a composition of around 17,000 years ago, but in fact it probably comprises a large number of artistic episodes from different phases. The great 'Hall of Bulls' is dominated by four huge black bulls up to 5 m (16 ft 5in) in length, the biggest figures known in Palaeolithic art. The cave also has numerous horse and deer figures; and one narrow passage with paintings on its

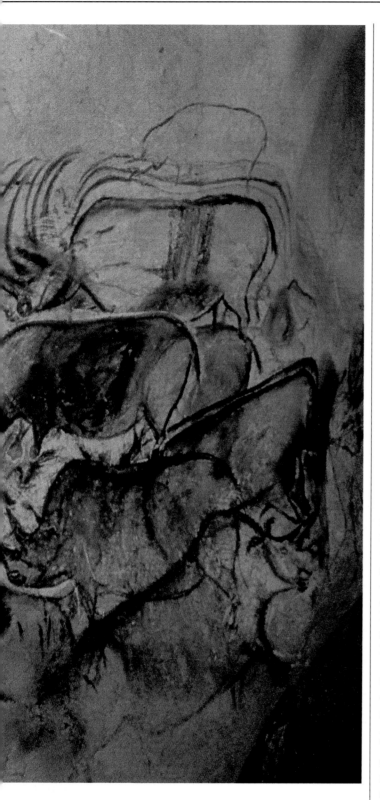

Instead a superb facsimile, Lascaux II, which enthrals hundreds of thousands of visitors every year, was opened nearby in 1983.

New finds continue to be made: an average of one new cave per year is still found in France and Spain, though caves are also known in Italy, and there are two in the Russian Urals. Most recently, the spectacular Grotte Cosquer was discovered by a diver near Marseilles — its entrance, on dry land at the time when the art was produced (27,000–18,000 years ago), was drowned by the rising sea-level at the end of the Ice Age. And at Christmas 1994 in the Ardèche there was the discovery of the remarkable Grotte Chauvet, whose early dates, forty-seven rhinoceroses and thirty-six large felines have forced a radical change in theories about cave art, which was previously thought to be dominated by horses and bison. Chauvet confirms, if confirmation were needed, that Palaeolithic cave art has nothing to do with hunting in any direct sense. It has complex meaning, probably religious in nature, or linked to mythologies.

In recent years, detailed analyses of pigments used in cave paintings have detected the frequent use of organic materials such as charcoal, and these can be directly dated by the radiocarbon method. The results, obtained in eight caves so far including Altamira, reveal a far greater complexity than had been thought. The caves are not random collections of individual images, nor are they single homogeneous compositions. Instead they seem to comprise episodic accumulations of compositions from different periods of the Ice Age, with retouching of images and re-use of panels.

In the 1980s and 1990s a series of discoveries have revealed that 'cave art' was also produced in the open air. Indeed this was probably the commonest form of art production in the Ice Age, but the vast majority of it has succumbed to the weathering of many millennia, leaving us with the figures that survived better inside caves. Only six sites are known so far, in Spain, Portugal and France, but they comprise hundreds of figures, mostly hammered into rocks, which by their style and content seem Ice Age in date. ∎

high walls and ceiling still preserves sockets that held beams for scaffolding.

The cave was opened to the public in 1948, but ten years later it became obvious that the 100,000 annual visitors were damaging the art with their breath, body heat and, especially, the algae and pollen carried in on their shoes: green patches were growing, and white crystals were forming on the walls. In 1963 Lascaux was closed; the algae were virtually eradicated, and the crystals kept in check, but the public could never again be allowed in en masse.

ICE AGE ART AND BURIALS
OF CENTRAL EUROPE

The predecessors of anatomically modern humans in Europe – the Neandertals – seem to have been an uncultured lot who left behind little in the way of artistic achievement. They may have manufactured some simple ornaments during their final period, and they apparently buried their dead, although the nature of their burials remains controversial. By contrast, from the time of their first appearance in Europe, modern human populations created highly sophisticated human and animal sculptures. One of the most striking examples of this early art is the female statuette, carved in green serpentine, found in 1988 at Galgenberg Hill on the Danube River in northeastern Austria and dating to almost 32,000 years ago. Other examples of portable sculp-

Although Ice Age cave art has never been found in Central Europe, apart from some traces of engravings on cave walls in southwest Germany, the region is rich in sophisticated portable art as old as the oldest cave art of western Europe. It includes ornaments, decorated stone and bone and a wide variety of small figurines made not only of stone and ivory but even of fired earth.

tures from the same period include an anthropomorphic figurine of ivory with a feline head from Hohlenstein-Stadel in Germany, and realistic small ivory carvings of woolly mammoth, a horse and other animals from Vogelherd cave in southwest Germany. The sudden florescence of art probably reflects a new emphasis on the use of symbols in human society, which may have conferred a significant organizational advantage over the doomed Neandertals.

If some ambiguity still surrounds the Neandertal graves, modern humans certainly buried their dead with clear intent and sometimes considerable fuss. The most impressive of the early burials is the mass grave uncovered in 1894 at Předmostí in Moravia by Karel Maska, a pioneer Stone Age archaeologist in central Europe. The remains of eighteen people – ten children

A shell necklace recovered from Dolní Věstonice.

The Galgenberg 'Venus' recovered in 1988 from an Ice Age camp site along the Danube in northeastern Austria and dated by radiocarbon to almost 32,000 years ago.

The richest collection of Ice Age sculpture and engravings has also been discovered in Moravia and in the adjoining region of Lower Austria. At several major sites in Moravia, Czech archaeologists have uncovered hundreds of animal and human figurines, many of them modelled in fired loess soil. The animals are often rendered with great skill and realism, and provide true portraits of species that vanished thousands of years ago, including mammoth, woolly rhinoceros and cave lion. Among human figurines, the 'Venus' statuettes are the most widely known. They are found in sites across much of the continent, although the most famous examples have been unearthed in sites such as Willendorf in Austria, which yielded a rotund limestone figure, and Dolní Vestonice in the Czech Republic whose 'Venus' was made of fired loess. The significance of their broad geographic distribution remains a mystery, but they are generally thought to possess religious meaning. These sites also contain other human images including some remarkable ivory sculptures and engravings of individuals – the first glimpse of a human face from the depths of prehistory. ■

A human head carved in mammoth ivory from Dolní Věstonice.

and eight adults – were excavated from a large oval pit beneath stone slabs and mammoth bones dating to between 30,000 and 25,000 years ago. Here, as well as in other Ice Age burials in Moravia, the dead were interred with ornaments and grave goods. At Brno, for example, a male skeleton was found with a necklace of shells and various other decorations and art objects. At Dolní Vestonice, a unique triple burial – of two young men with a young woman between them – was uncovered in 1986, and dates to 26,640 years ago.

The 'Venus of Willendorf' from the banks of the Danube.

ICE AGE ART AND BURIALS
OF EASTERN EUROPE

Before the appearance of modern humans in Eurasia – roughly 40,000 years ago – there is little evidence of ornamentation or art. Other than several isolated specimens from Neandertal sites, the earliest art known in eastern Europe has been recovered from Kostenki along the banks of the Don River in Russia. In the early 1950s, the late Soviet archaeologist Pavel Boriskovskii found stone pendants, perforated fox teeth, and other simple ornaments in deeply buried deposits dating to at least 35,000 years ago. Other slightly younger examples of early Ice Age art include bone fragments with incised geometric designs. Figurative art is extremely rare in eastern Europe until after 25,000 years ago, although some examples of both human and animal figurines have been found in western Europe that are 30,000 years old.

The well-known 'Venus' figurines are remarkably widespread across the European continent, from southwest France (see p. 56) to Siberia. The first Russian example was found in 1923 in deposits at Kostenki dating to roughly 24,000–22,000 years ago.

Ice Age cave art as found in western Europe is almost unknown in eastern Europe and Siberia – except for a painted cave in Romania and two in the Ural Mountains – but archaeologists in these regions have discovered a wealth of portable sculpture and engravings that tell us much about the lives of the people who inhabited these frozen plains and forests. Burials are rare but they offer further insight into the people and culture of this remote period.

Many other examples have been discovered elsewhere in Russia and the Ukraine, mostly carved in mammoth ivory or in limestone. Their styles vary, since these figurines seem to depict females of a wide variety of ages and physical types. They have generally been interpreted as objects of religious or ritual significance, although Soviet archaeologists of the 1930s also saw them as reflections of the political structure of matriarchal societies. Their continent-wide distribution is unique among Ice Age art forms, and may mark a large population movement at the beginning of the final major cold period of the Ice Age.

The classic 'Venus' figurines are unknown in Siberia, although female statuettes have been recovered from several locations there, most notably at the sites of Mal'ta and Buret' near Lake Baikal. These statuettes are especially interesting because they depict the well-insulated clothing, including headgear, that must have been essential for survival in Ice Age Siberia. Mal'ta and Buret' have also yielded a wealth of animal figurines, including ducks, swans, and other waterfowl. Animal art in the east European sites is more typically confined to the large mammals, such as mammoth, rhinoceros, lion and others, that were so important to the lives of these people. Although animals were sometimes modelled in a stylistic or impressionistic manner, they were often rendered with great realism and attention to detail.

Ice Age burials are rare in central and eastern Europe and Siberia. In a land where caves are uncommon, graves were exposed to the ravages of frost-heaving and scavenging animals. Most of the known burials date roughly to 30,000–

A female figurine, 47 mm (2 in) tall and carved in mammoth ivory, found at the site of Kostenki I in 1983. It was upright in a small, ochre-filled pit covered by a mammoth shoulder-blade. Note the rare depiction of eyes, nose and mouth.

20,000 years ago. The most spectacular examples are the multiple graves found in the 1960s near the Russian city of Vladimir by the late Soviet archaeologist Otto Bader. The burials at Sungir' include two adolescents and an older adult who were interred with a considerable amount of ornamentation comprising bracelets, pendants, necklaces, and rings, as well as with grave goods such as spears and stone tools. The graves, like those of Moravia, were liberally sprinkled with red ochre and charcoal. A child burial of comparable age at Mal'ta, although less elaborate than the Sungir' graves, also yielded sophisticated ornamentation in the form of a complex necklace. These burials suggest that – weather permitting – Ice Age people may have been dressed and decorated with more elegance than generally imagined by archaeologists or the popular media. ∎

RIGHT AND BELOW: One grave at Sungir', *c.* 24,000 years old, contained two youngsters, aged 8 and 13, head to head. They were accompanied by numerous objects of mammoth ivory and each body was covered with about 3500 ivory beads, presumably attached to now-vanished clothing.

THE FISHERS OF LEPENSKI VIR

Between 7000 and 8000 years ago, agriculture came to southeastern Europe. In the Carpathian mountains, where the Danube passes through a series of gorges called the Iron Gates, lived communities of fishers and hunters who took advantage of the natural abundance in this area. They built large settlements of trapezoidal houses and made unusual limestone carvings. In the end, they adopted agriculture, but for nearly a millennium they were a distinctive island in the midst of surrounding agricultural settlement.

In the gorges where the Danube cuts through the Carpathian mountains, on the border between Serbia and Romania, lie a series of sites belonging to the hunters, fishers and farmers who lived along the river over 7000 years ago. Perhaps the most famous of these sites is the enigmatic Lepenski Vir, located on a bend in the Danube on the Serbian side of the frontier.

The location of Lepenski Vir was well-chosen, for the bend in the Danube creates a large whirlpool that traps algae and lures fish to feed there. The gorge also shelters the site from extreme winds and creates a very uniform local climate. From about 6000 BC, for a millennium or more, the terrace along the river was occupied by successive communities who lived primarily on the bounty of the river in front of them and the hills behind them, but who in time adopted agriculture.

Lepenski Vir was discovered in 1960 by a group of archaeologists from Belgrade who were not particularly enthusiastic about the potential for it to be a rich site. Over the next couple of years, plans were developed for a hydroelectric damming project which would flood the Danube gorges, so Dragoslav Srejovic of the University of Belgrade took another look in 1965 and was astonished by the results of some trial trenches. Beneath the later layers which did not impress the archaeological party in 1960 lay traces of a hitherto unknown society. Excavations began in earnest in 1966 and were completed in 1968.

These excavations revealed a community of about twenty-five trapezoidal-plan houses which had their wide ends facing the river. The houses occurred in four basic sizes: 5.5, 9.5, 17 and 28 m² (59, 102, 182 and 300 ft²). Each had a central stone-lined hearth sunk into the limestone plaster floor, often surrounded by stone slabs. The roofs of the houses appear to have been somewhat lightweight lean-tos of saplings and twigs.

In many of the houses were enigmatic carved limestone boulders, with human-like faces but with fish-like mouths and abstract ornamentation thought to represent scales. These boulders, between 20 and 60 cm (8 and 24 in) high, are some of the earliest examples of 'monumental' three-dimensional sculpture. Although their purpose and symbolism is unclear, it is certain that they had a significant meaning for the inhabitants of Lepenski Vir. A number of burials were also found in and around the houses, reflecting an integration of settlement and cemetery.

From the animal bones, we know that fish from the Danube played a key role in the diet, and the rich aquatic life around the nearby whirlpool was probably this location's main attraction for settlement. Among the bones of land mammals, wild animals such as red deer and boar predominate in the early phase of the settlement, but by the later phases domestic cattle, sheep, goats and pigs were more important.

Lepenski Vir, and neighbouring settlements in Serbia and Romania like Padina, Icoana, Schela Cladovei and Vlasac, represent a series of complex specialized fishing communities in the Iron Gates region. At the same time, they were in the midst of the great transformation from hunting and gathering to agriculture. The rich aquatic resources of the Danube permitted them a level of security that made the switch to agriculture and stock-herding less urgent, but in the end they adopted domestic plants and animals by about 5000 BC. ∎

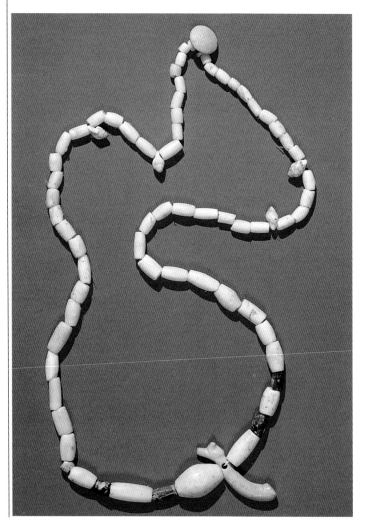

LEFT: An enigmatic fish-like sculpture found in one of the trapezoidal huts at Lepenski Vir.

BELOW: An abstract sculpture from Lepenski Vir that the excavator has named 'the deer in the forest'.

LEFT: Necklace with beads, made from *Spondylus* shell, stone and bone, found in a storage vessel at Lepenski Vir. The shell and stone (known as *paligorskite*) are believed to have reached the settlement through long-distance trade.

ÇATAL HÜYÜK

The Neolithic revolution brought about many basic changes to the ways in which people lived. Most obviously, people came to dwell year-round in villages that stored enough food from the annual harvest to get though the year. The stability of residence allowed people to accumulate wealth that the necessary mobility of earlier hunters had prevented them from owning. For the most part, the early villages were small, containing several dozen houses and several hundred people. Even by 4000 BC and later across much of the Near East, settlements typically were not larger than 2 or 4 hectares (5 or 10 acres) in area, and held only 500 to 1000 people. By this standard, Jericho (see p. 140) was unusual, and Çatal Hüyük was astonishing. Çatal Hüyük covered some 20 hectares (50 acres), a size that qualifies the place as a town, even by the standards of later Mesopotamian civilizations.

British archaeologist James Mellaart's excavations during the 1960s uncovered fourteen building levels that dated roughly to between 6250 and 5400 BC, with deeper levels left unexcavated. The town was composed of houses solidly packed together into a single mass of architecture, without any evident streets or alleys.

Set in the Konya Plain of south central Turkey, the Neolithic settlement of Çatal Hüyük was remarkable for its size. Moreover, the inhabitants possessed unusual wealth, much of it brought from great distances, and had a very rich and expressive ritual life.

Multiple burial below a house. At Çatal Hüyük, as in many cultures in different places and times in the Near East, people buried their dead beneath the floors of houses that continued to be used, thus making the dead a part of the living household. Many of the Çatal Hüyük tombs were used repeatedly as different members of the family died and were interred in the common crypt.

The mudbrick and timber houses contained rooms around an open courtyard, with entrances apparently through the roof. The typical residence contained around 23 m² (250 ft²) of floor space that was divided into one large room and a smaller storeroom. The main room was usually equipped with a variety of clay platforms, benches, hearths, ovens, bins, and other fixed equipment. Mellaart estimated that the town contained perhaps 1000 houses and a population of 5000 to 6000 people at any one phase of its existence.

By this time, farming and herding had come to supply most of the diet. At Çatal Hüyük, the ordinary strains of wheat and barley were supplemented by species that required irrigation to grow, implying that this Anatolian community had created a system of canals to water their fields. Among the animals domesticated cattle were particularly important. But the town's economy involved far more than farming. Potters made a crude ware, starting in an early phase of the town's history. Weavers made woollen and linen textiles, fragments of which have been preserved in burials. The many stone stamps, carved with geometric decorations, may have been used to decorate the textiles. Metal objects, including a lead pendant and copper beads from fairly early phases of the town, also appear in small numbers. These objects are among the oldest known examples of metallurgy in the Near East, and provide vital information about the beginnings of this important technology.

Remarkable as these discoveries are, Çatal Hüyük is best known for the indications of a rich ritual life. The bright murals that decorated the walls of many houses feature plain panels, textile patterns, landscapes, hunting scenes, and other elaborate motifs. Shrine rooms were distinguished from ordinary houses by elaborate ornamentation that focused on bulls. In many cases, pairs of bulls' horns were set in clay at the edge of platforms or benches, and sometimes multiple pairs of horns were embedded in a row in benches; and modelled bulls' heads might be fixed into the wall. Clay figurines, notably those of the mother goddess, give additional insight into the beliefs of the community.

The residents of Çatal Hüyük buried their dead beneath the floors and platforms of their houses. Families seem to have maintained their own 'family crypt', which they repeatedly opened to inter recently deceased relatives. Many of the bodies were prepared for burial by removal of the soft tissue, and the defleshed bones then were bundled together for interment. The bones where often sprinkled with red ochre (an iron oxide) or, less frequently, blue azurite or green malachite. Grave goods accompanied few of the dead into the afterlife, but when present the burial wealth often had exotic origins – turquoise, sea shells, high quality flint, copper, and the like. The skeletons indicate that, on average, the men died at thirty-four, and the women at thirty, years of age, and that many people suffered from an anaemia that may have developed from endemic malaria.

During the 1960s, when Mellaart excavated the site, Çatal Hüyük contradicted many expectations about the sophistication

of Neolithic societies. Since then, excavations at other sites have shown that Çatal Hüyük is extraordinary, but still not uniquely advanced for its age. The place may have profited from the development of trade routes that were coming to connect all the Near East, since Çatal Hüyük was able to control the traffic in obsidian, or volcanic glass, that went from central Anatolia to places as distant as Jericho. Trade certainly brought the exotic wealth that accompanied the privileged dead. It may also have stimulated the unusual concentration of people in the town, the growth of crafts, and the belief system expressed in art and ritual. ■

THE LAKE DWELLINGS OF
THE ALPINE FORELAND

In the Alpine foreland region of Switzerland, Germany, Austria, Slovenia, Italy and France, many lakes dot the landscape. Beginning about 4000 years ago, during the Neolithic period, and continuing into the Bronze Age, farming communities built settlements on their shores. The damp conditions along these lakes led to the preservation of not only the 'typical' archaeological finds of stone tools and pottery, but also of wooden artifacts and cordage and the structural remains of the houses themselves. First discovered in the mid-nineteenth century, these sites inspired the romantic vision of lakeside settlements that for many years dominated our perception of the earliest European farmers.

During the cold and dry Swiss winter of 1853–4, the water levels of many lakes in the Zurich region fell by 30 cm (12 in). At Obermeilen, this revealed a layer on the lake bottom, between 30

Since the middle of the nineteenth century, numerous prehistoric settlements have been found in and around lakes in the foothills of the Alps – in Switzerland, Germany, Austria, France and Italy. These 'pile-dwellings', as they are called today due to the construction technique used, provide a detailed glimpse into the lives of the early farmers of central Europe, as well as a lesson in the history of archaeology.

and 60 cm (12 and 24 in) thick (called the 'cultural layer'), which contained many posts, an enormous quantity of animal bones and antlers, and artifacts from stone, clay, wood, bone and antler. A local schoolteacher, Johannes Aeppli, who collected antiquities was notified and he in turn contacted Ferdinand Keller, the president of the Antiquarian Society of Zurich. It quickly became clear that the posts were the remains of houses, and the artifacts were the belongings of their inhabitants.

Keller proposed two alternative theories: (1) that the post dwellings were on the sandy shore, or (2) that the posts supported structures that were out over the water. He came to favour the

A Neolithic house, about 10 meters (32 ft) long, at the Egolzwil site, near Zurich, has a complex wooden floor construction and central hearth.

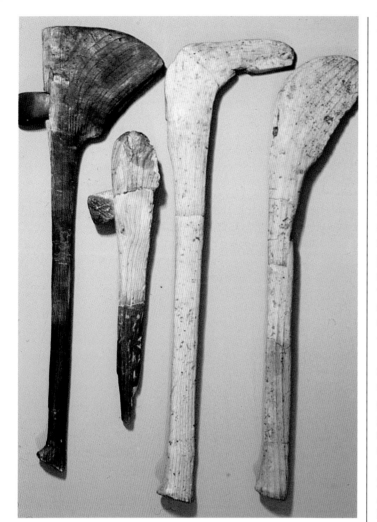

ABOVE: Although many stone axes are found on dry-land sites, the preservation conditions at the Alpine lake settlements have permitted recovery of the wooden handles that held the axe heads.

second idea, and illustrated it with a drawing of houses on a platform several metres offshore to which several gangplanks ran. It should be stressed that in Keller's mind these were not houses whose structural posts were driven down into the lake bottom. Instead, he viewed the posts found on these sites as the piles of platforms upon which houses were built. In his view, they were wooden islands, which he referred to as 'pile dwellings'. It is unclear where Keller got this idea, but possible sources include travellers' reports of such structures in Malaya and the East Indies and the writings of the ancient Greek historian Herodotus, who described similar constructions on a lake in Macedonia.

The concept of houses on platforms over the water was embraced by the romantic imagination of the public. Artists' renderings and models built in the late nineteenth and early twentieth centuries uniformly depict such wooden islands, and the sites were celebrated in literature and song. As more sites were excavated, however, archaeologists came to question the Keller theory and to argue that these settlements had really been built on the shore. The outcome of this debate was that by the early 1950s most archaeologists had reached the conclusion that, rather than

being set on piles over open water, the settlements were really built on land. Now the discussion is whether the houses had raised floors or whether, instead, the piles were footings which kept the houses from sinking into the muddy ground. Today, archaeologists differentiate between bog settlements and dry lakeshore settlements, but they have abandoned the idea of open-water settlements as envisioned by Keller.

Lakeside settlements can be found in all of the countries surrounding the Alps, although they are sometimes called in popular literature the 'Swiss Lake Dwellings' since that is where Keller first called attention to them. They originated in the Neolithic period and continued to be built during the Bronze Age. The houses were rectangular structures with hearths of clay. Tremendous quantities of artifacts are found among the structural remains, often numbering in the tens of thousands. In addition to plain, round-bottomed pottery and stone and antler tools, there are artifacts made of materials that are rarely preserved, including wood, cloth and twine. These sites normally yield much evidence about the prehistoric diet. In addition to the bones of domestic and wild animals, grains of domestic wheat, barley and peas along with a wide variety of wild fruits, nuts and seeds are found.

In many places around the foothills of the Alps there are museums which house quantities of these artifacts as well as open-air reconstructions of pile-dwelling settlements. A visitor to these regions may encounter sites being excavated, even in such unlikely places as downtown Zurich. New techniques of excavation and analysis (such as tree-ring dating) are making the investigation of these sites ever more informative, although highway and house construction along the lakes threatens many of the surviving sites. Even though the romantic vision of wooden islands has faded, the Alpine pile-dwellings will always occupy an important place in European prehistory. ■

ABOVE: Neolithic pottery characteristic of the lakeside sites of the Alpine Foreland. The handles presumably allowed them to be suspended from the rafters to keep the contents safe from moisture and vermin.

EARLY NEOLITHIC
LONGHOUSES IN EUROPE

Between 5500 and 4000 BC, the largest buildings in the world were in western and central Europe. Though they were as long as 40 m (131 ft), they were no more than 5–8 m (16 ft 6in–26 ft) wide. Groups of five or ten such houses were the first farming communities of the woodlands of central Europe. Their inhabitants brought an agricultural system based on domesticated plants and animals to an environment that had previously seen only hunting and gathering by mobile bands.

The Neolithic longhouses of central Europe are known only by traces left in the soil by their upright posts. In the earlier longhouses, individual holes were dug for each post, which left a separate round stain between 30 and 80 cm (12 and 31 in) in diameter. In later houses, rather than digging individual holes, the prehistoric builders excavated long trenches into which they set the upright posts, then backfilled the spaces between them. The outlines of the earliest houses were rectangular, but later houses often have plans in the form of elongated trapezoids.

In 1930 work on a park in Cologne in Germany revealed traces of a Neolithic settlement, and Werner Buttler began excavations. During the four years that followed, he found not only dozens of

The first farmers of western and central Europe lived in large rectangular houses, built from wooden posts set into the soil, that are sometimes as much as 40 m (131 ft) in length and on a given site are usually oriented in roughly the same direction. These structures, known as longhouses, appear to have been multipurpose; families lived, worked and kept their livestock inside them.

rubbish-filled pits but also hundreds of postholes that filled the areas between the pits. When the plans of the excavations were assembled and studied, these postholes were seen to form rectangular clusters, outlined by densely-spaced posts and sometimes a continuous trench, with a somewhat looser arrangement of posts inside.

Buttler believed that the pits were 'pithouses', while he thought that the rectangular structures were granaries and storehouses, based on the uses he had seen of post structures in the Balkans. Buttler's interpretation of the Köln-Lindenthal structures struck some archaeologists as extremely doubtful, and a debate ensued in the years just before and after World War II. By the early 1950s, the notion that the post structures found at Köln-Lindenthal and at other sites were actually houses had become accepted in archaeological literature. Longhouses are now routinely found on Neolithic settlements. Today the number of known houses probably reaches the thousands. It is always a moment of excitement, though, when the first posts or segments of a bedding trench are exposed. When the outline of the structure is traced out fully, it inspires awe and admiration for the accomplishment of its Neolithic builders.

Why longhouses? Why did they take an elongated form? We can only speculate about the answers to these questions. Clearly the pioneer farmers of continental Europe did not have the luxury of building farmsteads in a leisurely manner. Their houses needed to serve a va-riety of functions at once — dwellings, workshops, storehouses and stables — so they could not simply build a small house and then add outbuildings as time permitted.

Our direct knowledge of the

Early Neolithic longhouses are known from stains in the soil where the posts were set. Earlier houses (left) were rectangular with a complex pattern of posts. Later houses, such as the one at Oslonki (opposite), were often trapezoidal.

superstructure of the longhouses is very limited. We assume that the roof was pitched and probably either thatched with reeds or straw or covered with bark, although wood planks are another possibility. A clay model of a house with a pitched roof from Strelice in Moravia is often offered as evidence of the use of pitched roofs on early Neolithic houses. Such a pitched roof, in turn, indicates a mastery of carpentry and joinery, especially at the peak and the eaves, that is even more impressive in the absence of nails or other hardware.

Was there a wooden floor or was the interior soil the actual living surface? The assumption is the latter, but since the erosion of the habitation surfaces has eliminated the living surfaces we do not know for certain. Related to this question is the location of hearths. We do not know whether they were inside or outside the houses. A mixture of both locations seems likely, with interior hearths for day-to-day cooking and heating, with outside fires for roasting animals and firing pottery. Finally, can we be sure that the Neolithic longhouses were one-storey 'ranch-style' homes? Most archaeologists are reasonably sure that they were, although the possibility of lofts or attics in the pitched roofs cannot be excluded.

How long did these houses last? Timber, of course, rots, but how quickly? Various estimates have been made of the life of Neolithic houses in temperate Europe; some are as low as fifteen years, others as high as fifty. One point that is often forgotten is that these houses could be repaired, as would be the case with any timber structure today. The daub could be redone, and if necessary the walls could be taken apart down to the posts and reconstructed. The roof could be rethatched, and posts could be pulled out and replaced individually. With regular maintenance, the life of a Neolithic house could be prolonged for a long time, and fifty years or more does not seem to be an unreasonable estimate of their existence.

Although most archaeologists are convinced that Neolithic longhouses served primarily as dwellings, it is likely that they also had other functions. We know, for instance, that the earliest farmers of Europe kept domestic cattle, sheep, goats, and pigs; yet there do not appear to be structures that might have served as separate stables. It seems clear that Neolithic houses provided living space, but for how many people is not yet clear. Although during warm weather many activities could have occurred outdoors, during the winter most domestic activities like food preparation and manufacturing would have been moved inside. So the Neolithic houses also served as workshops and kitchens as well as living spaces. Moreover, parts may have been used as stables, at least during the winter, and very probably for storage of grain and raw materials.

In the vast forests of western and central Europe 7000 years ago, the longhouses are strong evidence of the power of humans to transform their habitat. The longhouses of Neolithic Europe are not simply important because they were the largest buildings in the world at that time; they also provide valuable information about Neolithic society. Their location in the landscape, the labour that went into their construction, their dimensions, and their associated pits and burials all shed light on the lives of the first European farmers. ∎

NEOLITHIC FLINT MINES

During the Neolithic and Bronze Age periods of European prehistory, before metal was widely available, most tools and weapons were made from stone. Because flint is a hard, shiny stone that is easy to work and can keep a sharp edge, it was a particularly popular material. For most purposes people were happy to work with flint found on the ground surface, but sometimes they preferred to use stone extracted from underground mines. By mining for flint it was possible to obtain larger nodules of better quality. Furthermore, if the flint was deep underground it was less likely to be flawed or to have been damaged by frost.

Neolithic flint mines exist all over Europe and range in size from a single pit to huge complexes of shafts and galleries extending over several hectares. Most of the largest flint mines are in northern continental Europe and southern Britain and are over 4000 years old. Some of the largest and best-known mines are Krzemionki in Poland, Grimes Graves in England, Spiennes in Belgium and Grand Pressigny in France.

How to mine flint in prehistory

If the source of flint is close to the surface, you would be able to quarry it easily by digging a shallow pit. If, however, the seam of flint is further under the surface, you would need to dig mine-shafts. The main tools would be stone axes and antler picks (these are commonly found at flint mine sites). You would probably need help digging, although once the main pits have been dug you would be able to extract flint from the seams alone. The chalk rubble from the shaft should be removed from the mine and dumped on the surface or in an abandoned mine-shaft nearby. When you reach the seam of flint that you want to quarry you could start to excavate radiating galleries extending from the pit in all directions. The antler pick would be useful for extracting the flint nodules from the soft chalk. Instead of carrying the chalk rubble to the surface, it could be deposited in abandoned galleries nearby. Now the flint would be taken to the surface where any lumps would be removed with a hammerstone, and then it would go to a prepara-

ABOVE: Prehistoric miners used antler picks to loosen the chalk around large nodules of flint.

LEFT: The interlinking galleries of the flint mines at Grimes Graves.

tion area. The raw flint could then be roughly shaped into 'blanks' for making axes and other tools. The manufacture of flint artifacts is potentially a multi-phase project, involving several stages of flaking, chipping and, if making an axe, grinding and polishing. Not all of these stages are necessarily carried out at the site of the mine, and the 'rough-outs' might be taken elsewhere for finishing. At Grand Pressigny in France, the flint was shaped into small blanks known locally as '*livres-de-beurre*' ('pounds of butter'), on account of their colour and shape, which were traded as raw material for the manufacture of knives and blades. As a result, the flint extracted from the Grand Pressigny mines was often made into tools hundreds of miles away from the source.

The importance of mining flint

In the Neolithic and Bronze Age, mining for flint was not simply a functional necessity. There is a lot of evidence to suggest that mining had ritual or religious significance, and that the flint extracted from mines was particularly valued by the people of the time. At many flint mines archaeologists have discovered evidence of sacrificial offerings, and it is possible that human burials in flint mines at Cissbury in England represent sacrifices. Chalk figures of, amongst other things, a pregnant woman and a phallus have been found at Grimes Graves (although these may be fakes). The mines themselves are often in places where they would be highly visible from the surrounding countryside and it has been suggested that mining flint might have been undertaken as a ritual activity. ■

HOUSES FOR THE LIVING AND THE DEAD

Skara Brae lies in the Bay of Skaill on the west coast of the main island of Orkney (known as Mainland). It is a complex of six houses connected by covered corridors. The settlement is remarkable not only for the survival of standing walls, but also because the fittings and furniture inside the houses still survive. This is mainly due to Orkney's bleak climate: in a place where very few trees can grow, most buildings and furniture are made of local flagstones. Whereas wooden furniture would have decayed through the years, the flagstone beds, dressers and cupboards of these 5000-year-old houses provide us with the best-known example of what a Neolithic house looked like.

The houses at Skara Brae were designed to offer maximum protection from the elements. They were built in hollows dug into an old midden with walls often over a metre (3 ft) thick. The

Some of the most complete and unusual Neolithic remains in Europe have come from the tiny storm-blown islands of Orkney, off the north coast of Scotland. One particularly fierce storm in 1850 revealed a group of ruins that further research showed to be the oldest and best-preserved prehistoric settlement in Northern Europe.

single doorway was only around a metre high, and was probably closed with a stone slab. In the centre of the floor was a large stone hearth and around it the 'fitted' furniture was built into the walls and floor. Stone beds were probably filled with furs and bracken to make them comfortable, and stone 'dressers' and alcoves in the wall would have held household goods and personal items. Of less certain purpose are the stone-lined square pits in the house floors. They were made watertight with clay along the joins and it has been suggested that the pits could have been used to soak limpets to ensure a constant supply of fresh bait for fishing.

Finds of pottery, bone and stone give us some idea of how this Neolithic community lived their everyday lives. They seem to have kept cattle and sheep as well as eating seafood, plants and wild game. They formed tools out of bone that were used to pre-

pare skins and furs, and made pots for storing food and other goods. In addition archaeologists have discovered a range of bone and ivory pins, and beads made from bone, shell, ivory and stone. Traces of red ochre in stone and shell cups might be evidence that people painted their artifacts or even their bodies. Red ochre is often found in Neolithic burials, and was perhaps associated with some religious rituals.

There seem to have been two main phases of occupation at Skara Brae between around 3100 and 2500 BC. After the settlement was abandoned – perhaps because of its vulnerability to storms – it was soon buried in sand and remained under the dunes of Skaill for more than 4000 years.

Maes Howe

The people who lived in villages like Skara Brae reserved their greatest skills and energies for the burial of their dead. The Neolithic and early Bronze Age monumental tombs of Orkney are truly spectacular. The biggest and most famous of these is the chambered tomb of Maes Howe. It is an artificial hill over 7 m (23 ft) high and 35 m (115 ft) across. A long passageway leads to the central chamber which is made of huge slabs of rock and has a high corbelled roof. Three alcoves lead off the chamber. The Neolithic people who built Maes Howe in around 2750 BC aligned the tomb so that the rays of the setting sun on the day of the winter solstice shine down the passage and illuminate the back wall of the chamber. ■

The elaborate bank and ditch around Maes Howe was first made in prehistoric times and probably rebuilt by the Norse in the ninth century AD.

BELOW LEFT: House 1 at Skara Brae. The function of the stone-lined pits near the dresser is not clear.

Runes at Maes Howe

The Norse invaders of Orkney were fascinated by the prehistoric tombs of the islands. 'Howe' is a Norse word meaning burial mound. The Norse believed that great treasure could be found in Howes, but that in order to remove it one had to brave the trolls and ghosts who lived in them. Nevertheless, some Christian Norsemen broke into the tomb in the twelfth century and left one of the largest collections of runic graffiti ever found, together with depictions of a dragon, a walrus and a serpent. Some of the inscriptions describe the removal of treasure from the tomb, but whether these statements refer to real events or are just empty boasts is difficult to tell. In any case, the tomb was empty of burials and grave goods when it was opened by antiquarians in the nineteenth century. Some rather earthier inscriptions also exist, such as this one praising the attractive widow Ingibiorg.

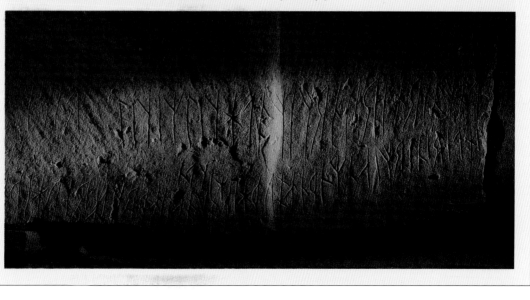

FLAG FEN AND
THE SWEET TRACK

Flag Fen, on the east side of Peterborough in East Anglia, England, is now an industrial area occupied by factories, warehouses and a new power station. But in prehistoric times this area, which marks the border between the flooded Fenlands and the dry lands to the west and north, was very important. For the people who lived there, the site gave them access to a wide range of resources – fish and waterfowl from the fens, and wild and domestic animals and birds in the dry meadows and woodlands. Then around 1350 BC, in the middle Bronze Age, the climate became wetter, the water level rose and the fens began to encroach upon the dry

Archaeologists usually have a limited range of materials to work from – most commonly stone, bone, pottery and sometimes metal, all durable substances that survive in the earth. Wood, textiles and other organic materials are not usually preserved, though in some conditions these biodegradable substances can last for thousands of years. The waterlogged peat deposits of northern Europe are particularly favourable to preservation and it is in these bogs that some of the most remarkable discoveries have been made.

land. It could have been the desire to protect their own land from their neighbours that caused the inhabitants of Flag Fen to construct a huge barrier, a kilometre (0.6 mile) long, with wooden posts. The barrier ran from the edge of the dry land on the west right across the flooded fen as far as the dry island of Northey to the east. Where it crossed the fen itself a massive wooden platform was constructed, about a hectare (2½ acres) in area.

Whether the platform was built specially to support the barrier, or whether it originally had some other purpose is still a mystery. But whatever the platform was built for, it seems to have been an

RIGHT: The Eclipse Track, dating to c.1500BC, is a wider structure than the Sweet track. It ran from the island of Meare to the Polden Hills in southwest England, and comprises over 1000 hurdles, primarily of hazelwood.

important centre of ritual activity in the Bronze Age. Archaeologists have found many metal and pottery objects and bones of humans and animals beneath and around the platform. The bronze objects were deliberately placed in the water at the edge of the barrier posts. Many had been broken before being deposited as offerings. In the Bronze Age, ritual deposits of metal, frequently broken, were often made in rivers and watery places, and water seems to have had a special religious importance to the people of that time.

Flag Fen was a particularly significant discovery because of its unique conditions of preservation. The special conditions enable archaeological specialists to study ancient wood, and they have found that lots of the wood in the platform appears to have been used previously at other nearby sites. Some are the structural timbers of Bronze Age buildings and can tell us something about how Bronze Age people built in other areas. Sites of this period are quite rare in Britain, so the archaeology of Flag Fen gives us valuable insight into a period that has generally been shrouded in mystery.

The Sweet Track

Flag Fen is not the only place where a miracle of preservation opens a window into prehistory. For example, excavations in the Somerset Levels in southwest England have revealed ancient wooden 'trackways' many metres below the modern land surface. The oldest of these, called the 'Sweet Track' after the man who found it, is more than 5000 years old. It was constructed in the early Neolithic period as a raised track to facilitate travel through the wetland environment. The Sweet Track runs for over 1.5 km (1 mile) and archaeologists working there have found not only quantities of worked wood, but also artifacts of wood and flint that were dropped or deliberately deposited along the track.

Many wooden tracks were laid through the Somerset Levels in the Neolithic and the Bronze Age. They were not all in use at the same time, but in the later Neolithic period several trackways formed a network of communication between islands and through the fens. ■

MALTESE TEMPLES

The temples are generally large buildings, sometimes with more than one storey. They have imposing concave façades and massive entrances leading to central courtyards. Other apse-shaped enclosures lead out from the courtyard like flower petals. Beyond these lie other chambers and niches, the entrances to which are often restricted by a slab of rock with a small 'porthole' in the centre. The stone blocks from which the temples are built are sometimes decorated with carved designs depicting plants and foliage.

Many early archaeologists were amazed at the architectural skill and the massive scale of construction of the Maltese temples. They believed that a 'primitive' culture would not have the organizational skill to undertake such enterprises, and concluded that the Maltese must have been influenced by the more 'civilized' cultures of the eastern Mediterranean. But we now know that the temples of Malta are actually older than the temples of the eastern Mediterranean, older even than the pyramids. Therefore, even though they knew nothing of writing, wheeled transport or the use of metal, the Neolithic inhabitants of Malta must have been sufficiently sophisticated in their own social organization to construct these extraordinary monuments without external help.

The Fat Lady

In the temple of Tarxien in Malta stands the lower half of a statue of a woman that must originally have been nearly 3 m (10 ft) high. All that remains

The tiny islands of Malta and Gozo, lying south of Sicily in the western Mediterranean, were first colonized by early Neolithic farmers sometime around 4000 BC. In the late Neolithic period these people developed the remarkable great stone temples of Malta, which are unique in Neolithic archaeology. From around 3000 BC until the arrival of metal technology around 2000 BC more than twenty of these magnificent religious monuments were built.

now is a pair of massive legs and a skirt. Statues and figurines of the 'fat lady' occur in many of the temples and in the tombs associated with them. By tradition these images are known as 'goddess' figures, but it is not certain that the woman depicted is always the same one, whether she was in fact a deity, and if so, whether she was connected in any way with other 'goddess' figures from different places and periods in European prehistory. The Maltese goddess figure is characterized by her obesity, particularly her fleshy thighs and hips. This might have been intended to emphasize her fertility or other feminine qualities, or her massive size might have been a reflection of her importance. ■

Inside one of the apses of the great temple at Mnajdra, Malta, showing the monumental doorway. The rounded wall slopes in towards the top, suggesting that the chamber at one time had a roof, perhaps a corbelled vault as at Maes Howe in Orkney (see p. 77).

Hal Saflieni

The temples of Malta were religious shrines, but did not function as burial places. The Neolithic inhabitants of Malta placed their dead in tombs that were cut into the actual rock, and the shape of the temples might be based on the shapes of these rock-cut tombs, which were often one or two irregularly-shaped chambers linked by short corridors and entered through a 'porthole' from above. One rock-cut tomb stands out amongst the rest. At Hal Saflieni, a series of interlinked chambers, known as a hypogeum, has been cut out of the solid rock. Even so, its twenty chambers are carved with roof beams, lintels and other features of buildings above ground, and the walls are painted with pictures of cattle. In this hypogeum the remains of perhaps 7000 people were found, so it is likely that it was in use for a considerable time.

The lower half of a statue at Tarxien, one of the most highly decorated temples in Malta. Other skirted female figures produced in Malta at this time are invariably in a seated position. Sitting or standing, this is the earliest known monumental statue in Europe.

LIKE A CIRCLE IN A
SPIRAL: MEGALITHIC ART

Not all megalithic monuments are decorated, but some parts of Neolithic Europe are particularly rich in megalithic art. Ireland, Brittany and Portugal are especially dynamic. In Ireland many of the decorated stones are in the great tombs of the Boyne valley, north of Dublin. They usually form part of the passages leading into the tombs, or they are kerb stones defining the outer edge of the tomb mounds.

Irish megalithic art is not representational, but certain motifs and designs seem to recur in many places. Spirals, concentric circles, lozenges, wavy lines and U-shapes are all common in the passage graves. In some tombs, such as Newgrange and Fourknocks, the designs are carefully integrated so that the entire surface of the stone is decorated. At other tombs, such as

Between 5500 and 4000 years ago the Neolithic people of Europe constructed great circles of standing stones, huge elaborate tombs and magnificent monuments that altered the shape of the landscape. These megalithic constructions have inspired awe and fascination through the ages. What they meant to the people of the Neolithic period is not completely understood, but the carved decoration many of them bear can provide clues to their rituals and beliefs.

Loughcrew, individual motifs bear no apparent relation to one another.

The Breton tombs have many of the same motifs as the Irish tombs, but in addition some of the megalithic art in Brittany contains figurative representations, most notably of axes and daggers, crooks and a shield-shape which has a human-like appearance and has been interpreted as an idol.

What does the art of the megaliths mean? Is megalithic art a unified phenomenon? Although there are big differences in local traditions, the recurrence of some of the motifs in different countries suggests that they had some widely acknowledged significance. Many archaeologists have interpreted the art in terms of its celebration of natural powers. Circles and spirals could symbolize celestial bodies, and the astronomical alignments of many of the megalithic tombs suggest that the sun, moon and stars were important to their builders. For example, the rays of the rising sun on the day of the summer solstice pass through a specially constructed opening above the entrance to the passage at Newgrange and light up the back of the chamber. Other scholars have been more interested in what the designs might say about human powers, and have suggested that the depiction of daggers and axes, for example, was intended to celebrate masculine authority.

A far more controversial theory concerns the possible relationship between megalithic art and the visual effects of altered states of consciousness. This theory maintains that the inducing of trance-like states, either by using naturally occurring hallucinogens or through hypnosis, was part of Neolithic religious rituals. The spirals and circles represented at Newgrange in Ireland or Gavrinis in Brittany might therefore depict the visions of a person in an altered state of consciousness. ∎

RIGHT: The great entrance stone of the tomb of Newgrange in Ireland bears spiral decoration all over its surface. After the design had been etched out by a small pointed pick – probably made of quartz or some other hard stone – the lines were rubbed with a stone to give a smooth finish.

LEFT: The passage of the Breton tomb of Gavrinis is extensively decorated with patterns of concentric circles and parallel lines.

THE ICEMAN

The Iceman constitutes the first prehistoric human ever found with his everyday clothing and equipment, and presumably going about his normal business; other similarly intact bodies from prehistory have been either carefully buried or sacrificed. He brings us literally face to face with the remote past.

The world's oldest fully preserved human body was found on 19 September 1991, by German hikers near the Similaun glacier, in the Ötztaler Alps of South Tyrol. At an altitude of 3200 m (10,600 ft), they spotted a human body, its skin yellowish-brown and desiccated. It was four days before the body, and its accompanying objects of leather, grass, flint and wood, were removed by Austrian authorities and taken to Innsbruck University. There were already suspicions that the corpse might be old, but nobody had any idea just how ancient.

The body was handed to the anatomy department for treatment, after which it was placed in a freezer at -6°C (10°F) and 98% humidity. Subsequent investigation determined that the corpse – called Similaun Man, Ötzi or, simply, the 'Iceman' – had lain 92 m (300 ft) inside the border of Italy, but most initial research has been carried out in Austria and Germany. However, apart from some body scans and radiocarbon dating, very little has yet been done with the corpse, while considerable work has been carried out on the objects that accompanied him. According to the investigators, he was probably overcome by exhaustion on the mountain – perhaps caught in a fog or a blizzard. After death, he was dried out by a warm autumn wind, before becoming encased in ice. Since the body lay in a depression, it was protected by the movement of the glacier above it for 5300 years, until a storm from the Sahara laid a layer of dust on the ice that absorbed sunlight and finally thawed it out.

He was a dark-skinned male, aged between twenty-five and forty, with a cranial capacity of 1500–1560 cc (91.5–95 in³). Only about 156–160 cm (5 ft 2 in) tall, his stature and morphology fit well within the measurement ranges of Late Neolithic populations of Italy and Switzerland. Preliminary analysis of his DNA confirms his links to Northern Europe. The corpse currently weighs only about 54 kg (120 lb).

His teeth are very worn, especially the front incisors, suggesting that he ate coarse ground grain, or that he regularly used them as a tool; there are no wisdom teeth, which is typical for the period; and he has a marked gap between his upper front teeth. His facial hair was shaved. When found, he was bald, but hundreds of curly brownish-black human hairs, about 9 cm (3.5 in) long, in the vicinity of the body and on the clothing fragments indicate that he had recently had a haircut. His right earlobe has a pit-like and sharp-edged rectangular depression, indicating that he probably once had an ornamental stone fitted there.

A jackhammer used in a crude attempt to dislodge him from the ice severely damaged the left pelvic area. A body scan has shown that the brain, muscle tissues, lungs, heart, liver and digestive organs are in excellent condition, though the lungs are blackened by smoke, probably from open fires, and he has hardening of the arteries and blood vessels. His left arm is fractured above the elbow: this almost certainly occurred during his recovery, when he was forced into a coffin. There are traces of chronic frostbite in one little toe. He has eight rib fractures, which were healed or healing when he died.

There are groups of tattoos, mostly short parallel vertical blue lines, half an inch long, on both sides of his lower spine, on his left calf and right ankle, and a blue cross on his inner right knee. These marks may be therapeutic, aimed at relieving the arthritis which he had in his neck, lower back and right hip. One fingernail was recovered and its analysis revealed that he undertook manual labour and that he underwent periods of reduced nail growth corresponding to episodes of serious illness – four, three and two months before he died. The fact that he was prone to periodic crippling disease may help explain how

The Iceman's body emerging from the ice, as he was first spotted on 19 September 1991 by a couple of hikers from Heidelberg at an altitude of 3200 metres (10,500 ft).

he fell prey to adverse weather and froze to death.

Archaeologists are particularly interested in the items found with him, which constitute a unique 'time-capsule' of the stuff of everyday life, many of them made of organic materials that were preserved by the cold and ice. An astonishing variety of woods, and a range of very sophisticated techniques of work with leather and grasses can be seen in the collection of seventy objects that have added a new dimension to our knowledge of the period.

The axe, 60 cm (24 in) in length, has a head of copper that was bound to the yew-wood handle with leather thongs. The bow, of yew wood, was almost 180 cm (6 ft)

long. One side is flat, the other rounded. Its odour at room temperature suggests it was smeared with blood or fat to keep it pliable. A quiver of deerskin contained fourteen arrows, only two of which were ready for use. Their 75 cm (30 in) shafts, made of two pieces, were of dogwood and viburnum wood, and had points of stone or bone fixed to them by pitch. The two finished arrows had double-sided points of flint and triple feathering whose placement meant the missiles would spin in flight and indicates an advanced ballistic design. The quiver also contained an untreated sinew (possibly for use as a bowstring), a ball of fibrous cord, bone or antler spines tied together with grass, and various objects of flint and bone, together with pitch – it may have constituted some kind of repair kit.

The dagger or knife has a sharp flint blade, only about 4 cm (1.5 in) long, set into an 8 cm (3 in) ash-wood handle. Polish on the blade indicates that it was used to cut grass. A woven grass sheath was also found. What was originally assumed to be a stone-pointed fire-striker was found to be a thick 'pencil' of linden wood with a central spine of bone, probably used for retouching and sharpening flint objects. A U-shaped stick of hazel and two cross-boards of larch are thought to be the frame of a backpack that may have contained some animal bones and residues of the skin of chamois and other small animals, found nearby: blood residues from chamois, ibex and deer have been found on some of the implements.

Other finds include a braided grass mat and a coarsely woven net of grass fibres (possibly a carrier-bag); a birch bark container with a raw blackthorn (sloe) berry in it, indicating that the Iceman died in the late summer or autumn; a leather pouch; a flat marble disc threaded onto a 'necklace' decorated with twenty leather straps; and two lumps of an agaric tree-fungus strung on a knotted leather cord: this kind of fungus grows only on birch trees, and has antibiotic properties, although it is also possible that the lumps were used as tinder, like the pyrites and charcoal also found in the collection.

The question of garments is more complex, since what is as-

Top: The body can only be examined for 20 minutes every 2 weeks to avoid deterioration. The artifacts will later be exhibited, but it is doubtful the Iceman himself will be displayed.

Above: The copper axe has deposits of large cooked or heated starch grains (probably barley) on its blade and where it is lashed to the shaft, showing he may have repaired it while eating porridge.

sumed to be his clothing was found in dozens of fragments, and many are still missing – perhaps removed by early visitors to the site. When found, the body wore only its leather leggings and well-worn size 5 or 6 leather shoes, all packed with insulating straw. The shoes had many lace-holes, and showed signs of constant repair. A rain-cloak of woven grass, similar to those worn by shepherds of the region until recent times, is thought to be present, as well as a fur cap with a leather strap. Opinions are divided over whether he wore leather trousers or a kind of fur-and-leather skirt.

Fifteen radiocarbon dates have been obtained from the body, the artifacts and the grass in the boots: they are all in rough agreement, falling within a range of 3365–2940 BC, averaging 3300 BC. ∎

VARNA: A COPPER AGE CEMETERY

Any discussion of the Copper Age cemetery of Varna in Bulgaria is inevitably laden with statistics: size, number, quantity, weight. In most cases, the statistics refer to gold, for the Varna cemetery has yielded the earliest major find of gold artifacts anywhere in the world. This site, dated between 4500 and 4000 BC, was discovered in 1972 during the excavation of a cable trench on the northern bank of a lake which was once a bay on the Black Sea. Between 1972 and 1986, an area of about 7500 m² (80,000 ft²) was excavated, about 75% of the estimated extent of the cemetery. Within this area, 281 graves were found that dated to the end of the Copper Age, although 20% of the graves were cenotaphs without actual human remains.

The burial rite was similar among all the graves. Rectangular pits ranging from 30 cm (12 in) to 2.5 m (8 ft) deep with sloping sides were dug. Into such a pit they then placed the body with

At the town of Varna on the Black Sea coast of Bulgaria, a Copper Age cemetery with nearly 300 graves has produced an astonishing amount of gold artifacts, including diadems, body ornaments and weapon shafts, as well as finely made objects of copper, flint and stone. Some of the graves were symbolic interments, without bodies but with lavish offerings like those in the regular burials, and the entire site reflects the growing differences in access to status and wealth during the period between the earliest farming communities and the subsequent Bronze Age.

the burial offerings or, in the case of the cenotaphs, just the artifacts for the symbolic grave. The pit was then filled, although with the inclusion of very little humus, making it very difficult for the excavators to locate the subtle discolourations that marked the locations of the graves.

Only twenty-three of the 281 excavated burials lacked grave goods. In about 60% of the graves, the number of offerings was between one and ten, while most of the remainder had somewhat more, including some that had hundreds of objects. The most spectacular features of the Varna cemetery are the gold artifacts, which occur in sixty-one of the graves. Interestingly, most of the gold is found in the cenotaphs, while of the graves with skeletons only a few were similarly provisioned.

Three of the cenotaphs – Graves 1, 4 and 36 – were extraordinarily rich. Grave 1 contained 216 gold objects that together weighed 1092 g (38 oz), while the 339 gold objects in Grave 4 weighed 1518 g (53 oz). Grave 36 had the most gold items – 857 – that together weighed 789 g (27½ oz). Three other cenotaphs – Graves 2, 3 and 15 – contained clay masks that had male features and were ornamented with gold.

Many of the Varna burials have skeletons in an extended position. Perhaps the richest of these was Grave 43, which contained the skeleton of a man about forty to fifty years old and about 1.75 m (5 ft 9 in) tall. Lying around and on top of the skeleton were nearly 1000 gold objects weighing a total of 1516 g (53 oz), along with other items made of copper,

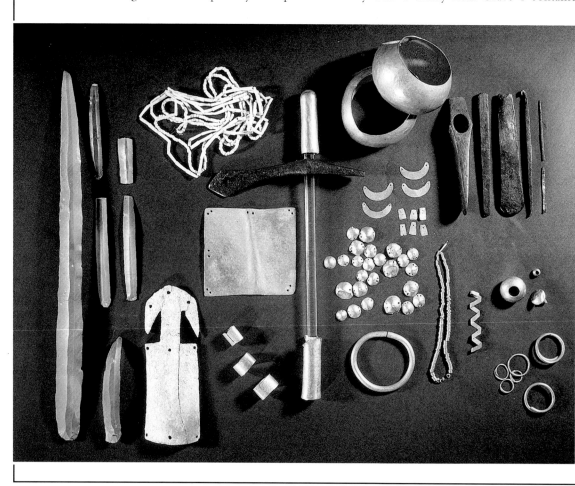

Collection of gold, shell, stone and bone objects found in a single burial at Varna.

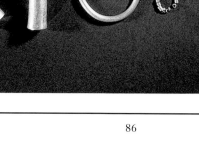

The greatest value of the gold artifacts found at Varna was as a symbol of the authority and power of its wearer. Its lavish use in body ornamentation is seen in this reconstruction of one of the rich burials.

stone, clay and the shell of the marine mussel *Spondylus*. Among the gold objects was a 'sceptre', whose wooden handle had been sheathed with gold and topped with a stone mace-head; large rings around the upper arms; numerous beads that had been strung together; and circles of gold sheet that ornamented the deceased's clothing. Other burials at Varna contained skeletons in a contracted position, with the knees drawn up to the chest and the head bent forward. There seems to be no difference between the grave goods found with the contracted burials and those in the extended position, so the significance of the variation is unclear.

While the gold artifacts are clearly the most memorable category of finds at Varna, it is important to remember that there were significant numbers of copper, flint and shell artifacts found in the burials as well. The copper is among the oldest found in Europe and reflects the growing sophistication in the control of high temperatures in the technology of this time. Many of the 160 copper artifacts are hammer-axes, while others are pins, rings and other ornaments. A variety of flint tools, made from long blades of high-quality material, were also found in the graves. Beads and arm-rings from *Spondylus* shells were particularly present in the graves with the masks.

The spectacular finds at Varna have been interpreted as signs of different degrees of access to status, power and wealth. Besides being used for ornaments, gold was incorporated into artifacts that clearly were symbolic in nature, such as the maces and masks. Moreover, it was used to highlight significant parts of the body, such as the face and genitals. It is evident that the gold and other high-quality artifacts had considerable prestige value.

We do not yet understand completely the society that produced the Varna cemetery. Nearby in northeastern Bulgaria there are large settlements, such as those at Ocharovo and Polyanitsa that have highly ordered, compact plans and are surrounded by palisades. Although it would be premature to say that this society was hierarchical, it is clear that it was highly organized, and maintained elaborate symbolic practices. ∎

LOS MILLARES AND ZAMBUJAL

The settlement at Los Millares is situated on a rocky hilltop, inland from the coast, and outlying bastions have been discovered at quite a distance from the main settlement site. Because the area around Los Millares was (and still is) very arid, it was probably important to its inhabitants to protect their land and crops. They went to some trouble to secure a water supply, and a channel was dug to bring water into the settlement area. The fields must also have been irrigated, or such a wealthy and long-term settlement as Los Millares could never have existed.

Outside the settlement of Los Millares is a large cemetery of more than seventy tombs with rich grave goods. The occurrence

The site of Los Millares in southeastern Spain is one of the most impressive fortified sites in prehistory. With its thick, bastioned walls and large cemetery, it was clearly of special importance in the Iberian Late Neolithic (sometimes called the 'Copper Age'), around 3000 BC, combining the monumental collective burial traditions of the Neolithic with the artisan economy and social competition of the Bronze Age. Archaeologists investigating the site found pottery and ornaments that convey something about the society's beliefs and represent some of the earliest evidence of organized metallurgy in Europe.

of settlement and funerary structures together at the same site is very unusual in late Neolithic archaeology. Here, burials were made in large collective tombs, many of which were plastered and painted inside. Some of the passage graves are divided up by large flat slabs with holes in, similar to the porthole stones of the Maltese temples (see p. 80). The grave goods in these tombs include imported objects of North African ivory and ostrich egg shell, as well as skilfully made pottery and copper objects. The profusion of such objects has been understood to indicate not only the development of specialization in craft production, but also the emergence of new hierarchies headed by people who based their status on the ownership of these prestige items.

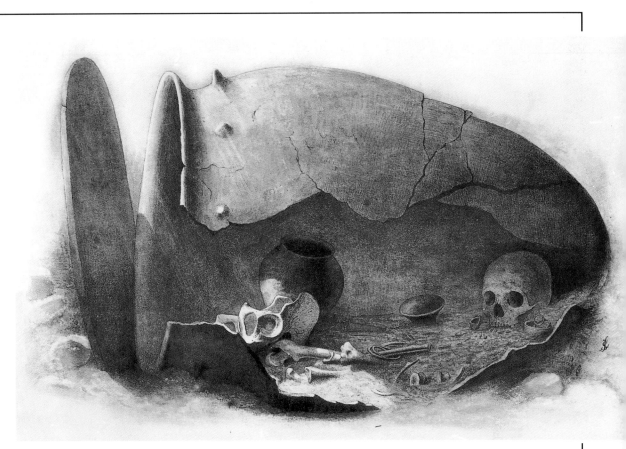

RIGHT: Urn burial from El Argar, as depicted in the 1880s by Louis Siret, one of the site's original excavators. The site of El Argar is later than Los Millares, but situated in the same part of southeast Spain.

BELOW: The massive defences of Los Millares. The main entrance has 5 major phases of construction. At the earliest stage the entrance consisted of simply a gap in the wall. The last phase involved the building of a barbican that projects more than 12 m (38 ft) outside the wall.

Los Millares has given its name to the 'Millaran culture' – a group of sites from the same region and period that share distinguishing architectural and artifactual features. Archaeologists used to believe that the Millaran culture in Iberia was influenced by the spread of ideas and technologies from the East, but the artifacts found at sites like Los Millares actually bear very little resemblance to Eastern ones. Refinements to the technique of radiocarbon dating have confirmed what some suspected all along – Los Millares is actually earlier than the cultures that were supposed to have influenced it! It seems likely therefore that changes in the Iberian Late Neolithic came from within the culture.

Zambujal

Zambujal, in Portugal, is another heavily fortified site. Like Los Millares, it is situated on a rocky promontory inland from the coast. The settlement is surrounded by three enclosing walls, one inside the other, that become thicker closer to the settlement. The inner wall, which is up to 17m (56 ft) thick in places, makes the monumental walls of Los Millares look positively flimsy. Outside the walls was a group of monumental tombs, similar to those at Los Millares. Many fine artifacts of bone, stone and pottery were found here, as well as tools and weapons made from copper.

Both Zambujal and Los Millares must have been important centres in Late Neolithic Iberia. The massive walls not only protected the settlements from attack, but emphasized how strong and how important they were. The outlying bastions might have been positioned to protect the crops growing in their precious irrigated fields, particularly those crops that were newly domesticated at this time, such as the olive tree, which requires many years of peaceful growth before they produce significant returns. ■

BRONZE AGE BARROWS

Bush Barrow is an early Bronze Age 'round bar-row' – a circular mound of earth and chalk raised over a burial. It is about 4000 years old and contains the remains of a single individual, lying extended on its back. Arranged around the body were a variety of grave goods. These were, briefly, a bronze and a copper dagger, several artifacts of gold including decorative plates and a belt hook, a bronze axe, a stone mace-head, some bone mounts (probably the remains of a decorated staff) and a large number of bronze rivets of unknown use.

This burial is different from the Neolithic burials that pre-ceded it in several respects. In particular it holds only one per-son, buried with many prestigious objects, as opposed to the burials of the Neolithic which were not characterized by rich grave goods and often contained the remains of several people. The Bush Barrow itself is part of a cemetery of round barrows in the parish of Wilsford in Wiltshire and though one of the best

The burial mound at Bush Barrow in Wiltshire, southern England, is the best example of what came to be known as a 'Wessex culture' burial. Modern archaeologists have interpreted the wealth of Bush Barrow and other Wessex burials as a way of emphasizing individual and regional prestige and power in the early Bronze Age.

known of the 'Wessex type' early Bronze Age burials, it is not unique. An exceptional richness in grave goods is par-ticularly concentrated in the Wessex area of southern Eng-land, but it is also found in Brittany, France, at the same period. In Brittany single burials under round mounds accompanied by very rich grave goods, in-cluding metal and imported objects, date to the same period (2300–2000 BC) as the rich Wessex barrows.

The grave goods, as beautiful today as they were 4000 years ago, point to a social transformation that took place at this time. At the end of the Neolithic period and the beginning of the Bronze Age there was a change from a society more concerned with the group as a whole to one in which certain individuals, families or regional groups were more powerful than others, and there was a high degree of social competition between these indi-viduals or groups. Burials of important people were accompanied by rich grave goods that emphasized their power, and the goods

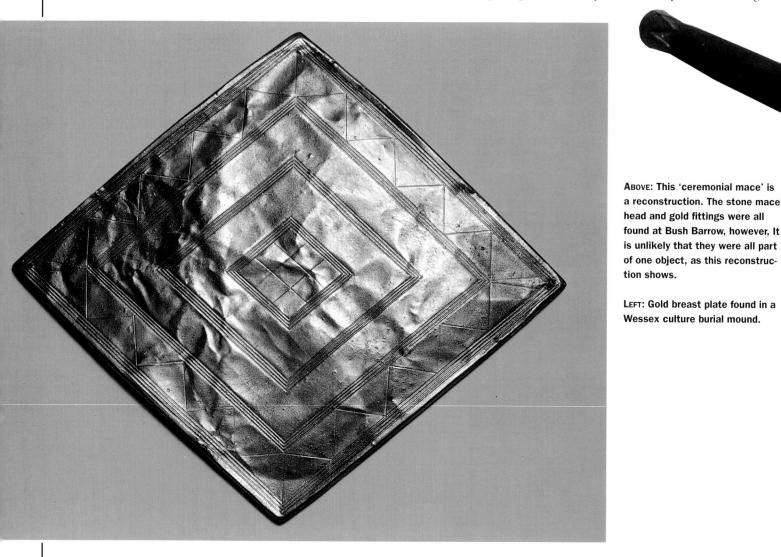

ABOVE: This 'ceremonial mace' is a reconstruction. The stone mace head and gold fittings were all found at Bush Barrow, however, It is unlikely that they were all part of one object, as this reconstruc-tion shows.

LEFT: Gold breast plate found in a Wessex culture burial mound.

ABOVE: Although the rich early Bronze Age graves were mainly concentrated in Wessex, occasional finds from other parts of Britain are of comparable quality. This little cup from Rillaton in Cornwall is less than 10 cm (4 in) high, yet it shows remarkable skill in its manufacture. The fact that it is too small to be of much use as a drinking cup suggests that it was valued for its beauty and finely crafted detail.

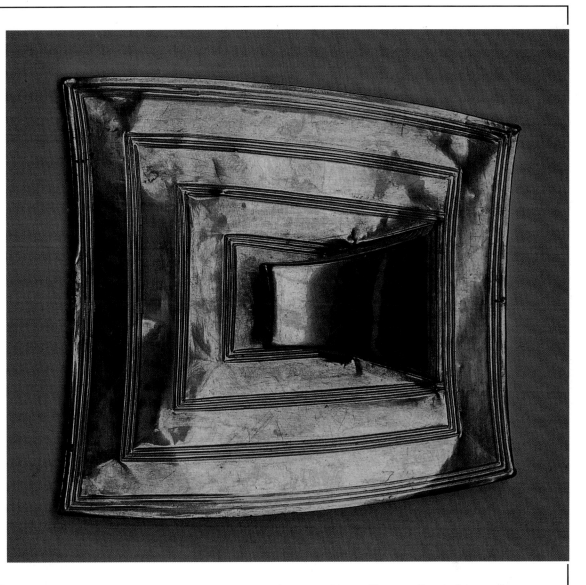

ABOVE: Gold belt hook recovered from a Wessex culture burial mound.

were probably selected because of the special meaning they embodied. The bronze dagger, for example, seems to have been particularly important. It is often found in these rich burials, depicted in Bronze Age art (carved on the great stones at Stonehenge, for example), and imitated in other materials such as flint. A person's burial rite not only contributed to the expression of that person's individual identity, but involved in structuring relationships between the living as well. ■

EVANS AT KNOSSOS

Although it seemed likely that the island of Crete might prove one of the centres of Aegean civilization, it was not until 1900 that Arthur Evans was able to start his excavations at Knossos. As a result he discovered the earliest literate society in Europe and revealed the remains of Minoan civilization.

In 1887 Heinrich Schliemann (see p. 98) visited Crete and became convinced that Knossos would repay investigation. There had already been excavations on the site, undertaken by the aptly named Minos Kalokairinos in 1878. Kalokairinos had cleared one of the storerooms of the palace that was lined with clay jars. Schliemann entered into negotiations with the Turkish landowner but they could not agree a price and so he returned to Troy.

Seven years later, in March 1894, Arthur Evans saw Knossos for the first time and was no less impressed, but his attempt to buy the land was also frustrated. However, Evans was more determined than Schliemann and eventually, in 1900, he was able to excavate at Knossos.

The son of the prehistorian John Evans, Arthur Evans must have seemed destined to become an archaeologist. Yet he first made his name as a journalist, becoming the special correspondent of the *Manchester Guardian* in Bosnia. But he also made a study of the antiquities of the Balkans. He saw an exhibition of the finds from Troy and subsequently met Schliemann in Athens in 1883. Evans believed that the prehistoric Greeks must have been literate. He thought that the designs engraved on sealstones, which he had examined in Athens, might be hieroglyphic symbols. Since Crete was known as a source of these seal-stones, he went there and was shown Knossos.

Evans was not an experienced excavator but he was assisted by Duncan Mackenzie who had been a member of the British team at Phylakopi on Melos in 1896–9. The excavations began on 23 March 1900 and within a week they had found a 'kind of clay bar, rather like a stone chisel in shape, though broken at one end, with script on it and what appear to be numerals': Evans had already proved that this was a literate society. Moreover, it seemed that the pottery was 'prae-Mycenaean' and so earlier than Schliemann's discoveries at Mycenae. The presence of a gypsum throne suggested that this must be a palace.

Since Minos was the legendary ruler of Knossos, Evans called the complex which he had uncovered the Palace of Minos and the civilization therefore became known as the Minoan. As he had surmised, the Minoan civilization was older than the Mycenaean. The first palace at Knossos had been constructed around 2000 BC. It was rebuilt and underwent a number of modifications before it was destroyed by fire in the fourteenth century BC. The plan of the palace, dominated by a large central court, at first seemed haphazard and complex, literally labyrinthine. But careful

ABOVE: An ivory figurine of a bull-leaper from Knossos. Although the body is abnormally elongated to stress the youth's athleticism, the muscles and veins are realistically rendered.

LEFT: One of the frescoes from the Palace at Knossos restored so that the images of male and female bull-leapers are visible.

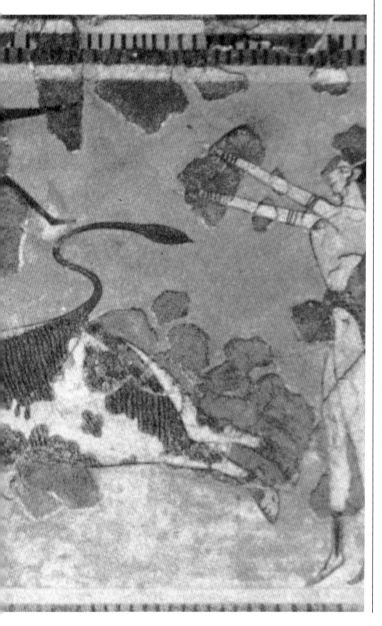

study revealed that the blocks of rooms were arranged around the court so that the palace had been designed inside out. Moreover, the rooms at first-floor level often determined the plan of those below. It was also evident that the palace was multi-functional. There were elegant residential suites, gypsum-paved and fresco-decorated, and spacious rooms, which might have served as the state apartments, on the first floor. But the enormous capacity of the storerooms exceeded the needs of those who were resident in the palace and must have supported a large retinue. There were specialist craftsmen based in the palace, and also bureaucrats whose records were written on clay tablets. The palace was also a cult centre. Evans identified a number of shrines and it is likely that the large paved courts were used in religious ceremonies, some of which are depicted in the frescoes that Evans found and carefully restored. ■

THE DECIPHERMENT OF LINEAR B

The excavation of the Minoan palace at Knossos on Crete proved that prehistoric Greek societies were literate, as Arthur Evans had suspected. In the ruins of the palace he found clay tablets that had been written by the palace scribes. He recognized three different scripts and from their context on the site it seemed that they were used in succession. The first of these scripts, the Minoan hieroglyphic, appeared on Crete when the early palaces were built. Evidently the palaces were major political and economic centres that needed a system of written records so that their administration could control transactions. The scribes who developed the first Minoan script borrowed a number of signs from Egyptian hieroglyphic, but it is

The clay tablets that Arthur Evans discovered at Knossos (see p. 93) demonstrated that the Minoans were literate, and in due course the Mycenaean palaces also produced texts written in the Linear B script. It was evident that these were administrative documents, but it was not until 1952 that the script was deciphered as an early form of Greek by architect Michael Ventris.

clear that their language was quite different. Minoan hieroglyphic remains undeciphered and may well remain incomprehensible unless a much larger archive of tablets is discovered. Nor can we read the next Minoan script which is known as Linear A. This was in use at the time of the second palace and is found throughout Crete and even on some of the islands in the Cyclades. Since the number of signs is approximately one hundred it is evident that the script is not alphabetic. Nor is it a pictographic script, in which each sign denotes a word: the signs must represent syllables. There are also numerals that can be understood, since the Minoans adapted the Egyptian system, and it would seem that most of the tablets written in Linear A were inventories.

The third script dates from the final phase of the palace at Knossos. Arthur Evans found over 4000 tablets written in Linear B. Subsequently tablets have been discovered at Chania, another site on Crete, and in the Mycenaean palaces at Mycenae, Pylos, Thebes and Tiryns in mainland Greece. Linear B evidently evolved from Linear A and is also a syllabic script. Evans could identify numerals and also ideograms – single signs that indicated what was listed on the tablet – but he could not decipher the script.

In 1936 Arthur Evans gave a lecture on his discoveries that was attended by Michael Ven-

LEFT: Portrait of Michael Ventris taken in 1954 soon after he accomplished the decipherment of Linear B.

ABOVE RIGHT: Clay tablet from the Mycenaean palace at Pylos. The Linear B inscription records offerings of oxen, sheep, wheat, cheese and wine to the god Poseidon.

tris, then aged fourteen. He was already fascinated by languages and decided that he would study these undeciphered Aegean scripts. Four years later, when he was still only eighteen, he published his first article on the subject in which he argued that the language of the scripts was Etruscan. The war then intervened but he did not lose his interest in Linear B and he circulated the results of his research as a series of 'Work Notes'. He devised a grid that indicated which signs were linked and he gradually refined this as more texts became available. However, he still believed that the language was Etruscan. In 1951 he noted 'the remote possibility that the Knossos and Pylos tablets are actually written in Greek', but added 'I feel that what we have seen so far of Minoan forms makes this unlikely.' Ventris did not seriously consider that the language of the tablets might be Greek until June 1952, but he soon became convinced that he had deciphered Linear B. As he was, in fact, an architect by profession, he enlisted the aid of a philologist, John Chadwick, and together they published an article in which they set out details of the decipherment. Scholars were rather sceptical at first, but it happened that Carl Blegen, the excavator of the Mycenaean palace at Pylos (see p. 100), tried out the proposed decipherment on a tablet that he had found the previous summer. Not only could he read most of the tablet, but the identification of a number of words was confirmed by ideograms. Blegen was satisfied that Ventris had succeeded and in due course most scholars also accepted that Linear B was an early form of Greek. Translation of the tablets was a slow process, however, and so the death of Michael Ventris in a car accident in 1956 was a great loss for scholarship. Nevertheless he had transformed Aegean archaeology. ■

Clay tablet from Pylos, baked by the fire that destroyed the palace in the 13th century BC, and one of a series documenting a system of land tenure.

THE COLLAPSE OF THE MINOAN CIVILIZATION

Around 1500 BC, the island of Crete suffered a catastrophe that ended the brilliant Minoan civilization. Palaces, villas and towns were destroyed by fire. Only the palace at Knossos (see p. 92) escaped unscathed, but it also lay in ruins less than a century later. In archaeology it is seldom clear why civilizations have collapsed and Minoan Crete is no exception. In 1939 the Greek archaeologist Spyridon Marinatos suggested that the cause might have been

When Spyridon Marinatos argued that the eruption of the Thera volcano might have caused the collapse of the Minoan civilization there was considerable scepticism. In his quest for evidence he discovered a prehistoric town buried beneath the volcanic ash at Akrotiri on Thera, and consequently disproved his own theory.

the eruption of the Thera volcano. The island of Thera, also known as Santorini, is just 100 km (62 miles) north of Crete and there was certainly a major eruption at this time. In his excavations at Amnisos, a Minoan harbour town on the north coast of Crete, Marinatos found that large blocks of stone had been torn out of position and he wondered whether a massive tidal wave had swamped the site. Of course this could not have caused the fires but it was clear that huge amounts of hot ash and rock were blasted out of the volcano and might have enveloped Crete. It was certainly a spectacular theory and archaeologists were sceptical and felt that Marinatos should provide further proof.

He decided that an excavation on Thera might reveal more about the effects of the eruption but he faced a major problem in that the island was covered by a thick layer of volcanic ash. Nevertheless, some prehistoric finds had been reported, especially from fields around the village of Akrotiri in the south of the island. Marinatos was shown hollows where the ground had collapsed and was told that the farmers could not plough because of the mass of stones. He guessed that there were structures under the ash and so in 1967 he began his excavations at Akrotiri.

He found a prehistoric Greek Pompeii, a town that had been buried by pumice

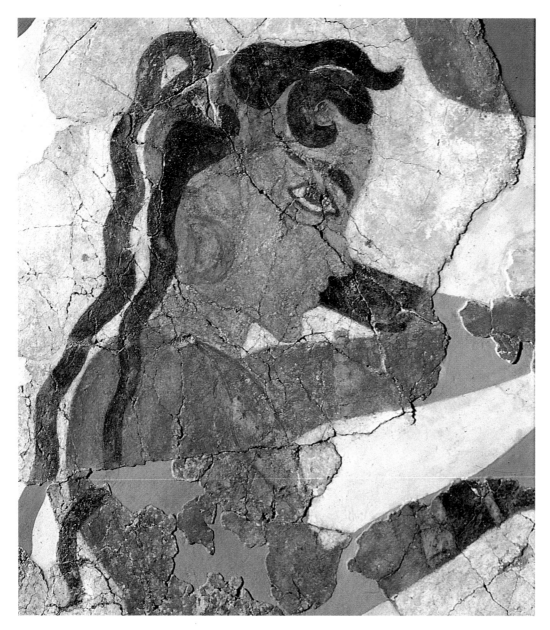

LEFT: Detail of a fresco from one of the houses at Akrotiri which depicts two youths boxing. The distinctive hairstyle may be an indication of their age.

One of the two-storey houses at Akrotiri that has been preserved under the volcanic ash.

and ash when the volcano erupted. The houses were remarkably well preserved, their stone and timber walls often two storeys high. Brilliant polychrome frescoes still decorated some of the rooms, depicting the Theran landscape and religious and military scenes. Plaster of Paris poured into cavities in the ash revealed beds and tables. In the basements of the houses were the jars in which food had once been stored. But there was no trace of the inhabitants. They must have been aware that the volcano was about to erupt and had fled. We can only hope that they left the island because they would not have survived otherwise.

In 1974 Marinatos was killed in an accident at Akrotiri but his spectacular discoveries had focused attention on the possible link between the eruption of Thera and the collapse of the Minoan civilization. The inhabitants of Akrotiri were certainly well aware of their Cretan neighbours. The houses have Minoan features and the frescoes closely resemble those at Knossos, but this was not a Cretan settlement. Most of the pottery was locally produced but there were Minoan imports and they have a special significance because the pottery found in the destruction levels on Crete is quite different and clearly later in date. There can be no doubt that Akrotiri was abandoned at least twenty or thirty years before the sites on Crete were destroyed. Ironically it was Marinatos who had demonstrated that there could be no link between the eruption and the destructions at other locations. The collapse of the Minoan civilization remains a mystery. ■

SCHLIEMANN AT TROY AND MYCENAE

In the nineteenth century it seemed unlikely that the Homeric epics were based on fact but Heinrich Schliemann was convinced that archaeology could reveal a prehistoric Greek civilization, and his discoveries at Troy and Mycenae vindicated this belief.

When Heinrich Schliemann first visited Greece and Turkey in 1868, most scholars believed that the *Iliad* and *Odyssey* were poetic fantasies. It was not thought likely that the heroic age of Greece, so vividly described by Homer, might have a historical basis. Yet ancient Greek writers were not so sceptical. The siege and sack of Troy lay in the distant past even for them but they could see the monuments of this era: for example, at Mycenae Pausanias describes the fortifications, supposedly built by giant Cyclopes since the blocks of stone were so enormous; the lion gate, and the graves of Agamemnon and his followers, who were murdered on their return from Troy. Travellers in Greece in the eighteenth and nineteenth centuries also saw and recorded some of these monuments but they did not make the connection between these remains and Homer.

Heinrich Schliemann was born in Germany in 1822. His father was a pastor and apparently kindled his son's passion for Homer when the boy was just eight years old. However, Schliemann's scholarly ambitions were thwarted by family circumstances and he settled in Russia where he made his fortune as a merchant. Eventually he was able to retire and could at last pursue his interest in classical antiquity. In the course of his travels around Greece and Turkey his faith in Homer as a historical source was confirmed, but he needed proof; so in 1870 he began preliminary excavations at Troy.

The precise location of Troy was in fact disputed. Most scholars favoured the site of Balli Dag, but Frank Calvert, a local antiquarian, persuaded Schliemann that he should excavate at Hisarlik, and the results of the first season encouraged Schliemann to undertake a major campaign there. Between 1871 and 1873 he and his team of 150 workmen drove a series of vast trenches through the mound at Hisarlik. The site they uncovered was extremely complex – containing layer upon layer of levels – but Schliemann believed that he could distinguish four successive cities, the second of which had been destroyed by fire. Surely this was Homer's Troy, the city of Priam, besieged and sacked by the Greeks. In May 1873 Schliemann glimpsed gold in one of the trenches. An early lunch break was called and the workmen dismissed. Schliemann, apparently accompanied by his Greek wife, Sophia, then excavated a hoard of gold, silver and bronze objects that were promptly smuggled out of Turkey. The Turkish authorities were furious, since they should have been given some of the finds, but 'Priam's Treasure', which disappeared from Germany at the end of World War II and has recently resurfaced in Moscow, made Schliemann famous and vindicated his belief in Homer.

He could not continue his excavations at Troy, however, and so he turned his attention to Greece. In the Homeric epics, Mycenae is the city of Agamemnon, the leader of the Greeks at Troy, and is described as 'rich in gold'. It was only natural that Schliemann should take an interest in Mycenae, especially as the mas-

ABOVE: Heinrich Schliemann's Greek wife, Sophie, seen wearing some of the elaborate Early Bronze Age jewellery from 'Priam's Treasure', which was found at Troy in 1873.

LEFT: Bronze dagger with inlaid gold and silver figures from one of the shaft graves at Mycenae. The scene represents a lion hunt, with the hunters protected by huge shields covered in oxhide.

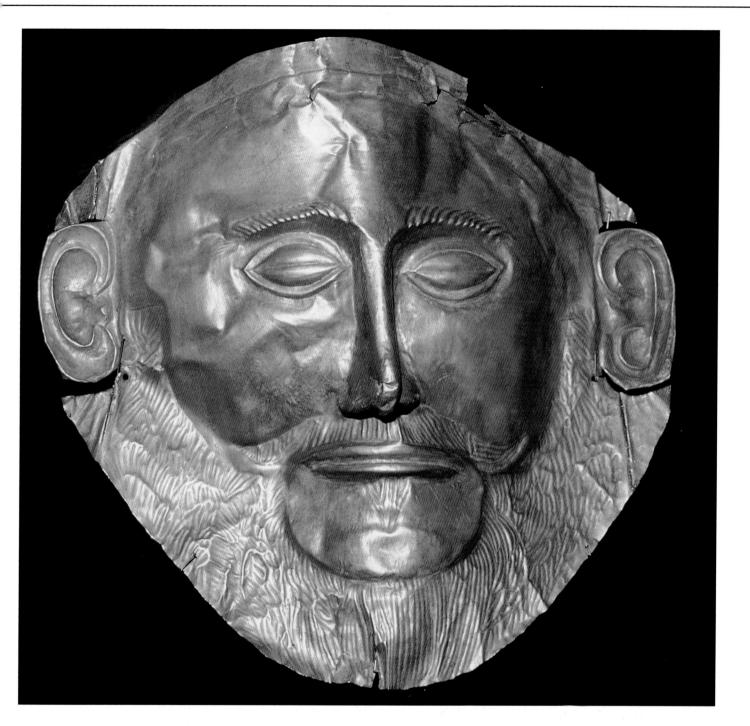

The 'Face of Agamemnon', a gold funeral mask from one of the shaft graves at Mycenae.

sive 'Cyclopean' fortifications and stone tholos tombs could still be seen. The identity of Mycenae was not in doubt. Pausanias had written that Agamemnon and his companions were buried inside the fortifications and Schliemann therefore concentrated on the deep deposits just beyond the lion gate. Once again his intuition was rewarded. In July 1876 he discovered the shaft graves, deep pits cut through the rock and earth, in which the early rulers of Mycenae had been buried in spectacular style. Their offerings included gold, silver and bronze jewellery, plate and weapons. When he found a gold mask in one of the graves, Schliemann declared that he had gazed on the face of Agamem-non, but the shaft graves date from the early years of the Mycenaean civilization, the sixteenth century BC. If there was a historical Agamemnon, he would have lived and died at Mycenae in the thirteenth century BC.

Nevertheless the discovery of the shaft grave circle was a triumph for Schliemann. In 1880–81 he excavated at Orchomenos where he investigated the Mycenaean tholos tomb known as the 'Treasury of Minyas', praised as 'one of the greatest wonders of the world' by Pausanias. In 1884 he uncovered the Mycenaean palace at Tiryns and was back at Troy in 1878–9 and again in 1889-90 when he clarified the stratigraphy of the site and demonstrated that there were seven 'cities'. He would certainly have continued his excavations at Troy, but in December 1890 he fell ill in Naples and died. ■

BLEGEN AT PYLOS

When Homer lists the Greek forces at the siege of Troy, the contingent led by Nestor, king of Pylos, is surpassed in size only by the army of Agamemnon, the leader of the expedition. Throughout the *Iliad* and *Odyssey* old Nestor is a prominent figure, dispensing sage advice, and so it was only natural that Heinrich Schliemann, having proved that Homer's tales were not poetic fantasies through his excavations at Mycenae, Tiryns and Troy (see p. 98), should have sought the palace of this mighty ruler. It was evident that Pylos must be in Messenia, the southwestern province of the Peloponnese in southern Greece, but even ancient Greek geographers were not sure of the precise location. Their confusion became proverbial, 'there is a Pylos in front of Pylos and there is still another Pylos', and Schliemann was no more successful in his quest for Nestor.

Interest in Messenia was rekindled when two Mycenaean tholos tombs were discovered early this century. The tombs had been robbed but their impressive stone vaulted chambers must once have contained rich offerings. A joint Greek-American expedition was therefore formed to explore western Messenia for Myce-

Archaeologists were sure that there must be a Mycenaean palace in Messenia, Greece, not least because one of the most powerful Greek chiefs at Troy was Nestor of Pylos, but it was not discovered until 1939 by Carl Blegen. His careful excavations have revealed the best-preserved of the Mycenaean palaces and an archive of Linear B tablets that document the Bronze Age Greek economy.

naean sites. One of the leaders of this expedition was Carl Blegen, who had directed the American excavations at Troy in 1932–8. In 1939 he examined a number of sites around the Bay of Navarino but was particularly struck by the remains on the hill of Epano Englianos.

Although there were no traces of the massive stone fortifications like those that enclosed and protected the Mycenaean palaces of Mycenae and Tiryns, Blegen decided to undertake trial excavations. He started on 4 April 1939 and by the end of the first morning he had discovered Mycenaean pottery, stone walls, fragments of painted plaster and clay tablets inscribed in the Linear B script. He felt sure that this must be a Mycenaean palace, a conviction that grew as the excavation season progressed. Unfortunately, 1939 was not the best year he could have chosen for his discovery. Because of the outbreak of World War II and the subsequent civil war in Greece, it was not until 1952 that Blegen could return and resume his excavations at Pylos, which continued until 1966.

The architectural complex he uncovered closely resembled the palaces at Mycenae and Tiryns, especially the frescoed throne

for wine and olive oil, and we know that some of the oil was used as a base for perfume. Two rooms by the main entrance were set aside for the palace scribes, who kept their records on clay tablets. In due course these tablets would have been pulped, but when the palace was destroyed by fire around 1200 BC the tablets were baked hard, and so preserved.

Blegen found over 1000 tablets that are covered in the Linear B script that Michael Ventris sensationally deciphered in 1952 (see p. 94). The tablets are administrative documents that record the minutiae of the palace economy: the rations drawn by textile workers, the bronze supplied to smiths, even the offerings given to the gods.

room, dominated by a large circular hearth. The residential rooms included a bathroom; the terracotta tub still in place. The ruler was evidently a generous host since the palace pantries contained thousands of cups and plates that must have been brought out for feasts and banquets. In the storerooms there were rows of clay jars The tablets confirm that this was Pylos, or *pu-ro* in Mycenaean Greek, and the king is mentioned, but he is not Nestor. It is possible that person never existed, except as a fictional hero, but who can blame Carl Blegen for publishing his discovery as the 'Palace of Nestor'? ∎

ABOVE: Reconstruction of the courtyard in front of the throne room complex at Pylos. Residential apartments open off the portico at the far end of the court.

RIGHT: Plan of the palace at Pylos. The throne room is in the centre, flanked by storerooms in which olive oil and wine were kept.

LEFT: Reconstruction by the artist Piet de Jong of the throne room in the palace at Pylos, showing the colourfully decorated walls and ceiling. In the centre of the room is an immense ceremonial hearth.

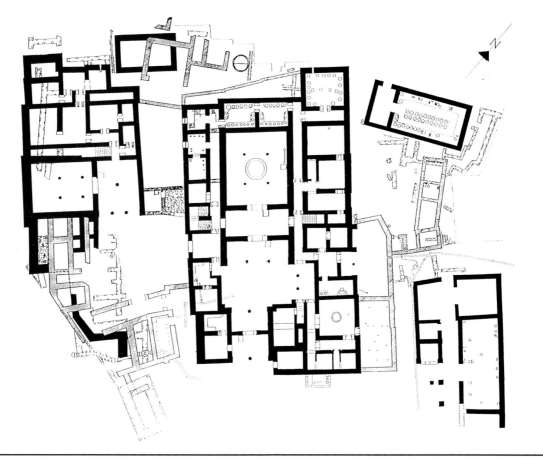

THE ULU BURUN SHIPWRECK

The discovery and excavation of a fourteenth-century BC shipwreck off the southern coast of Turkey has provided a wealth of information about Bronze Age trade in the eastern Mediterranean. The ship carried a large consignment of copper and other raw materials, as well as a remarkable array of objects.

In the later second millennium BC there was a huge increase in the volume of trade between the states of the Eastern Mediterranean, partly prompted by the need for raw materials, in particular copper and tin from which bronze tools and weapons were manufactured. The products of skilled craftsmen were also exchanged, especially between the rulers of these states. Objects of gold, silver, ivory and faience were given as gifts in order to secure or maintain political alliances. It is clear that much of this

Hundreds of wrecks have been identified by underwater archaeologists in the Mediterranean, but few are as early as the ship that went down off cape Ulu Burun on the southern coast of Turkey in the fourteenth century BC. It is likely that the ship had left Cyprus and was bound for the Aegean. The crew had no doubt sailed this route before, but the Mediterranean is unpredictable and stretches of this coast can be dangerous. The ship foundered and lay undisturbed until 1982.

foreign trade was conducted for the benefit of the rulers and their entourage, but texts from the Near East indicate that there were also merchants who operated for their own profit.

The texts providing information about trade and foreign emissaries are depicted on the walls of Egyptian tombs, but most of our evidence comes from the objects themselves. These tell us what was traded, but not how. Shipwrecks are useful because they provide a snapshot of ancient trade. The Ulu Burun wreck was found by a Turkish sponge diver in 1982. He reported what he had seen and it was then examined by archaeologists from the Museum of Underwater Archaeology at Bodrum and the Texas University Institute of Nautical Archaeology based at Bodrum. A team led by George Bass, who had already investigated a number of other wrecks around the coast of Turkey, began excavations at Ulu Burun in 1984. As the ship lies in 45 m (150 ft) of water, the divers can spend no more than twenty minutes on the site at a time. Moreover, the seabed shelves quite steeply and is covered in rocks, so it is no wonder that the excavation is still in progress. Nevertheless, there have been some spectacular discoveries.

Most of the ship has disintegrated but a section of the hull is preserved. Fir was used for the planks and the keel which are fastened by mortise-and-tenon joints. The bulk of the cargo consisted of rectangular copper ingots. There were over 250 ingots on board, 6096 kg (6 tons) at least. Scientific analysis has shown that the copper was mined on Cyprus, which was the main source of this vital metal, so much so that the Greeks called the island 'copper'. The ship also carried ingots of tin, although it is still not clear where this had originated. Texts suggest that the source may have been in Afghanistan. More exotic raw materials included ingots of blue glass that the Mycenaeans used for jewellery. The Linear B tablets suggest that perfume would have been produced from the ton of terebinth resin on the ship, and furniture from the logs of Egyptian ebony, and from the elephant and hippopotamus ivory.

Organic remains are often much better preserved underwater than on land and this is certainly true of the Ulu Burun wreck which has produced acorns, almonds, figs, olives and pomegranates. It is not clear whether the foodstuffs would have been traded or eaten. Some of the pottery was certainly for use on board but there was also a large jar in which a consignment of Cypriot pots had been carefully packed. Gold and silver jewellery, bronze tools and weapons have also been recovered from the wreck.

There has been much speculation about the 'nationality' of the ship but this seems rather fruitless since the finds include Mycenaean, Cypriot, Canaanite, Kassite, Egyptian and Assyrian objects, and the personal possessions of the crew were equally cosmopolitan. It is quite possible that much of the cargo was a royal consignment, destined for a Mycenaean palace, but there may also have been merchants on board, one of whom used a wooden writing tablet to note deals. ■

ABOVE: Hinged wooden writing table found in the Ulu Burun shipwreck. The leaves were covered with wax on which notes could be inscribed and then erased.

OPPOSITE: A gold chalice and some of the jewellery recovered from the wreck. The jewellery exhibits the cosmopolitan character of the cargo.

HALLSTATT: AN EARLY IRON AGE MINING CENTRE

In the early Iron Age, a remarkable community arose high In the Austrian Alps whose livelihood was based on salt mining. The nineteenth-century discovery of the cemetery and salt mines at Hallstatt has since provided details of life in this period, particularly of wealth, status and trade.

High in the Alps near Salzburg in Austria, one of the most extraordinary Iron Age sites in Europe lies in a narrow valley above the town of Hallstatt. The late-spring Alpine flowers covering the meadows just below the entrance to modern-day salt mines grow across the surface of one of the richest cemeteries of Iron Age Europe, where over 2000 graves have been excavated. Deep in the adjoining mountain are traces of Iron Age salt mining in which the salty, moist conditions preserved numerous wooden, leather and fur artifacts. The finds at Hallstatt date to the early part of the Iron Age, between 700 and 500 BC.

The archaeological story of Hallstatt began in 1846, when the mining engineer Johann Georg Ramsauer began excavating the Iron Age cemetery, using miners as labourers. Each grave, of which Ramsauer excavated 980 between 1846 and 1863, was cleaned, sketched, and described in writing. Examples of the remarkable artistic documentation, by the painter I. Engel, can be seen on display at Hallstatt today. Unfortunately, Ramsauer's meticulousness did not extend to publication. The master documentation from his excavations disappeared after his death only to resurface in a Vienna used-book store in 1932. The materials were finally published in 1959, a century after their excavation. Subsequent excavations, including those of the Duchess of Mecklenburg early in the twentieth century, raised the total of graves at Hallstatt to about 2500.

The Hallstatt burials reflect the extraordinary wealth of the community. Both cremation and skeleton burials are known, with cremations appearing to merit the greater quantities of artifacts. Buried with the dead were weapons – including swords of iron and bronze, daggers, axes and helmets; bronze bowls, cauldrons and cups; ceramic vessels; bronze, gold and iron ornaments; and beads of amber and glass. The inhabitants of Hallstatt were part of a trading network that encompassed central Europe and reached beyond to the Baltic and the Mediterranean. The sword handle from Grave 573, for instance, was made from ivory inlaid with amber.

The wealth of Hallstatt was based on salt mined in the adjacent mountains. In recent centuries, salt-miners have encountered numerous traces of prehistoric activity, including galleries with timber shoring and a range of organic remains preserved by the salt. These include miners' tools such as picks, shovels and mallets; torches used for illumination in the dark passages which sometimes reach 330 m (1090 ft) below the surface of the mountain; packs made from leather stretched over wooden frames, which the miners used to haul the blocks of salt to the entrance of the mine; and clothing made from hides and fur. In 1734 miners found the preserved body of an Iron Age counterpart who had been killed in a cave-in. (Unfortunately, they interred the corpse in a local cemetery, where it has no doubt decayed.)

The mining centre at Hallstatt fits into a broader pattern of mining, metallurgy, trade and accumulation of wealth and prestige in Europe at this time. Elsewhere, great fortified sites with large cemeteries are found at Sticna and Magdalenska Gora in Slovenia, while in Poland to the north, the Iron Age settlement at Biskupin (see p. 108) flourished. Further west were the communities who produced the spectacular 'princely' burials, such as those found at

Detailed watercolour paintings of each of the cremation burials were made by Ramsauer's illustrator, Engel, showing the positions of urns with burnt bone and other grave offerings.

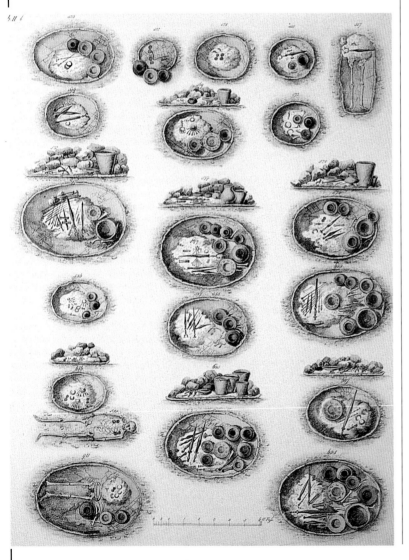

The miners at Hallstatt used leather rucksacks to transport tools into the mine and to carry out salt. Due to the extraordinary preservation provided by the salt, leather items such as these have been found preserved in ancient mine shafts.

Bronze buckets, or *situlae*, are often found in Hallstatt burials. They are carefully crafted with a single handle and lavishly decorated.

Hochdorf (see p. 106), with lavish Mediterranean imports. This flowering of production and trade in the early Iron Age formed the basis for the subsequent emergence of the earliest true towns in Europe a century or two later.

Today, a visitor to Hallstatt can tour the modern mines and the damp passageway 300 m (984 ft) below ground and can see the location of the cemetery. The numerous finds from both the cemetery and the mine-workings can be seen in the Naturhistorisches Museum in Vienna. ■

HOCHDORF: A 'TUT'S TOMB' OF THE IRON AGE

O ne of the most spec- tacular finds of the late 1970s in Central Europe was the high-status bur- ial at Hochdorf, in the German state of Baden-Württemberg. The tumulus at Hochdorf was unrobbed, extraordinarily rich, and fully excavated in 1978 and 1979. It dated to the late Hallstatt period, between 550 and 500 BC, and is one of a number of such burials from this period in Central Europe that have been termed 'princely tombs'. In southern Germany, near Stuttgart, a Celtic mountain stronghold at the Hohenasperg was surrounded by a ring of such 'princely tombs', but almost all of them had been robbed in antiquity or in modern times. In 1977, however, an amateur archaeologist, Renate Liebfried, notified the State Antiq- uities Office of Baden-Württemberg of the existence of a burial mound about 10 km (6 miles) west of the Hohenasperg.

Although the Hochdorf tumulus has been estimated to have been 6 metres (20 ft) high in its original state, by the mid-1970s it had become eroded so that it was hardly visible above the surface

An unrobbed burial mound at Hochdorf demonstrates the wealth and luxury enjoyed by the Iron Age élite. Gold, bronze and iron ornaments and vessels, along with furniture and a wagon, accompanied the man buried in the main burial chamber. Residues in drinking vessels indicate the consumption of mead, while luxury goods reflect trade with Mediterranean settlements.

of the ploughed field in which it was situated. Intensive archaeo- logical prospecting in the area since the nineteenth century had failed to even identify it as a prehistoric burial mound. It was only in February 1977 that it was possible to identify the Hochdorf mound as an Iron Age tumulus with a stone ring, of a scale similar to that of the other 'princely tombs' in the region. By this time, erosion and ploughing threatened to destroy the mound, and it was decided to excavate it completely in a com- prehensive campaign.

The excavations began on 5 July 1978 and lasted until 30 No- vember. The following year, they began on 7 June and also lasted until November. The total cost of the fieldwork was about 440,000 DM (nearly $300,000 by exchange rates at that time). Excavations were very difficult, due to the richness of the burial goods and their density in the tomb, so in some places whole blocks of soil were taken out intact and excavated delicately in the laboratory. Conservation work on the artifacts was also very painstaking, and lasted until 1985.

The excavation of the tumulus, 60 m (197 ft) in diameter, re-

The bronze recliner on which the body was found.

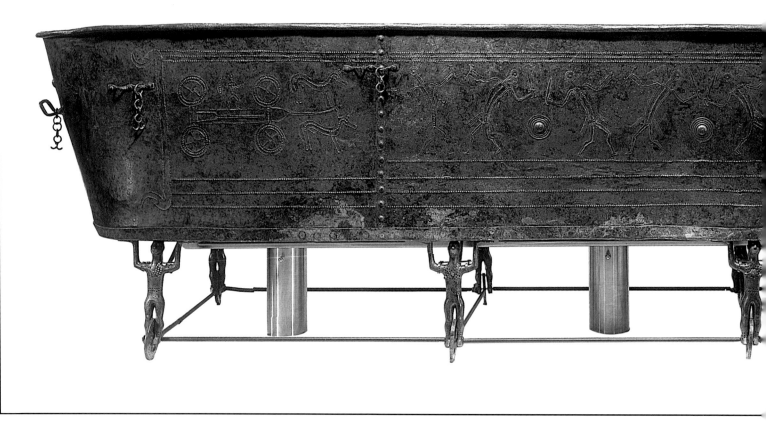

A reconstruction of the tomb's interior at the time of the Iron Age burial.

vealed a central burial shaft, 11 x 11 m (36 x 36 ft) and about 2.5 metres (8 ft) deep. Inside this shaft were two wooden structures, one within the other. The outer one was constructed of oak timbers and was a box 7.5 m² (80 ft²). Inside this was another box, 4.7 m² (50 ft²) and 1 m (3 ft) deep. The space between these was filled with stones, which were also heaped over the whole tomb, about fifty tons in all. Unfortunately, this weight caused the roof of the burial chamber to collapse shortly after the burial, before the corpse had even decomposed. At the north side of the mound, a low stone wall served as a gate into the central burial

chamber before it was secured with the stones. Finally, when the mound was built up, manufacturing by-products and residues from the working of gold, bronze and iron were included in its fill, indicating that there were workshops close by the tomb, which apparently produced many of the grave goods.

The burial chamber of the Hochdorf tumulus had an extraordinary level of preservation, not only of metals but also of wood, leather, and textiles. The primary burial was of a man about 1.8 m (5 ft 11 in) tall. On his head was a conical birchbark hat. Around his neck was a gold hoop and on his chest was a small bag with a wooden comb, an iron razor, five amber beads and three iron fishhooks. He was lying on a bronze recliner, which has no known parallel in Celtic Europe, upholstered in furs and textiles. The seat was supported by bronze figures of eight women with up-stretched arms, and scenes of wagons and dancers are embossed on the large bronze surfaces of the back and sides of the recliner. Numerous gold ornaments decorated the clothes and even the shoes of the deceased, including fibulae, cuffs, and bands of hammered gold.

Nearby was a large bronze kettle, believed to have been manufactured in a Greek colony in southern Italy, which was decorated with three lions, and nine drinking horns hung on the wall of the chamber. Mead residue was found in the kettle, which also contained a small gold bowl. On

Golden snake fibula (enlarged), which decorated the clothing of the buried man.

the other side of the burial chamber was a four-wheeled wagon, made of iron-sheathed wood, with harnesses for two horses. Wagons are common elements in Celtic 'princely tombs', but the iron sheathing is unique. Including its tongue, the wagon is 4.5 m (15 ft) long, with massive ten-spoke wheels supporting a rather lightweight platform.

The Hochdorf tumulus offers rare evidence of Celtic royal life and death. We can speculate about the power structure during this period: were there 'dynasties' or did the 'princes' fulfil a different, possibly religious, function? Strongholds like the Hohenasperg appear to have maintained their status over several generations, but what was their true significance? Was the occupant of the Hochdorf burial chamber really as high-status an individual as the spectacular trappings of his burial suggest? The Hochdorf tumulus is in many respects a 'King Tut's Tomb' of Celtic archaeology but, as was the case in dynastic Egypt, the full understanding of the society of this period will require the analysis of a great many other pieces of evidence. ■

BISKUPIN: A WATERLOGGED IRON AGE SETTLEMENT

The site of Biskupin, about 60 km (37 miles) northwest of the city of Poznan, is one of the most fascinating settlements in Europe from the first millennium BC. Since the settlement was waterlogged, the plan of the wooden houses and streets was preserved in marvellous detail, along with artifacts from organic materials rarely found on dry sites. The area around Biskupin is characterized by numerous small lakes left by the last Ice Age. On peninsulas jutting into these lakes and on the short streams that connect them numerous prehistoric settlements from many different periods have been found.

In 1933 a local schoolteacher named Walenty Szwajcer noticed

Excavations at Biskupin in north-central Poland have revealed the waterlogged remains of a fortified settlement of the Early Iron Age. Over one hundred houses in thirteen rows were separated by timber-paved streets and surrounded by a rampart and palisade. Large quantities of preserved wooden implements and other artifacts illustrate the activities of the inhabitants of the settlement.

timbers protruding from the peaty surface of a peninsula in Lake Biskupin. Drainage had lowered the water level of the lake, and the surface of the peat had subsided. Szwajcer reported his discovery to the Great Poland Museum in Poznan, and the following summer the director of the museum, Professor Józef Kostrzewski, began excavations at the site.

Over the following six years, Kostrzewski uncovered a tangled mass of waterlogged timbers. As the excavations expanded these timbers took on regular arrangements and gradually the outlines of walls and streets emerged. Scattered among the timbers were thousands of artifacts made from pottery, stone, metal, and wood that dated the site to the early half of the first millennium BC, around 700 years before Christ. Clearly, the peninsula at Biskupin had masked the traces of a prehistoric town that could be excavat-

A reconstruction of part of the settlement; looking down the 'main street' towards the gate, past 2 rows of houses

ed almost in its entirety. By 1939 thirteen rows of houses had been uncovered, with walls preserved to a height of more than a metre (3 ft). Between them were streets paved with logs, while surrounding the entire settlement was a rampart made from timber cribbing filled with earth and stone. At the lake shore, a wooden breakwater kept the base of the rampart from being undercut by wave action.

Kostrzewski's excavations were very large and technically advanced for their time. For example, in 1935 a balloon borrowed from the Polish Army was used to take photographs of the excavated area from heights of up to 150 m (492 ft). Botanists, zoologists and geomorphologists were engaged to analyze the rich organic finds and sediments. The Biskupin project also provided the subject for one of the first films ever made about archaeological excavations.

The outbreak of World War II interrupted Kostrzewski's excavations, and in 1942, German archaeologists carried out some limited investigation of the site. Following the war, excavations were resumed by Kostrzewski's student, Zdzislaw Rajewski of the State Archaeological Museum in Warsaw, which assumed control of the project. The excavations at Biskupin were given high priority by the postwar Polish government, which attached much importance to establishing the continuity of cultural traditions in this area.

The settlement at Biskupin covered about 2 hectares (5 acres), surrounded by a rampart about 4 m (13 ft) thick built from timber cribs filled with stones and plastered with clay. A breakwater of oak logs protected the rampart from wave erosion. Just within the walls ran a circular perimeter street paved with logs. Off this main street branched eleven parallel streets across the centre of the settlement, separated by rows of timber houses. The houses had party walls and consisted of a uniform module of an anteroom beside the door and a central area with a stone hearth.

The inhabitants of Biskupin were farmers and herders who used fields and pastures on the firmer ground south of the peninsula. Millet, wheat, barley, rye and beans were the main crops. The animal bones found in the settlement indicated that pigs were important food animals, but cattle were kept for milk and as draught animals as well as for meat. The waterlogged deposits permitted the recovery of an extraordinary range of products made from wood, bone and cloth, in addition to grindstones and metal ornaments and tools.

When inhabitants of Biskupin died, their cremated bones were buried in an urn in a cemetery across the lake. Kostrzewski and Rajewski estimated its population at between 1000 and 1200, although other specialists believe that a more realistic estimate would be approximately 200. Unfortunately, the settlement

Professor Jósef Kostrzewski and Doctor Zdzislaw Rajewski in the field laboratory of the expedition, 1936.

at Biskupin was doomed by the progressively moister climate in the middle of the first millennium BC. The settlement was flooded, forcing its inhabitants to relocate.

In 1949 a museum was established at Biskupin to house the finds from the excavations, and reconstruction of a segment of the rampart and some of the streets and houses began in 1968. Since then, Biskupin has been developed as a tourist attraction. The interiors of the houses have been furnished to illustrate the activities of their inhabitants, and the museum depicts the history of settlement in the Biskupin area. ∎

Aerial view of the excavations at Biskupin, 1937.

ETRUSCAN TOMBS

The earlier explorers of the cemeteries under the olive groves in the Tuscan estates saw them simply as providing goods that could be sold. In this way, large quantities of Athenian figure-decorated pottery went into European private and public collections. Perhaps one of the most famous of these collectors was Lucien Bonaparte, Prince of Canino, on whose land near Vulci a spectacular tomb was discovered in 1828.

The area of modern Tuscany, to the north of Rome, was the heartland of the Etruscans. Although there are few substantial remains above ground, extensive cemeteries cut into the relatively soft local tufa have provided an important insight into this culture. Large chamber tombs were carved into the rock, and many of the tombs had their walls decorated with elaborate wall paintings. The tombs, which were cut as if they were rooms for the living, were also the repositories of a range of objects such as ceramic drinking vessels or elaborately engraved bronze mirrors.

lis at Norchia is evidence of his enthusiasm: 'We turned a corner in the glen, and lo! a grand range of monuments burst upon us. There they were – a line of sepulchres, high in the face of the cliff which forms the right-hand barrier of the glen, some 200 feet above the stream – an amphitheatre of tombs!' Dennis's writings are an important commentary on the topography of ancient Etruria and continue to be used.

The Etruscans were made popular by the English traveller George Dennis through his book, *Cities and Cemeteries of Etruria*, first published in 1848, following his travels throughout Etruria between 1842 and 1847. His description of a visit to the necropo-

Some of the most important discoveries were the elaborate paintings decorating the tombs found at places such as Tarquinia. In the nineteenth century painters recorded these scenes, many of which show a taste for the banquet. The Tomb of the Leopards at

Tarquinia (early fifth century BC) included scenes of reclining banqueters and of dancers, who move along the long walls of the chamber. In the Tomb of the Augurs, also at Tarquinia (late sixth century BC), one scene shows two men – one bearded and the other beardless and thus presumably younger – wrestling beside a stack of metal bowls, the intended prize, and being overseen by an umpire. The illustration may be a representation of the funeral games for the deceased. The Etruscan taste for banquets is also reflected in the Tomb of the Reliefs at Cerveteri (early third century BC) which has a series of couches cut out from the rock, with cushions for the 'comfort' of the reclining banqueters, who in reality were to be the corpses.

Although the Etruscan language was for some time a mystery, recent developments have assisted with its reading. One of the most important breakthroughs was the discovery of an Etruscan book, consisting of some 1200 words, which had been reused to bind up an Etruscan mummy now in Zagreb. The book related to a religious calendar that contained details of various rituals. A second

Wall paintings in the Tomb of the Leopards, Tarquinia, show reclining male and female banqueters being served.

One of the 3 gold plaques written in Etruscan and Phoenician that helped with the understanding of the Etruscan language.

example comes from Pyrgi, the coastal harbour of Cerveteri, in three gold tablets that record a dedication to the Etruscan goddess Uni by somebody called Thefarie Velianus. Two of these gold plaques are written in Etruscan and the third is in Phoenician, and as such provide the Etruscan equivalent of the Rosetta Stone. Sadly, most Etruscan inscriptions are relatively short, often simply identifying the owner of an object or the person buried in a tomb. ■

VERGINA

Although it had been hoped that the mound had been unexplored, the first tomb struck was found to have been looted in antiquity. It was nevertheless important as it was found to contain wall paintings, in relatively good condition, of the seizure of Persephone by Hades. Near this tomb was discovered another tomb with a vaulted ceiling, which was decorated above its entrance with a painted frieze 5.56 m (18 ft) long showing a hunting scene.

The small town of Vergina in northern Greece had been identified as the site for Aigai, the ancient capital of the Macedonians. As it was known that this was the area where the local kings were buried, Greek archaeologist Manolis Andronikos decided to explore the Great Tumulus, a mass of earth some 14 m (46 ft) high and 110 m (361 ft) in diameter.

It was soon realized that the two slabs that formed the monumental doorway into the tomb were undisturbed, and therefore it seemed likely that it was intact. So the archaeologists decided to enter the tomb by removing the keystone of the vault – a method known to have been used by ancient robbers of tombs. As the top of the tomb was being cleared, the excavators found what appeared to be the remains of an altar made from sun-dried bricks. When the tomb was opened, it became obvious that it was completely undisturbed. Bronze armour, for example, was found

propped up against the wall; elsewhere on the floor of the chamber was a group of silver vessels. At the rear of the chamber and facing the door was a marble box, a sarcophagus. It was clear that the tomb had contained wooden furniture that had rotted, and fragments of gold and ivory appeared to have come from an ornate shield. Ivory and glass inlays also seem to have come from a couch, which incorporated small relief portrait heads.

One of the most important finds was discovered inside the marble sarcophagus – it contained a gold chest or larnax, weighing some 11 kg (24 lb), which carried on its lid a star, the symbol of the Macedonian royal family. Inside were found the cremated remains of an individual that had originally been wrapped in a purple cloth; a gold oak wreath had been placed on top.

As the excavation continued, a second chamber at the front of the tomb was explored. This, too, had contained wooden furniture, as well as gilded bronze armour, and a gilded silver bow-

LEFT: Gilded silver bow and arrow case decorated with scenes showing a battle which appears to be taking place in a sanctuary. It seems to reflect the sacking of a city.

ABOVE: Medical forensic techniques were used to reconstruct the face of the man who was cremated and whose remains were placed in a gold box ('larnax') in the Royal Tomb.

OPPOSITE: Gold larnax from the main burial chamber of the Great Tumulus. The top is decorated with a star-burst, the symbol of the Macedonian royal family.

and-arrow case. The antechamber also contained a gold larnax, inside which was found a gold and purple cloth used to wrap some further cremated remains. These appear to be the bones of a woman, probably in her mid to late twenties.

Such rich remains found under such a large tumulus point to the fact that this is likely to have been the tomb of a member of the Macedonian royal family. This theory is further supported by the appearance of the royal star on the gold larnax in the main chamber and on three gold discs found in the antechamber. A gold and silver diadem, found placed in a helmet in the main chamber, is the type of object known to have been worn by Hellenistic kings. The stylistic date of the paintings and the objects found within the tomb place it in the mid-fourth century BC. If this is indeed the tomb of a king, these features would lead to the suggestion that the remains within the gold larnax were none other than those of Philip II, the father of Alexander the Great.

A medical forensic team have been able to make an attempt to reconstruct the face of the individual who was buried in the tomb. He was probably aged between thirty-five and fifty-five, and stood some 1.67 to 1.72 m (5 ft 6 in to 5 ft 8 in) tall. There were clear signs of a injury to the eye, a wound known to have been sustained by Philip II. Comparisons between the reconstructed face and portraits of the king tend to support the identification. ∎

BOG BODIES:
FACES FROM THE PAST

On 8 May 1950 two men were cutting peat at Tollund Fen in Denmark when they were horrified to see a human face protruding from the peat. What they had first assumed to be the buried remains of a murder victim turned out to be of quite a different significance and the local police sent for archaeologist Peter Glob. The body, which became known as the Tollund Man, was lying naked except for a leather cap and belt, with his legs drawn up in the foetal position. His eyes were closed and his lips pursed as though in peaceful prayer or meditation. That tranquillity was shattered when the peat round his neck was removed, and the rope by which he was hanged about 2000 years ago was discovered.

The Tollund man owes his survival to the special properties of the peat bog. In most soils the fleshy parts of the body quickly

The rope noose is clearly visible around the neck of Tollund man.

Archaeologists study people in the past, but it is only rarely that we can gaze upon their actual faces. Because of the special qualities of peat bogs, bodies of people who lived and died over 2000 years ago have been almost perfectly preserved in them. These 'bog bodies' not only allow us to learn more about Iron Age life, but also provide fascinating evidence of the ritual and religious structures through which these people understood their world.

decay leaving only the bones of the dead individual; but in peaty conditions it sometimes happens that the flesh and skin are preserved while, ironically, the bones of such bodies often become spongy or decay altogether. The Tollund man was not the only ancient body to be recovered from a bog. Hundreds of 'bog people' have been discovered in Northern Europe. Most of the remains were discovered by local peat cutters decades or centuries ago, and the bodies have been lost or reburied. But modern scientific techniques can yield important evidence about the lives and deaths of these people from the past. By analyzing their gut contents we can learn about their diet and even the season of death (since some plants are only available at certain times of the year). The bodies themselves can tell us their sex and age, indicate diseases and medical conditions they might have suffered from, and, of course, provide details of the way these people died.

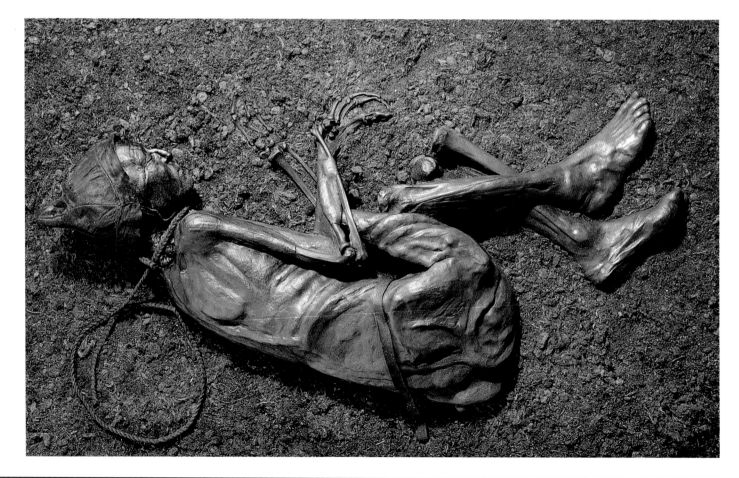

The head of Tollund man is particularly well-preserved. The stubble on his chin could be post-mortem growth.

Most of the bog people we know about died violent deaths, often from strangulation (hanging or garotting), blows to the head, or stabbing (and sometimes from more than one of these). It is possible that they were being punished for a crime, but there is some evidence to suggest that their deaths were ritual sacrifices. Perhaps the grain porridge found in the stomachs of some of the bodies were ritual meals. The nature of the deaths could be special sacrificial methods of execution. In addition it is likely that many of the victims were of high social standing: their hands are well-kept and without callouses, and they were groomed and stripped before being deposited in the bog.

Not only bodies are found in bogs. During the Iron Age other ritual deposits were made in bogs and waterways, so it is likely that these places of earth and water had some special meaning to Iron Age people. ■

The Gundestrup Cauldron

This magnificent silver cauldron was found in pieces in a bog at Gundestrup in Denmark, within sight of the place where two women and one man were buried in the bog during the Iron Age. Although it was found in Denmark it is not of local manufacture; it probably came from southeastern Europe some time after 200 BC. The cauldron is elaborately decorated inside and out with relief work. Each of its thirteen plates features a central Celtic deity surrounded by scenes from mythology, real and fantastic animals and scenes of sacrifice. We can never know for certain how this beautiful cauldron came from southeast Europe to end up in a bog in Denmark, but its placement in the bog was certainly deliberate, and it was probably intended as a votive offering. The cauldron dates to the same period of prehistory as the majority of the bog burials.

THE ATHENIAN AGORA: THE HEART OF DEMOCRACY

The agora was conceived as a sacred space, marked with stones (*horoi*) on which were inscribed, 'I am the marker of the agora'. Perhaps from the end of the sixth century BC a series of buildings were constructed that appear to be linked to the newly established democracy. Many of these were erected along the west side of the agora; they include the *bouleuterion* where the council of 500 met. Nearby was the *tholos*, a circular building, the meeting place for fifty members of each of the ten tribes who held control of the city in rotation. Near these public buildings was found the long stone base that would have carried the bronze statues of the eponymous heroes after whom the Attic tribes were

A long-term excavation in the heart of Athens, Greece, has uncovered the political heart of the city, the agora. The earliest remains, however, stretch back into prehistory. On the north slope of the Acropolis above the agora were found some twenty wells that date from the Neolithic period. During the Late Bronze ('Mycenaean') Age a series of chamber tombs and graves were cut in the area.

named. Another important square structure in the south-west corner of the agora may have been a law court (the *heliaia*) which could include up to 2500 members. Other buildings included a fountain house, the *enneakrounos* ('nine-spouter'), provided by the tyrant Peisistratos in the late sixth century BC.

Near the temple of Apollo was found the casting bit for a bronze statue, inside which were found the remains of the mould for the casting of what appears to have been the cult statue for the temple: a striding naked youth (*kouros*). This was not the only evidence for ancient bronzeworking to be found at the agora. On the hill behind the public buildings was the temple of Hephaistos. Although the pair of cult statues (Hephaistos and the goddess Athena) no longer remain, an inscription records the purchase of copper, tin, lead, wood and charcoal for their production.

The Athenian agora, in the middle ground, with the reconstructed Stoa of Attalos, left, and the Acropolis, top right.

The temple of Hephaistos and the agora.

Although in the Hellenistic period (323–1st century BC) the Greek world was dominated by the kingdoms formed in the wake of Alexander the Great's conquests, Athens itself received benefactions from these same rulers. One of the grandest examples from the agora was a long two-storeyed colonnade (*stoa*) flanking one side of the open space, which was given by Attalos II, the King of Pergamon in northwest Asia Minor. This building has been reconstructed and now houses displays of the finds as well as offices for the excavation; as such it helps to define the ancient space of the agora and sets the tone for the other less substantial remains.

The Roman period saw many changes to the agora. One of the most important was the filling of the open space by buildings, reflecting the way that the city had lost an element of its autonomy as it was now incorporated into the Roman Empire. This included the construction of a concert hall (the *odeion*) by Agrippa, the son-in-law of the emperor Augustus, who visited the city between 16 and 14 BC. The excavators – primarily a team from the American School of Classical Studies, which began work here in 1931 – were intrigued to find the remains of a fifth-century BC temple in the centre of the agora. Masons' marks show that it had been dismantled and removed from its original site (perhaps at Acharnai in the Attic countryside) and reconstructed in the open space. There are indications that it may have been used for the worship relating to the family of the Roman emperor. Other architectural fragments found during the excavations also appear to have been derived from similarly dismantled structures in Attica.

Although much knowledge has been gained by archaeology, the finds have been enhanced by contemporary descriptions which have helped to identify buildings and fill in the gaps. One of the most important documents comes from the travel-writer Pausanias, who, writing in the second century AD, described the paintings in the 'Painted Stoa' which included the battle of Marathon, and the bronze statues of the 'Tyrant-slayers', Harmodios and Aristogeiton. Remains of this open-fronted and colonnaded building, perhaps 36 m (118 ft) long, have been found on the northern edge of the agora. ■

APHRODISIAS

Excavations, most notably those by Turkish archaeologist Kenan Erim, have greatly enhanced our knowledge of the city: for example, through the discovery of inscribed archives that record the links between the city and Rome. One letter from Augustus dating to 31–27 BC related to a request from the island of Samos to receive the privilege of freedom; the emperor refused and noted that only Aphrodisias could receive such an honour. Presumably Aphrodisias was keen to promote its own position over that of rival communities.

The benefactions of private individuals were clearly important. Caius Iulius Zoilos, a former slave who was probably freed by the

The exploration of the city of Aphrodisias, a 500-hectare (1235 acre) classical city on a tributary of the Meander River in southwestern Turkey, has made an important contribution to our understanding of civic life in the eastern Roman Empire. Most of the surviving remains, including the agora (civic centre), the *odeion* (theatre and concert hall) and the temple of Aphrodite and baths, belong to the Roman period.

emperor Augustus, was a major benefactor. Inscriptions record work in the theatre as well as the dedication of the temple of Aphrodite. He himself was celebrated in a relief that appears to come from his mausoleum in the city; fragments were found built into the later city walls. In it Zoilos is shown twice: once in the guise of a Greek, and once in the dress of a Roman citizen. Personifications of the city and people of Aphrodisias, as well as 'manliness' and 'honour' crown him, reflecting the way that he has brought distinction to his home city.

Although the city was technically free, citizens established the cult of the Roman imperial family, building a temple (*sebasteion*)

RIGHT: The city of Aphrodisias was named after the goddess Aphrodite, whose temple is shown here. The building was extensively refurbished in the Hadrianic period.

BELOW: Detail of a sarcophagus from Aphrodisias.

LEFT: The theatre of Aphrodiasis was the venue for some of the cultural events that formed part of the city's religious festivals. A number of important inscriptions were displayed there.

that was approached along a courtyard flanked by two colonnaded buildings. These porticoes were the setting for a series of reliefs celebrating the achievements of the imperial family. Inscriptions record that the project was undertaken by two separate families who were responsible for different parts of the complex that were dedicated to Aphrodite, the 'August Gods' (i.e., the Imperial Family) and the personification of the People (*Demos*). The colonnaded buildings were three storeys high, each in a different architectural order (Doric, Ionic and Corinthian). The middle and top floors carried sculptures in low relief reflecting mythological, ethnic and imperial scenes. The imperial scenes mostly show members of the Julio-Claudian family from Augustus to Nero. Augustus is shown next to a victory trophy with a winged Victory (*Nike*). Another shows Claudius subduing a personification of Britannia that reflects his victorious invasion in AD 43.

Wealthy members of the community also left money to the city in order to fund festivals, and details have been provided by a series of inscriptions. For example, in the late second century AD money was left for a musical contest by one Flavius Lysimachus. The establishment of the games named in his honour – which occurred in a four-yearly cycle – is evidenced by prize lists which include a choral flautist, a tragic chorus, ancient comedy, and a boy harp-singer. Such events no doubt exhibit the taste of the benefactor, and are likely to have taken place in the city's *odeion*. However, the purely athletic festivals would have been held in the stadium. A study of this structure shows that different groups in the city – including the association of gardeners, and the goldworkers – had different parts of the seating assigned to them, the best being reserved along the south side where they would be shaded from the sun by a canopy. Such allocated seating may reflect the underwriting of the construction of the stadium by these same groups. ■

MEDITERRANEAN SHIPWRECKS

Many of the ship-wrecks discovered were identified by the easily recognizable cargoes of clay transport containers or *amphorae*. In the ancient world these were the normal means of transporting liquids such as wine and olive oil, although inscriptions found on them indicate that some contained fish sauces and even nuts. The wreck off Albenga, Italy, dating to the first century BC may have carried 500 tons or more of wine in transport amphorae. The first wreck to be discovered at Grand Congloué by the French oceanographer Jacques Cousteau in the 1950s was found to be carrying some 400 wine amphorae from Italy, others from Rhodes and nearby Cnidus, and 7000 pieces of Campanian pottery. The amphorae from some of these wrecks appear to have come from a single source, as some carried names

The invention of the aqualung and the growth of sports diving have led to the discovery of an increasing number of ancient shipwrecks. In the Mediterranean alone some 1000 pre-medieval wrecks have been recorded. Even remote deep-water sites are now being explored thanks to the introduction of robots. Excavations of these underwater sites have also raised important questions about the ancient economy.

stamped into the handles. Thus a second wreck at Grand Congloué was found to be carrying 1200 amphorae, all stamped with the name Ses(tius); each amphora contained about 26 litres (5.7 gallons) of wine, suggesting the cargo was at least 31,200 litres (6860 gallons).

It is known from the writings of Cicero that the Sestii owned a villa at Cosa in northwest Italy, where there are facilities for amphora production adjoining the harbour. It thus seems likely that this was the port from which the Grand Congloué ship departed. Amphorae bearing the Sestius stamp are distributed

Sarcophagi from the Roman wreck off Taranto in southern Italy. Marble sarcophagi were transported in a semi-finished state around the Mediterranean to serve the funerary tastes of the élite.

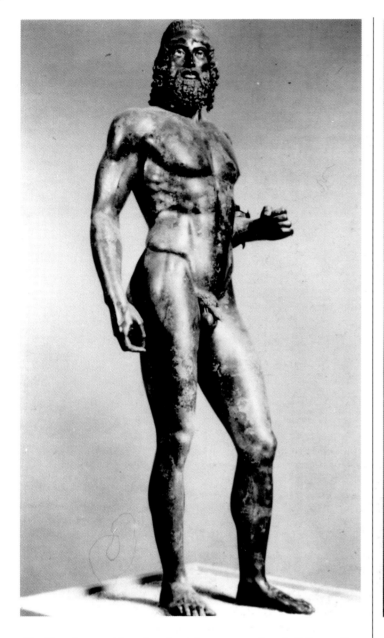

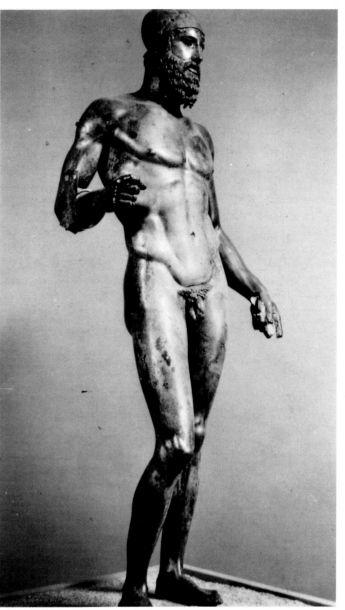

The Riace bronzes. These two Greek bronzes were found off the small coastal town of Riace in southern Italy. They seem to represent two warriors, as parts of the shield can be found on the left arms of both men. They may have been looted by the Romans from a monument in a Greek sanctuary.

widely along southern Gaul, and even up the Rhône valley.

There are a few wrecks that date to earlier centuries. An archaic wreck off Giglio Island, near the coast of Etruria, was found to contain Etruscan amphorae in which were found olive stones; the presence of small figure-decorated ceramic containers (*aryballoi*) from Corinth suggests that perfumed oil was another part of the consignment. A fourth-century BC wreck off Cyrenia on the north coast of Cyprus was found to be carrying transport amphorae and millstones, as well as almonds.

A number of Bronze Age shipwrecks in the Mediterranean have also been explored. One at Kas-Ulu Burun (see p. 102) off western Turkey is dated to the fourteenth century BC, and was carrying at least 250 copper ingots. A similar wreck dating to

*c.*1200 BC has been excavated off Cape Gelidonya on the southern coast of Turkey. Once again much of the cargo consisted of copper ingots.

Underwater sites in the Mediterranean have also yielded some of the few surviving bronze statues from antiquity. Whereas on land they might have been looted and melted down for their metal, underwater they have been preserved. The Antikythera shipwreck was carrying a number of bronze statues, some from the fifth and fourth centuries BC. These are likely to have been removed from a sanctuary or public space, as the ship itself appears to date from the first century BC and was also carrying pieces of marble sculpture which appear to have been made in a classicizing style. Two life-size statues, apparently of the fifth century BC, were found off the small south Italian coastal resort of Riace. They seem to represent two warriors. Some of the wrecks from which these statues may have come could well date to the Roman period when Greece was being plundered to provide great works of art for Roman connoisseurs to display in their villas in Italy. ∎

POMPEII AND HERCULANEUM

The site of Pompeii, near Naples, Italy, was discovered in 1594 when an irrigation channel was dug across the site to provide water for the estate of Count Muzzio Tuttavilla, although it was not until 1637 that the German Holstenius proposed the identification. The site of Herculaneum was discovered in the early eighteenth century when the Prince of Elbeuf acquired a site that had been yielding ancient marbles and started to dig for more. Opening a tunnel, he happened to chance upon the theatre. Some of the finds were distributed as diplomatic gifts, such as some marble statues known as 'the Vestal Virgins' which were given to the Prince of Saxony. The excavations resumed in 1738 under the control of the Kingdom of the Two Sicilies. It soon became fashionable for members of the European social élite to call at the site during their visits to Naples, and often it appears that

The sudden volcanic eruption of Mount Vesuvius on 24 August AD 79 buried the Roman towns of Pompeii and Herculaneum, as well as a number of luxury villas such as Oplontis. The burying of Pompeii by volcanic ash, and the submersion of Herculaneum by mud meant that different types of objects were preserved from the two sites, and that different strategies had to be adopted to explore them.

special 'discoveries' were engineered to be uncovered for the benefit of these VIPs. One aspect of the discoveries that was immediately striking was the way that the forms of long vanished human bodies were preserved in the ash. The nineteenth-century Italian archaeologist Giuseppe Fiorelli found that a special mixture of plaster could be inserted into the space, and when it was set the form of the human corpse or even of a guard dog could be preserved.

The solid mud which engulfed Herculaneum made it less easy to explore the site. One method was to dig tunnels, which al-

BELOW: Interior of the Villa of the Mysteries, Pompeii.

RIGHT: Stucco wall decoration in one of the rooms of the Suburban Baths at Herculaneum. The original wooden door, just visible, is still in place.

lowed buildings to be explored when a wall was struck. The Scottish architect Robert Adam, a visitor to the site in 1755, recorded his visit:

> We traversed an amphitheatre with the light of torches and pursued the tracks of palaces, their porticoes and different doors, division walls and mosaic pavements. We saw earthern vases and marble pavements just discovered while we were on the spot and were shown some feet of tables in marble which were dug out the day before we were there. Upon the whole this Mediterranean town, once filled with temples, columns, palaces and other ornaments of good taste is now exactly like a coal-mine worked by galley slaves.

The excavations have been extremely important in our understanding of small towns in Italy in the first century AD. The well-preserved wall-paintings, for example, find no comparable parallels in the rest of the Empire. Likewise the range of wooden artifacts, either carbonized at Herculaneum, or recoverable viathe plaster technique at Pompeii, provide valuable

BELOW AND RIGHT: Bodies in plaster cast.

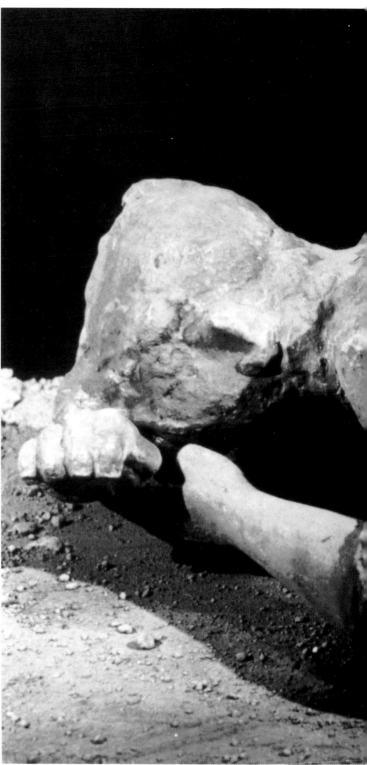

information about couches, doors, and even loaves of bread.

The discovery of what is in effect a sealed deposit means that the cities can be studied in considerable detail. Take, for example, the bronze statue of Lucius Mammius Maximus found in the theatre at Herculaneum on Christmas Eve 1743. He can be identified by a bronze plaque attached to the marble base of the statue itself. Inscriptions elsewhere in the city record him making dedications to the female members of the Julio-Claudian family, and another records his benefaction of a market in the city. At Pom-

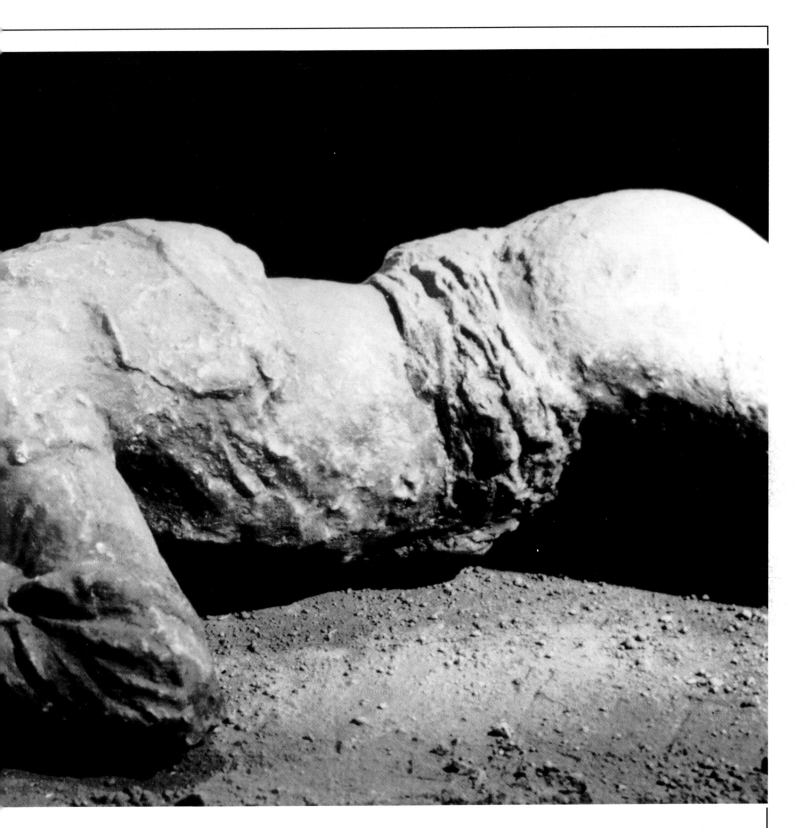

peii, Eumachia, daughter of Lucius, is known to have dedicated a building ('in her own name and that of her son Marcus Numistrius Fronto') near the southeast corner of the forum to serve as a headquarters of the collegium of the wool-traders and fullers. Her husband was one of the civic magistrates in AD 2/3, and his name suggests family links with the Lucanian region of Italy. A portrait of Eumachia has been identified in the building, and her tomb has been located in the cemetery outside the city, although it appears that she was never in fact buried there.

Some of the most spectacular finds in the cities relate to the paintings and mosaic floor decorations. In the case of paintings – since walls rarely survive intact, and then only from the final phase of a building – it is possible to appreciate the taste of the wealthier members of Pompeian society. Some of the most exotic come from the Villa of the Mysteries just outside Pompeii. The figures, which decorated the *oecus* of the villa, are associated with a Dionysiac cult. As such, they represent the initiation process for women. ■

VINDOLANDA

The fort was established in the latter part of the first century AD, when Rome started to consolidate the northern parts of Britain. It was one of a string of forts established along the Roman road – later known as the Stanegate – which ran across the neck of Britain between the Tyne and the Solway. Recent discoveries by British archaeologist Robin Birley, who has been excavating here since 1969, have brought to light a large temporary building dating to the first half of the second century adjoining the early fort. It has been suggested that it might have served as the palace of Hadrian when he visited the region to oversee the construction of the fixed frontier.

In spite of the wealth of literary texts and inscriptions from the Roman Empire, it is rare to gain an insight into the lives of private individuals of the period. The waterlogged nature of the site has ensured the survival of wooden writing tablets, on which writing was cut through wax, and of thin wood slivers bearing writing in ink which can now be read with the help of infra-red photography. Such documents may be compared to the papyri known from the eastern part of the Empire in Syria and Egypt. Over 1500 documents have been found, of which about 200 have readable texts. The letters provide valuable information about individuals within the province, and to date some 140 new names have supplemented what was previously known from inscriptions and from the few Roman literary texts that mention Britain.

The documents include roster lists, private correspondence, and records and supplies for the garrison. For example, a roster list for the First Cohort of Tungrians, dated 18 May, shows that the nominal strength was 752, including six centurions. Of these 456 (including five centurions) were absent, serving as guards at Corbridge and for the provincial governor, presumably in London. However, a number of the remaining 296 soldiers are listed as sick, wounded, and 'suffering from inflammation of the eyes'. One letter notes the sending of socks and undergarments to the recipient.

A number of letters relate to Sulpicia Lepidina, the wife of Flavius Cerialis, commander of the ninth Cohort of Batavians who were garrisoned at Vindolanda. There are two letters in the corpus that were sent to her

Although the workings of the Roman army are relatively well known, the exploration of the small fort at Vindolanda (the modern Chesterholm) just to the south of Hadrian's Wall in northern England has brought considerable information to light about life on Rome's northern frontier. Work has concentrated on the civilian settlement just outside the fort rather than on the military occupation.

from Claudia Severa, the wife of Aelius Brocchus, presumably another local commander; a third letter is in the same hand. One of the letters is an invitation: 'On 11 September ... for the day of the celebration of my birthday, I give you a warm invitation to make sure that you come to us, to make the day more enjoyable for me by your arrival, if you are present.' It is clear that the wives and children of the garrison commanders lived in the garrison. The handwriting also indicates that the wives were literate.

The documents also provide an insight into the problems of transport and supply. A letter to a certain Lucius, a *decurio* (or cavalry troop commander), mentions the gift of fifty oysters from an as yet unidentified place, Cordonovi. Another letter from somebody called Octavius to his brother Candidus records the problems of moving 5000 modii of grain and 170 hides; 'I would have already been to collect them except that I did not care to injure the animals while the roads were bad.'

The presence of ration lists allows consumption to be compared to the type of remains that have been found in the archaeological record. For example, lists of food consumed by the garrison included a variety of meat: ham, pork and venison. Although the consumption of meat by soldiers had been known from similar lists in Egypt, it had been thought that this was exceptional. These letters are borne out by the discovery of animal bones in the excavations at Vindolanda and at other military sites which support the view that meat was indeed part of the soldier's diet. ■

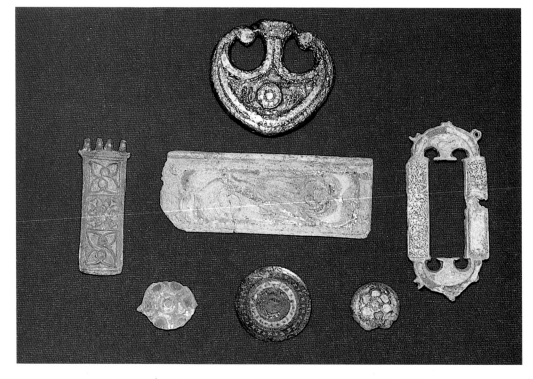

ABOVE: Aerial photograph of Vindolanda. The fort appears in the top of the picture; the administrative building at the centre. The civilian settlement is outside the walls.

RIGHT: Fragment of a wooden writing tablet from Vindolanda. This formed part of a letter mentioning sandals, woollen socks and two pairs of underpants.

LEFT: Belt attachments with coloured enamel inlays. These were excavated in the civilian settlement.

SUTTON HOO

Unlike the Viking ships at Gokstad and Oseberg (see p. 132), the wood of the Sutton Hoo boat had not been preserved. The vessel survived only as 'ghost' stains in the sand and in rows of nails that had once held it together. The finds from the ship, however, included beautiful artifacts of gold and silver, as well as coins and weapons, many of which are in perfect condition.

From the coins it is possible to date the Sutton Hoo burial to some time after AD 620, and it is most likely that it took place before 650. This means that the Sutton Hoo burial is at least two hundred years earlier than the Viking boat burials at Gokstad and Oseberg. At that time England was ruled by a number of Anglo-Saxon kings, and many people suspect that the Sutton Hoo burial was for a member of one of the Saxon 'royal families'.

The burial included a sword decorated with gold and garnets, a helmet, several other weapons, a shield with dragon and bird de-

The Sutton Hoo boat burial is the most spectacular Anglo-Saxon find ever made – some have called it the greatest find in all of British archaeology. It was discovered under a mound at Sutton Hoo near the Suffolk coast. When the mound was opened in 1939 archaeologists uncovered grave goods of unparalleled richness.

signs made from bronze gilt foil, three bronze hanging bowls, drinking horns with silver fittings, a large silver bowl and a set of smaller ones, nineteen pieces of gold jewellery inset with garnets, a purse full of coins and numerous other objects of gold, silver and other materials. Amongst all this wealth, however, no actual body was found. Whether there ever was a body or whether the Sutton Hoo burial is a 'cenotaph', or empty tomb, has been the subject of much controversy among archaeologists. The acid conditions of the sand are such that it is possible for a body to be entirely eliminated, including the bones and teeth. Tests for the chemical traces of a body have been carried out, but the results were not conclusive. The burial contains none of the personal items, such as pins and rings, that one might expect to be buried with a body. However, the iron fittings for a coffin were discovered marking out an empty rectangle in the middle of the area of the grave goods. It is

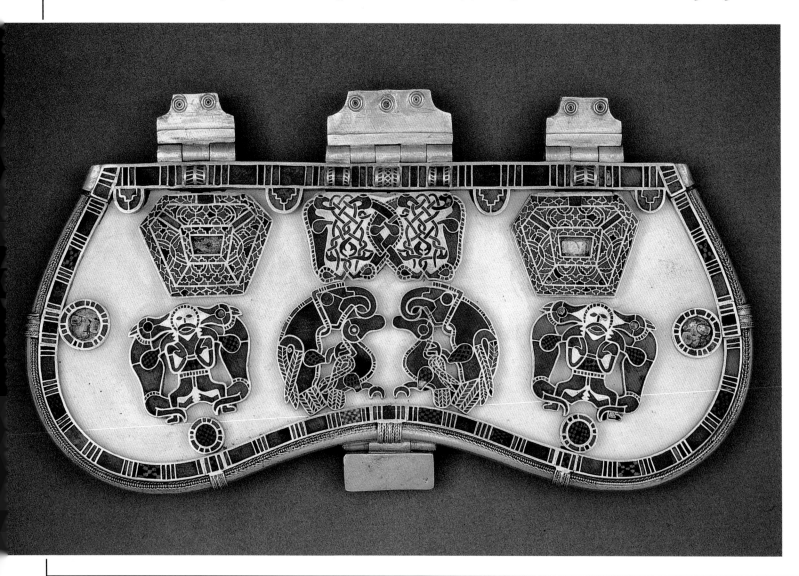

The Sutton Hoo ship under excavation in 1939. Rows of nails are visible along the length of its sides.

BELOW: The great buckle is made of solid gold and weighs nearly 0.45 kg (1 lb). It is decorated all over with interlacing patterns featuring animals and birds.

LEFT: This exquisite purse lid is decorated with gold, garnet and millefiori enamel.

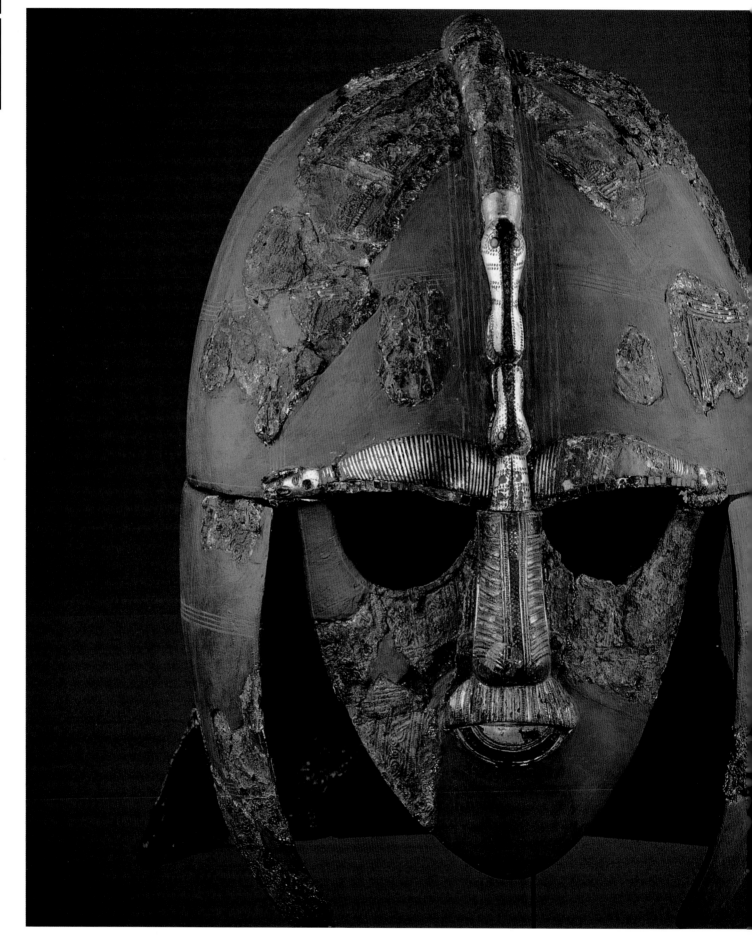

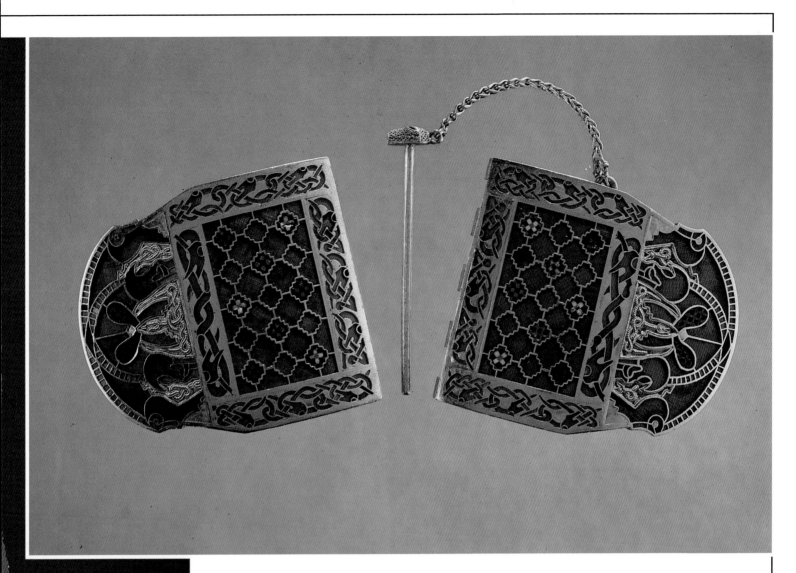

therefore likely that the ship originally contained a body which has since completely dissolved, along with the wood of the coffin, in the acid sand.

The grave goods were not only impressively rich but also interesting for the range of craft traditions that they represent. The objects come from Egypt and from Scandinavia, from southeast Europe and western Asia. The artistic style of the English-made jewellery and weapons mixes Saxon and Celtic in a distinctively 'British' style.

Many scholars have wondered who the individual buried at Sutton Hoo could have been. Whoever it was must have been rich and of high social status with access to imported artifacts and the finest Saxon work. Contemporary chronicles and histories tell us the names of some of the East Anglian royal family of the time and something about their lives, but in the absence of personal artifacts it is impossible to say for certain who was buried at Sutton Hoo.

However, the name of the person buried is perhaps less important than the change in our view of the early Anglo-Saxons that the discoveries there brought about. Instead of being crude warriors, the Anglo-Saxons could now be seen as rich in material wealth and artistic skills, as an economic force in a wider European network, and as respectful and imaginative in the treatment of their dead. ■

VIKING SHIPS

In 1880 a mound in Southern Norway near the town of Oseberg on the Oslo Fjord was excavated, leading to the discovery of a complete Viking ship, dating from about AD 900. This 'Gokstad ship' was 25 m (83 ft) long and 6 m (20 ft) wide across the middle. It was equipped with both oars and sails. The hull of the ship was made of overlapping horizontal planks (clinker-built). The details of its construction reveal something about the success of the Vikings. The ship was slim and shallow with a deep keel. This means that it was easy to direct, even in shallow waters. Viking ships were large and fast enough to cross oceans, but also sufficiently manoeuvrable to be sailed inland along rivers. The ship would have had no need of protected harbours and could make

We tend to think of the Vikings as piratical destroyers, raiding the peaceful settlements of western Europe. Their reputation for violence is well-deserved, but these sea-borne Scandinavians also developed a sophisticated social and economic culture. From the eighth century AD they sailed out not only to pillage and plunder, but also to trade and to colonize. The Vikings were international merchants, bringing back goods from the Far East and possibly the New World to their trading centres at Birka, Hedeby and elsewhere.

landfalls wherever there was a shallow beach onto which it could be carried. The victims of Viking raids were often surprised to be attacked from shores with no harbour, or from rivers that were assumed to be unnavigably shallow.

On the Gokstad ship was a wooden burial chamber containing the skeleton of a man. The burial had been pillaged by grave-robbers, and we can only guess at its original splendour. Despite the removal of weapons and personal ornaments the burial contained the remains of at least twelve horses, six dogs and a peacock – a very exotic possession. The man was furnished with a sledge, some small boats and other equipment, including a huge cauldron.

In 1903 another boat burial was discovered at Oseberg which surpassed even the Gokstad ship in its richness. Like the Gokstad ship, the Oseberg ship was exceptionally well-preserved. The two vessels are of similar dimensions, but the prow of the Oseberg ship is beautifully carved. It also has a burial chamber that contains the remains of two women, one old and one young. Some Norse scholars have suggested that the young woman could be Queen Asa who died in the middle of the ninth century. Some of her personal objects had been stolen by grave-robbers (possibly not long after her death, as many Norse sagas include episodes of grave-robbing), but archaeologists still found three sledges, at least ten horses, a saddle, two oxen, several beds with bedding and other textiles, domestic equipment and an elaborately carved cart.

The magnificent boat burials of the pagan Vikings, the poetical descriptions of ships and seafaring in Norse sagas and the frequent depictions of boats in their art suggest that, for the Vikings, their ships not only carried them from place to place, but also defined their identity and encapsulated their values. ■

The Smiss stone from Gotland shows a ship under full sail. Pictorial representations of ships are often found in monuments and art of the Viking period and give us an idea of their importance to the Norse people.

RIGHT: The ornamental carving on the Oseberg ship's prow is clearly visible on this photograph of the ship under excavation in 1904. Note also the clinker-built construction of the hull.

BELOW: The Norse tradition of boat burial includes not only the spectacular burials like those at Oseberg and Gokstad, but also simple burials in little rowing boats or even, like these burials from Lindholm in Jutland, just a representation of a boat. These boat-shaped stone settings were erected in the late Viking period.

NOVGOROD: A MEDIEVAL CITY IN RUSSIA

The excavations at Novgorod, about 160 km (100 miles) south of St Petersburg in northwestern Russia, began in 1929 under the direction of Artemii Artsikhovsky; since 1951 they have been more or less continuous. Indeed, it was assumed that they would continue indefinitely, but whether this will be possible is unclear in light of current economic conditions in Russia. For nearly fifty years, however, the Novgorod excavations were among the largest in Russia. The waterlogged deposits resulted in an extraordinary degree of preservation of wood, especially of house walls and timber streets, but also of leather and wooden utensils, musical instruments and even toys. Analysis of tree rings in the larger timbers has permitted the development of a chronology that can date structures with a precision of the order of fifteen to twenty-five years.

Many of the structures are workshops that specialized in the manufacture of leather goods, jewellery, shoes, metal and glass objects, and other crafts. Novgorod was linked to a trading network that encompassed much of northern Europe and extended even to the Indian Ocean. Domestic buildings at Novgorod were log

Excavations at the medieval Russian town of Novgorod have revealed many layers of construction, which began in the ninth century AD. The soil under Novgorod is clay, so the timber buildings and streets that were constructed in the eight centuries that followed became waterlogged and preserved. Among these structures were over 100,000 artifacts, including 700 unusual birchbark manuscripts on which the everyday life of the inhabitants of Novgorod was recorded.

cabins, built using combinations of several basic modules, possibly with two or even three storeys. They were separate buildings, each with a yard enclosed by a stake fence which isolated the complex from the street. The streets were surfaced with timbers, using a method that involved laying three or four thin poles along the length of the street upon which were laid split logs of about 40–50 cm (16–20 in) in diameter side-by-side across the width of the street. At Saints Cosmas and Damian Street, a total of twenty-eight paving levels have been identified dated by their tree-rings. The earliest street at this location was laid in AD 953 and the latest in 1462.

Perhaps the most extraordinary finds at Novgorod have been over 700 birch-bark manuscripts, known as *beresty*, which were written between the middle of the eleventh century and the early fifteenth century. The first of these was discovered in 1951 in a level dating between AD 1369 and 1409, but more were later found in earlier levels. The *beresty* were pieces of birchbark that were boiled to remove the coarse outer layers. The fine inner layers were then inscribed without ink using styluses made from bone or metal. The contents of the beresty describe numerous aspects of life in Novgorod, from dull household records to legal, governmental and commercial discussions. They reveal a level of literacy hitherto unexpected in medieval Russia and, moreover, indicate that a large segment of the population could read and write to some degree.

Approximately 2% of the area of ancient Novgorod has been excavated, so archaeologists have estimated that there are over 20,000 *beresty* remaining to be found, buried in the medieval layers under the modern town. *Beresty* have recently come to light in other towns in northwest Russia, such as Pskov, and these documents will be a continual source of new information about medieval Russia. When combined with the huge number of artifacts and the preserved houses and streets, they offer a wealth of information about the life of this region about a thousand years ago. ■

The waterlogged preservation in the deposits of Novgorod has permitted the recovery of objects of everyday life, such as this child's leather shoe, which are rarely found at other sites.

ABOVE: An example of one of the *beresty*, or birch-bark manuscripts, from Novgorod.

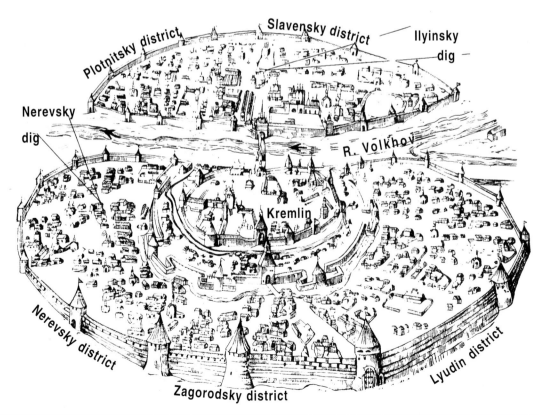

Plotnitsky district

Slavensky district

Ilyinsky dig

Nerevsky dig

R. Volkhov

Kremlin

Nerevsky district

Zagorodsky district

Lyudin district

LEFT: The central feature of medieval Novgorod was its *kremlin*, or citadel, but most of the excavations have taken place in the surrounding residential districts. The birch-bark manuscripts were first found in the Nerevsky district.

Western and Central Asia

MOUNT CARMEL AND THE PALAEOLITHIC AGE

The Palaeolithic cave sites of Tabun, el Wad, Skhul and Kebara have attracted archaeological investigation since the 1920s and 1930s. Dorothy Garrod, the first female professor at Cambridge University, began the work at Tabun, el Wad and Kebara, while a collaborator excavated at Skhul. In the 1950s and later, excavators returned to these same sites and investigated additional ones, bringing new techniques of excavation and dating to bear. Despite these later advances, Garrod and her peers at the Mt Carmel caves made several enduring contributions to the Palaeolithic archaeology of the Near East. The stratigraphic excavations detected the changes through time of stone tool forms and

Mount Carmel is a rugged outcrop of limestone on Israel's coast, just south of Haifa. The limestone contains many caves in which the Palaeolithic inhabitants left remains of their presence during the past quarter of a million years. Excavation of these sites has revealed the stone tools, hunting patterns and the physical characteristics of these early people. As a group, the Mount Carmel sites establish a baseline for Palaeolithic archaeology and make important contributions to understanding the evolution of modern humankind.

technology, and established a sequence of periods that reflected these changes over at least 200,000 years. At the beginning of this sequence, the Lower Palaeolithic, the inhabitants of the cave were primitive, not modern, *Homo sapiens*, and were very similar to the Neandertals of Europe. These primitive people used tools like the handaxe, and scrapers made from flakes of stone, that were very similar to the ones being used in Europe. The following Middle Palaeolithic period also contained many similarities with contemporaneous Europe. During this time a special preparation technique called Levallois was often used to control the size and shape of the stone flakes that could then be turned into tools. And in the Upper Palaeolithic period tools were often made on standardized long, narrow blades of stone in a manner so similar to a stone tool industry in France called the Aurignacian that the Upper Palaeolithic materials at Mt Carmel and other Near Eastern sites were

General view of the Mt Carmel caves. Cave sites like Tabun, el Wad and Skhul have occupation deposits both inside the cavern and at the top of the talus slope that formed at the cave's entrance.

given this name too. In the last phases of the Palaeolithic, the blade tools grew much smaller and were broken into geometrically shaped segments that could be mounted in handles as knives, sickles and other compound instruments. This 'Epipalaeolithic' period included the Natufian culture, whose habits and circumstances led to the first farming at places like Jericho (see p.140).

Bones also figured prominently among the finds in the Mt Carmel sites, bones both of animals and of people. Dorothea Bate studied the animal bones that Garrod had excavated, and her analysis made as basic a contribution to knowledge of the period as Garrod's study of the chipped stones had. For Bate, the animal bones were significant in two different ways. Most obviously, they represented the animals that human hunters had killed and brought home to share and eat, including various kinds of goat, deer, gazelle, boar, wild horses and wild cattle. The habits of these animals gave clues about where the prehistoric people went to hunt, and so helped to infer the behaviour patterns of the people. But, ingeniously, Bate also used the habits of the animals to help date the periods of the Mt Carmel Palaeolithic. She noted that high proportions of gazelle indicated open desert vegetation and a drier climate, whereas high proportions of fallow deer reflected a more wooded landscape and a wetter climate. The fluctuating ratio of gazelle to deer in the Mt Carmel caves indicated three episodes of wetter conditions, which Bate proposed to correlate with glaciation events in the better known Ice Ages in Europe. In this indirect way, she laid the foundation for dating the Palaeolithic of the Near East, even before the advent of radiocarbon and other laboratory methods.

The Mt Carmel caves also held the skeletons of Neandertals and of early modern people. These fossils have contributed important information to the story of human evolution. Garrod and her collaborators found eleven skeletons in the Tabun and Skhul caves. Many of these remains had both Neandertal characteristics, like a very heavy brow ridge, and modern characteristics, like a higher forehead and a chin. The combination of physical traits seemed to reflect an evolutionary transition to modern human beings. The renewed excavations in the Mt Carmel caves and in other Palaeolithic sites in Israel during the past thirty years added significantly to this inventory of fossils, and compounded the complications of their interpretation. The fossils from the Qafzeh site, near Nazareth, repeated the combination of Neandertal and

A Natufian burial at el–Wad. By the end of the Palaeolithic, interment of the dead in formal graves, accompanied by objects of wealth, had become common. In this case, the deceased was decorated with a headband of sea shells.

modern anatomical characteristics that had first been seen in the Skhul specimens. Most physical anthropologists today classify these specimens as early examples of modern humans, despite the persistence of some older, Neandertal, traits. Moreover, recently developed dating techniques indicate that the Skhul and Qafzeh fossils are roughly 100,000 years old, making them contemporaneous with the Neandertals found in the Tabun cave. From this evidence it seems that populations of Neandertals and of modern *Homo sapiens* co-existed for a very long time in the Near East. ■

JERICHO

The British archaeologist Kathleen Kenyon undertook the most thorough and careful of these excavations during the 1950s. Although Kenyon and the earlier diggers were most interested in understanding its Biblical associations, the most important scientific results of the Jericho excavations concern its beginnings and the rise of farming as a way of life.

The oldest Jericho belonged to the Natufian culture, which dates roughly to 10,500–8500 BC, at the end of the Ice Age. The Natufians were the first people in Palestine to build villages that several hundred people occupied for most of the year. The vil-

Jericho, an oasis in the Jordan River valley, is best known for the story of Joshua and the trumpets that brought down the city wall. Joshua's victory was part of the Israelite movement into the Promised Land, which archaeologists place at the beginning of the Iron Age, around 1200 BC. Excavations over the past century have revealed the Iron Age town, as well as its Bronze Age predecessors.

lagers lived in round, single-roomed houses that were dug partly into the ground, and used heavy equipment that was too burdensome to carry over long distances. These people collected and stored large amounts of wild wheat and barley, and probably experimented with planting these cereals.

The Neolithic period followed the Natufian culture. In the nineteenth century, the name 'neolithic' (new stone) denoted the invention both of a new kind of stone tool technology (polished stone axes) and of pottery, and scientists believed that pottery and farming went together. But in the Near East, and in many other early farming cultures around the world, farming began before the invention of pottery. In order to make the seeming anomaly of a food-growing culture without pottery very plain, the early phases came to be called the Pre-Pottery Neolithic (PPN), which was divided into two phases: PPNA (8500–7300 BC) and PPNB (7300–6300 BC). The Pre-Pottery Neolithic communities lived from a combination of farming, animal herding, hunting and gathering wild plant foods. Human manipulation of plants and animals produced changes in the shape and size of the wild species, changes that indicate domestication of the species. Among the crops of PPNA agriculture were several species of wheat, barley and lentils, while domesticated goats appeared during the PPNB period. Kenyon's work at Jericho provided some of the first evidence for very early farming in the Near East, to which other sites in the Levant, Turkey and Iraq have since added much information. But Jericho and the Levant lagged behind other parts of the Near

The stone tower of the Pre-Pottery Neolithic period. Civic engineering on such a large scale was completely unexpected for the period nearly 9000 years ago.

A Neolithic burial with skulls beneath a house in Jericho.

East in animal herding – sheep, cattle, pigs, and goats appeared earlier in the mountains of Turkey and Iraq than in Palestine. In other words, Jericho was part of the first farming, but adopted animal keeping later, from the neighbouring region to the north. In combination, these plants and animals still form the basis of life across the Near East and Europe today.

In addition to the lack of pottery, Pre-Pottery Neolithic Jericho presented several unexpected features. Already during the PPNA a stone wall and a large ditch cut into bedrock surrounded the 4 hectare (10 acre) settlement. The 3.6 m (12 ft) high town wall was enhanced by a tower, 9 m (30 ft) high, built of solid stone and entered through an internal staircase. Although Kenyon believed the monumental stonework to have been built in defence of the settlement, more recent thinking relates it to diversion of flood waters. The houses of Jericho and of other PPNA villages were built of stones or mudbricks and were often partially sunk into the ground, similar to the habitations of their Natufian predecessors. The oval structures normally contained a single room with a plastered floor and a hearth. In the PPNB settlement that followed, the typical house was rectangular and elaborated with a thick plaster floor that was often polished and painted. The shift from circular to rectilinear architecture established the typical Near Eastern village of today with residences thickly packed, higgledy-piggledy, along winding lanes.

The PPNB culture was most remarkable for the burials beneath the floors of houses. The skeletons often lacked skulls, which had been separated before burial and used as the base for a death-mask of clay or plaster modelled over the bone, often inset with cowrie shells for eyes, and, in at least one case, decorated with a painted moustache. These portrait skulls might be buried near the body or in groups, or might be kept in the room above the burial. Many archaeologists believe that the portrait skulls were part of an ancestor cult. Kenyon and the earlier excavators at Jericho found remains of nearly life-size human figures in plaster, the faces of which were very similar to the portrait skulls. These plaster statues may have played a role in the same ancestor cult, or may have represented deities. Plaster was also formed into a kind of pottery, foreshadowing the more regular use of clay for ceramics during the Pottery Neolithic period that followed. ■

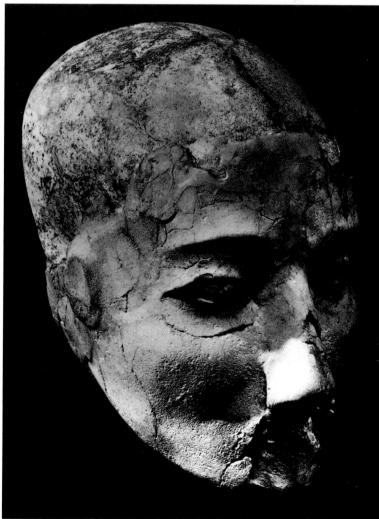

Plastered portrait skull from Jericho. While many examples of plastered heads are not well preserved, others are in good condition. This example retains almost all the plaster covering, and indicates the care taken in the preparation of these portraits.

UR

The earliest traces of human occupation in the Tigris-Euphrates river valley of southern Mesopotamia date to around 5500 BC, when villagers using a particular style of painted pottery first appeared in the archaeological record. From this time until the first written texts, the continuity of occupation remained unbroken. By around 3500 BC, these people were building elaborate temples, which they filled with exotic stone and metal objects. At about this time, the need to keep track of more complicated economic transactions led to the invention of a primitive writing that developed into a literary instrument within the next thousand years. Around 2700 BC, kings began leaving inscriptions boasting of their deeds, priests began recording their myths, and accountants kept track of the finances of palaces and temples. These Sumerians laid the foundations of the Mesopotamian civilization.

The Sumerians were discovered during the 1870s, but they remained poorly known until after World War I, when excavations throughout southern Mesopotamia revealed their houses, palaces, temples, burial practices and wealth. The most famous of these excavations was Sir Leonard Woolley's work at Ur, in the deep south of Mesopotamia. Woolley dug at Ur from 1922 until 1934, during which time he gained a comprehensive understanding of the city's history from its prehistoric beginnings nearly 7000 years ago to its final abandonment around the time of Christ. He dug

When the British scholar Sir Leonard Woolley dug at Ur, during the 1920s and 1930s, he made some of the most spectacular discoveries in the history of archaeology. Woolley uncovered evidence for the biblical Flood and for Ur's prehistory, as well as excavating the city's main religious buildings and entire residential neighbourhoods. He also found the tombs of the kings and queens of the Sumerian ruling family, along with other notables, which contained an incredible array of precious and finely crafted objects, and vivid indications of human sacrifice.

up an entire city quarter in which winding lanes passed by houses that focused inward on courtyards that dated to around 1800 BC, the time of Hammurabi the Babylonian law-giver (see p. 146), and of Abraham the Biblical patriarch. He also worked out the history of the ziggurat, finding evidence for the great construction by Ur-Nammu, the first king of the powerful Ur III dynasty around 2100 BC, and traced the later remodelling of the ziggurat down to the time of the Babylonian empire of Nebuchadnezzar.

However, Woolley's most important finds at Ur belong to the Sumerians and their prehistoric antecedents. In a deep sounding,

RIGHT: Skull of an attendant wearing a headdress. The court attendants sacrificed to accompany their master in death were also dressed in expensive finery when they ended their lives. Many of the women wore headdresses of gold and semi-precious stones brought from distant lands.

BELOW: The ziggurat of Ur-Nammu. The ziggurat, or staged tower, was first developed during the fourth millennium BC and became a standard feature of the Mesopotamian cities. Although this ziggurat may cover an older structure, the visible ziggurat at Ur was originally the work of Ur-Nammu, who founded the Ur III dynasty that soon expanded into an empire during the twenty-first century BC. The form of the ziggurat was modelled on a mountain and represented the abode of a god – at Ur it was Nanna, the moon god.

ABOVE: Imagined scene in the Death-Pit. The scene in the royal graves at Ur moments before the climactic acts of sacrifice are now represented only by the rows of skeletons and objects. But this evidence attests to the serried lines of ladies-in-waiting, soldiers, ox-carts and their drivers, if not to the imaginable thoughts of the victims and the rituals of the officiants.

RIGHT: Inlaid lyre with golden bull's head. When Woolley found many of the delicate objects in royal tombs, the wooden parts had decayed, leaving the metal parts, stone and mother-of-pearl inlay, and other durable pieces that were loose but in place. By careful preservation, he was able to reconstruct the form and decoration of many objects like musical instruments, gaming boards, and inlaid panels. The front panel of the sound box of this lyre is decorated with inlaid scenes of animals and heroes.

he came upon the remains of flimsy huts and painted pottery that marked the first occupation of Ur, around 5000 BC. These huts were buried beneath a thick deposit of river silt that seemed to match the story of the Flood recorded both in the Bible and in Mesopotamian myths. Thick deposits of garbage from the town then built up over the silts near the ziggurat. Starting around 2500 BC, and continuing for the next 500 years, the people of Ur buried their dead in this garbage.

In the first several hundred years, the dead kings of Ur were buried with elaborate rites in this Royal Cemetery. To be sure, many commoners were buried here, too – Woolley found nearly 2500 graves in this cemetery, most containing only the body accompanied at most by a pot or two. Other burials of commoners did contain greater riches, like metal weapons and tools, stone vessels, beads and other jewellery of semi-precious stones, and other objects that had to be imported into resource-poor Mesopotamia. The royal graves were subterranean chambers, often with vaulted roofs, and were entered through a ramp or pit. Identified by cuneiform inscriptions, these were the tombs of Meskalamdug, Akalamdug, the queen Pu-abi, and others, members of the ruling house of Ur around 2500 BC.

These famous tombs contained not just the dead king or queen but also the remains of wagons and oxen and the skeletons of many attendants. These people and animals apparently had been sacrificed to serve the dead royalty in the afterlife. The kings of Ur seem to have required a lot of attention. One grave contained sixty-eight female and six male subordinates, laid out in rows with their finery still ornamenting their bones; and, in another grave, soldiers with their weapons and ox-cart drivers and their animals guard the outer passage, while nine women with gold headdresses attend the burial chamber itself.

As befits a king, even the royal tombs that had been robbed in antiquity still held beautiful precious objects. The royal tombs, and Woolley's careful excavation of them, yielded some of the most celebrated pieces of Sumerian art; one example is the 'Standard of Ur', a panel inlaid with nacre and lapis lazuli, showing scenes of warfare and peace. Gaming boards, figures of a ram caught in a thicket, and lyres were ornamented with geometric designs and figured scenes in the same inlay technique with mother-of-pearl, carnelian, and lapis lazuli. The decoration of one lyre made a visual joke by depicting a band of animals playing musical instruments. The electrum helmet of the king Meskalamdug is as much an expression of the mastery of the smith's craft as of the tangible wealth of Ur's kings. The myriad of more common objects, like gold and silver jewellery and vessels, ostrich eggs inlaid with asphalt, cylinder seals of semi-precious stones, cosmetic containers, and other goods merely punctuated the message of riches and power. ■

BABYLON

Babylon, more than any other city of ancient Mesopotamia, remained part of the western historical tradition. It gave its name to the tower of Babel, and later was the place of the Jewish exile, and featured in the Biblical story of Daniel and the writing on the wall. Greek scholars and soldiers knew the place and left first-hand descriptions of the massive city wall, the temple of Bel, and the Hanging Gardens, the latter counted among the seven wonders of the world. The city passed into the western tradition as a symbol of oppression and iniquity, and its fate of destruction has served to remind all secular authority of the ephemeral nature of power. Babylon's location had never been forgotten – medieval Arab and, in more recent centuries, European travellers described its remains, sometimes in lurid and fanciful language, and often with the classical authors in hand. But systematic excavation of the place did not begin until the end of the nineteenth century, when the German archaeologist Robert Koldewey started digging up the city of Nebuchadnezzar. Although the Assyrian palaces at Nineveh (see p. 150) had been uncovered for half a century, the archaeology of southern Mesopotamia was still little explored. Koldewey changed this situation through his extensive excavations between 1899 and 1917, which uncovered many of Nebuchadnezzar's buildings.

The German excavation showed that Babylon was not one but two cities. The outer city spread over 7 km² (3 miles²) and was surrounded by a massive triple wall with towers placed at regular intervals. As Herodotus had described it, the wall was wide enough for a chariot pulled by a team of four horses to turn around. The outer city wall merged with two other compounds. The northeast

Babylon was a small town until around 1900 BC. The famous law-giver Hammurabi (1792–1750, see p. 142) made it the capital of his imperial kingdom and elevated the city's god, Marduk, to the national god. Hammurabi's success had established the city as the political centre of Babylonia, and over a thousand years later Babylon hosted another powerful dynasty that overthrew Assyrian domination and created an empire. Its king, Nebuchadnezzar (604–562 BC), completely remodelled the city and erected a massive palace, the Hanging Gardens, the ziggurat and the temple of Marduk.

corner held a palace whose modern name, Tell Babil, reflects the ancient name. The western side was given over to the inner city, itself covering almost 5 km² (2 miles²) and divided into two parts by the Euphrates River. Enclosed within its own massive walls, the inner city held Babylon's royal and sacred buildings, and served as the centre of Nebuchadnezzar's empire. Most of the monumental buildings lined a major avenue, the Processional Way, that stretched southward from the Ishtar Gate through the inner city. The Ishtar Gate, named after the goddess of love and of war, was a high-arched affair decorated with figures of animals. The main palace, just inside the Gate, contained hundreds of rooms arranged around large courtyards. An equally large fortress adjoined the palace outside the inner city wall, enclosing additional royal apartments and a museum in which Nebuchadnezzar kept his collection of Mesopotamian antiquities. A group of underground rooms with vaulted ceilings and equipped with wells and asphalt water-proofing may represent the foundations of the Hanging Gardens of Babylon, at least in Koldewey's view. Nearly 1 km (0.6 mile) farther south along the Processional Way, two adjacent plazas contained the city ziggurat and the temple of Marduk. The ziggurat, the characteristically Mesopotamian stepped tower and prototype of the tower of Babel (see p. 142), was about 91 m (298 ft) on each side, though its original height is unknown. The temple of Marduk, whom the Greek called Bel, also contained shrines dedicated to other gods. The Greek authors reported that the statue and other equipment of the Marduk cult used over 20 tons of gold, and that the rituals required over 2 tons of imported frankincense each year. ■

LEFT: General view of the city. Koldewey opened up an enormous portion of the inner city, including the monumental gateway seen in this photograph.

RIGHT: A reconstruction of the Ishtar Gate. The gateway was decorated with dragons and bulls whose shapes were composed of moulded bricks laid into the wall. The bricks were glazed blue, red, yellow or white so the figures stood out against a coloured background. This decorative technique was employed in other buildings of the city, like Nebuchadnezzar's throne room, and was later borrowed by the Persians for their royal buildings (see p. 154).

EBLA AND CUNEIFORM WRITING

Palace G is the most important of the Early Bronze Age buildings revealed so far at Ebla. The excavation has uncovered a large courtyard framed by a massive wall and staircase on one side and by a series of rooms on another. The palace contained many exciting artifacts, like fragments of carved wooden furniture, stone inlay in the Sumerian style, cylinder seals also derived from Sumerian prototypes, stone vessels imported from Egypt, and a 22-kg (48-lb) stock of lapis lazuli that must have come from eastern Afghanistan. In 1974, the excavators in this part of the site also came upon a small group of clay tablets, an unusual find for Early Bronze Age Syria. However, the discoveries of the next season completely overshadowed these first finds – an archive room in which about 15,000 tablets lay on the floor.

The cuneiform scripts of the ancient Near East were deciphered during the first half of the nineteenth century. The trilingual in-

When Italian archaeologists began in 1964 to work at Tell Mardikh, the ancient Ebla – a Bronze Age city not far from Aleppo in north-central Syria – they revealed some moderately interesting Middle Bronze Age temples and other well-preserved buildings. Then they began to uncover remains of an Early Bronze Age palace. Built around 2500 BC, it still contained the state records, nearly 20,000 cuneiform tablets. Until the discovery of these archives most scholars had complacently assumed that Mesopotamia held unrivalled economic and political superiority over the Near East during the Early Bronze Age.

scriptions from Persepolis (see p. 154) and Behistun allowed scholars to read first the cuneiform script used for the Old Persian language and then the written form of the east Semitic Akkadian language. This accomplishment let Assyriologists read the many tablets being recovered in the excavations of palaces at Nineveh (see p. 150) and other places in Mesopotamia; and when excavations at places like Ur (see p. 142) discovered the much older tablets written in the Sumerian language, these too could be understood. The Eblaite language was a west Semitic tongue, more closely related to Hebrew and Arabic than to Akkadian, the language of Mesopotamia. The Ebla scribes borrowed some signs that stood for whole words in Sumerian, but also used signs to represent the syllables of their language. Since Eblaite was closely related to well-known languages and the script was already familiar, deciphering the Ebla tablets was comparatively easy.

The quickly won ability to read the Ebla cuneiform opened a world that hitherto had been unsuspected. Most of the tablets were the records of the palace official who kept track of livestock and grain, the textile and metals industries, foreign trade, temple offerings, and other transactions of the state economy. The texts described a very rich, powerful kingdom whose economy was based on cultivation of cereals, olives, and grapes, and on tending vast herds of two million sheep and half a million head of cattle. The sheep supplied the enormous amounts of wool that large teams of weavers turned

The variety of cuneiform used for the Ebla tablets is most similar to that used at sites like Fara and Abu Salabikh in Mesopotamia. The Ebla scribes may have trained in Mesopotamian schools, and certainly itinerant scribes from Mesopotamian cities passed through Ebla.

into textiles, which in turn helped to support Ebla's strong foreign trade. As was often the case in ancient Mesopotamia, the state involved itself in many aspects of the economy, keeping lists of labour available in villages, distribution of rations to workers, distribution of seed to villages, inventories of palace property, and the like. A smaller number of texts were state legal records, including official correspondence, decrees, and treaties; and a few tablets held examples of Mesopotamian literature, like a new episode in the myth of Gilgamesh, and school exercises like word lists and math problems.

The Ebla discovery sparked tremendous excitement and controversy that has not yet abated, and several basic features of the texts remain unresolved. One issue concerns the date of the palace, the archive, and the kingdom of Ebla. The style of writing suggests a twenty-sixth century BC date, a time when numerous city-states in Mesopotamia were vying for regional domination. However, the archaeological evidence suggests that the palace was used late in the twenty-fourth century BC, a time when Mesopotamia had been unified into an empire that quickly spread outward across many regions of the Near East, including Ebla. Deciding the date of the Ebla kingdom influences the way its records are read today. Another issue concerns the size of the kingdom. Many names of towns and lands have been read as places in Palestine, Lebanon, central Turkey, and northern Iraq, and some schol-

ars believe that Ebla held commercial dominion over these regions. Other scholars read the same Eblaite documents in a very different way, arguing that the places are villages near Ebla within Syria, and that the kingdom was more localized in extent. But whatever the eventual answer to these questions, the continuing excavations at Tell Mardikh are revealing the unexpected kingdoms of Syria that were contemporaries of the Mesopotamian city-states and their equals in sophistication and wealth. ■

Wood is not commonly well preserved in the ruined cities of Near Eastern civilizations, making its abundance in Ebla unusual. Most of these pieces were once the carved ornamentation of tables and other furniture, and consist mostly of geometric borders and representations of lions often attacking other animals, and of human warriors and other figures. The illustration, which may represent the king, is wearing a turban and a flounced garment that was Sumerian in origin, and holds a double-headed axe across his chest, perhaps an emblem of office.

NINEVEH AND ASSYRIAN PALACES

French and British diplomats founded Mesopotamian archaeology during the 1840s when they began to uncover ancient Assyrian palaces with their monumental sculptures and artwork. When in 1842 Paul Emile Botta, the French consul in the city of Mosul, began digging at Nineveh it was the first ambitious excavation of a Mesopotamian site. Soon disappointed by the results, Botta switched his attention to the nearby site of Khorsabad, where he laboured for several years to uncover the palace of the Assyrian king Sargon (721–705 BC). The Englishman Austen Henry Layard, an officer attached to the embassy in Istanbul, began his famous work in 1845 at Nimrud, where he uncovered the ruined palaces of the kings Assurnasirpal (883–859 BC), Shalmaneser III (858–824 BC) and Esarhaddon (680–669 BC). Layard also worked at Nineveh, succeeding where Botta had given up when he found the palaces of Sennacherib (704–681 BC) and Assurbanipal (668–627 BC). In less than a decade, Botta and Layard had excavated three Assyrian capital cities, and had filled museum displays in the Louvre, Paris, and the British Museum, London, with objects of the ancient civilization previously known only through the descriptions of biblical prophets and chroniclers.

The Assyrian triangle is the section of northwestern Iraq that is formed by the Tigris River and one of its major left bank tributaries as they flow together through the rolling piedmont plain of northern Mesopotamia. This triangular portion of Assyria hosted early farming villages, at Nineveh and elsewhere, some 8000 years ago. Here the kings of the powerful Assyrian empires of biblical renown founded new royal cities and built their spectacular palaces.

The Assyrian capitals have continued to attract attention since Botta and Layard. The English in particular worked on and off at places like Nineveh and Nimrud well into the twentieth century. For example, the *Daily Telegraph* supplied funds for George Smith, a self-taught cuneiform expert, to go to Nineveh in the 1870s in search of clay cuneiform tablets that contained missing sections of the Mesopotamian version of the biblical story of Noah and the Flood. Smith found the missing tablets within a week of beginning work, and reported his discovery in the newspaper. Sir Max Mallowan, the archaeologist husband of the mystery writer Agatha Christie, made important discoveries in Assyrian mounds during the twentieth century, among them the prehistory of Nineveh, and the carved ivories and other objects at Nimrud.

Although Nineveh was the traditional seat of the Assyrian throne, the Assyrian kings repeatedly established new royal cities at places like Nimrud and Khorsabad. The powerful and bloodthirsty king Assurnasirpal II founded Nimrud, and inaugurated his new capital with a banquet attended by 50,000 guests, among whose number figured the vassal rulers of the Assyrian empire. Designed to over-awe, the place contained the enormous and richly appointed palace of Assurnasirpal himself and those of several successors to his throne, like Shalmaneser III and Esarhaddon. Khorsabad was basically a fortified palace town, called Dur-Sharrukin, or Fort Sargon, that later Assyrian kings abandoned. These places provided many of the best known examples of Assyrian palace and temple architecture and artwork.

The Assyrian palaces were like small fortified towns, protected by thick outer walls and elaborate gateways. Often the palaces were set into the main city walls, apart from the residences of ordinary citizens. Inside, the palaces were formed in blocks of rooms and corridors that encircled large courtyards. These blocks housed the various activities that supported the royal family and the Assyrian state, and included the throne room and other ceremonial space, cult rooms, residential quarters, kitchens and other work spaces, and extensive storage facilities. Much of the palace space was highly ornamented. Large stone statues, some 3.6 m (12 ft) high, of human-headed winged bulls guarded the main doorways of the palace. The walls of the ceremonial rooms and passages were fitted with alabaster panels carved with scenes and descriptions of the king's deeds in warfare, hunting, and ritual observances. The carvings were visual propaganda that displayed the king as the source of Assyrian power and prestige, and also as the giver of life and the protector of cosmic order. The guardian figures and the alabaster reliefs that Botta and Layard found at Nineveh, Nimrud and

Reconstruction of the Khorsabad palace. The Assyrian palaces, enclosed by strong walls, were small cities within cities, complete with residences, work and recreational spaces, temples and ziggurats.

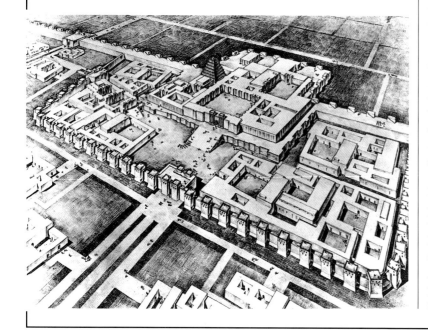

Statue of a human-headed guardian winged bull from Khorsabad. These massive statues, placed on each side of doorways and gates, are among the most typically Assyrian art and later appeared in Persian copies at places like Persepolis (see p. 154).

Khorsabad now grace the Louvre and the British Museum; and the numerous reliefs – Layard claimed that he had found nearly 3 km (2 miles) of wall reliefs in Sennacherib's palace at Nineveh – provided an invaluable source for understanding Assyrian history.

The Assyrian palaces also contained many important objects on a less monumental scale. Assyrian kings like Sennacherib and Assurbanipal assembled libraries of cuneiform tablets that recorded the religious, literary, and scholarly traditions of Mesopotamia. The decipherment of the Akkadian cuneiform script in the 1850s made available the invaluable information of these texts, and resulted in the bilingual dictionaries that eventually allowed tablets in Sumerian to be read. Other archives of tablets recorded the administrative and economic affairs of the palace household and of the Assyrian government; and the palaces were full of other objects like carved ivory fittings for furniture, carved stone altars and stelae, the cylindrical seals that marked ownership, vessels of metal, ivory, stone and pottery, and the many other artifacts of daily palace life. ■

BELOW: Example of an Assyrian wall relief from Nimrud. Assurnasirpal II, the builder of Nimrud, affirmed many Assyrian ruling patterns, including regular and aggressive military campaigning and the glorification in art and chronicles of royal accomplishments. Nimrud, built and decorated on a grand scale to impress the king's subjects, contains many fine examples of carved alabaster panels that once decorated the palace walls with narrations of the king's prowess.

MOHENJO-DARO AND THE INDUS CIVILIZATION

In 1924 John Marshall, the Director of the Archaeological Survey of India, announced the discovery of a new civilization, the remains of which members of his staff were excavating at Harappa and Mohenjo-daro in northwestern India, modern Pakistan. Traces of this Harappan civilization had been noticed more than a century earlier, when civil engineers using the burnt bricks of Harappa as a source of ballast for a railroad line turned up several seals engraved with the symbols of an unknown script. But during the nineteenth century archaeologists believed that Indian civilizations went back only to 1000 BC, or perhaps slightly earlier, and expert opinion placed the strange seals from Harappa around the time of the Buddha. Almost immediately after Marshall's announcement, Mesopotamian archaeologists recognized that a few Indus artifacts had been found in Mesopotamian sites, a discovery that implied a far older date for the newly discovered civilization.

Archaeologists have now recorded hundreds of Harappan cities,

The Indus, or Harappan culture, was the first great civilization of the Indian subcontinent. This Bronze Age civilization, dating roughly to 2500–2000 BC, expressed itself in large cities like Mohenjo-daro and Harappa, and in innumerable villages scattered throughout the Indus River valley in modern Pakistan, and also southward through Gujarat and eastward to Delhi in modern India. Although dug over half a century ago, Mohenjo-daro still gives us the most complete picture of the way of life of the Indus people.

towns and villages, and have undertaken serious excavations at several score. But despite the long time that has elapsed since Marshall and his collaborators finished their decade of work at Mohenjo-daro, this city remains the most extensively explored site of the Indus culture. Mohenjo-daro, like many Indus cities and towns, was laid out in two distinct parts: a citadel and a lower town separated by empty space (or by a wall in other settlements). The citadel contained a group of public buildings set on a massive brick platform that covered about 8 hectares (20 acres) and rose some 6 m (20 ft) above the Indus flood plain. The buildings erected upon the platform formed an administrative centre. Made of burnt brick, these facilities included a large, ventilated granary, a large asphalt-lined 'bath', probably used during ritual purification, a suite of rooms that Marshall called priests' quarters, and a large colonnaded hall. The lower town, where people lived and worked, extended across nearly 101 hectares (250 acres) and held perhaps 40,000 people.

ABOVE RIGHT: A Harappan seal with Indus inscription and figure of a humped bull. The Indus script remains undeciphered despite many attempts to read it. The inscriptions are all fairly short, usually no more than five or six signs, and probably represent proper names and titles.

LEFT: View of the citadel at Mohenjo-daro. The Great Bath occupies the foreground and the Buddhist stupa dominates the background. The stupa, a domed brick structure that holds sacred relics, capped the citadel several thousand years after the Indus city was abandoned.

The main streets were up to 9 m (30 ft) wide, and formed a regular, apparently planned grid-work. Covered drains, connected to the toilets of private houses, ran under the streets in a surprisingly sophisticated sewer system. The city blocks held residential apartments, barracks and workshops. The individual residential units, formed around courtyards, contained anywhere from one to dozens of rooms, with staircases leading to the roof or upper stories.

Various artisans practised their crafts in workshops that clustered together in different sections of the city. These craftsmen made the ordinary goods of the Indus civilization: the pottery painted with designs of plants, fish and animals; the standardized flint knives; the bangles cut from large sea shells; the carnelian beads etched in white geometric patterns by an alkaline solution; and the square stamp seals made of soapstone. The seals normally bear a short inscription in the Indus script, as do amulets, and, less regularly, several other kinds of objects. Despite many attempts to read the script, it remains undeciphered. Many scholars believe that the Indus tongue belonged to the Dravidian language family, which today is represented by Tamil and other languages of southern India.

The Indus civilization remains mysterious three quarters of a century after its discovery. Although its cities and towns are spread over the 1206 km (750 miles) between the Indian Ocean and the Himalayan foothills, the architecture, art, and other artifacts of the Harappan culture are extremely similar, sometimes identical, across this large area. The architecture gives the impression of town planning and of a regimented society, yet no palace or anything that could be described as royal has been discovered. Many scholars see religion as the organizing theme of Harappan society, which priest-kings ruled by their association with rituals and the gods. Some elements of Indus art seem to evoke a spirit typical of later India. These similarities suggest that later Hindu India contained many attitudes derived from the Indus people. Indeed, archaeological investigations in recent years have indicated more and more strongly the continuities in pottery styles and other common objects between the Indus civilization and the Iron Age of the Buddha that emerged in India over a thousand years later. ∎

Statue of a Harappan priest-king from Mohenjo-daro. While statuary is not a common aspect of the Indus culture, this piece shows that the Harappans could create art in this medium. Made of soapstone, the bearded man wears an emblem tied to his forehead, and a cloak decorated in a trefoil pattern that may represent stars. The statue was originally painted with different pigments, and the trefoils had been filled with red paste.

PERSEPOLIS

During the middle decades of the sixth century BC, Cyrus the Persian defeated the Medes, the Lydians and the Babylonians and created an empire that extended from Bactria in Central Asia to the Mediterranean Sea. His successor, Cambyses, added Egypt to the empire, but soon after died while dealing with an attempted coup d'état. Darius then came to the throne under suspicious circumstances, and had to put down a general rebellion. Despite this shaky start, Darius consolidated the empire, organizing it into *satrapies*, or provinces. His son and successor, Xerxes, failed in his attempt to add Greece to the empire, and the famous battles at Thermopylae, Marathon and Salamis came to represent the struggle for freedom in the face of overwhelming odds. The Persian empire endured until Alexander the Great returned the favour by invading Asia and defeating the Persian king in the decade between 333 and 323 BC.

Cyrus built a royal retreat at Parsagadae, in Persis, and this place hosted the coronation of many later kings. When he came to power, Darius began construction of a new city, which the Greeks called Persepolis. This new city centred on a large stone terrace that covered 435 by 310 m (1400 by 1000 ft, or about 32 acres) and rose 15.5 m (50 ft) above the surrounding plain. A massive double staircase gave access to the platform. Many of the important buildings upon the terrace were themselves set on plat-

The Persians created a world empire during the sixth century BC, when their armies conquered the lands from Central Asia to Egypt and western Turkey. Although they came from the highlands of southwestern Iran, they established their capital in Babylon and then in the nearby Susa. The Persian kings, however, did not forget their homeland of Persis (the area of modern Shiraz), where they built and visited ceremonial cities, and where they had built their tombs. One of these ceremonial places was Parsagadae, and another, somewhat younger and better preserved, was Persepolis.

forms, with access through additional staircases, giving the entire complex a multi-levelled effect. The buildings include the so-called Treasury, the palaces of Darius and Xerxes, and the Apadana, or 'Audience Hall'. Many of these monumental structures were colonnaded halls and are now survived by the standing pillars that dot the site. Large statues of winged bulls guarded a number of doorways, just like in Assyrian palaces (see p. 150). The staircases and walls were decorated with reliefs that depicted the king and his courtiers, the Persian army and government officials, and processions of tribute-bearers from the various parts of the empire. The end of Persepolis was also the end of the Persian empire. Alexander the Great occupied Persepolis in 330 BC, and after a night of revelry put the place to the torch, some say in revenge for the burning of Athens 150 years before.

The Persian kings left other highly visible monuments in western Iran. Darius, Xerxes, and several later kings were buried at Naksh-i Rustam, a rock face near Persepolis where burial chambers were cut into the cliff. The tomb entrances were carved as the façade of a columned building, with reliefs and inscriptions overhead that presented the dead king as lord over the subject peoples of the empire. Darius also carved on a cliff face, at Behistun in western Iran, a long inscription repeated in three languages, that justifies his accession to the throne and recounts his struggle to suppress the civil war after Cambyses' death. The accompanying relief shows the defeated and bound rebels brought before Darius for judgment.

Persepolis, Behistun, and the other royal Persian monuments were not lost and forgotten, as so many ancient cities were. Like the Parthenon in Athens, Persepolis remained open to the elements through the centuries, and European travellers returned home with descriptions and drawings of the ruins. Indeed, careful copies of the cuneiform inscriptions, made in the eighteenth century, laid the basis for deciphering these scripts of the ancient Near East. The trilingual Behistun inscription provided the key for reading the older Akkadian language (see p. 148), and thereby unlocking the secrets of ancient Mesopotamia. Most scholarly work on the Persian

General view of Persepolis, showing the terrace and many of the individual buildings marked by columns.

monuments has focused on the historical implications of the architecture, art and inscriptions. These studies use the monuments to ask questions about the development and organization of the empire, its ethnic composition, the impact of Greece on Persian architecture and art, and so forth. Archaeological excavation has played a role in this endeavour, by clarifying many architectural details. Excavation has also discovered archives of tablets, coins, foundation inscriptions, and the objects of daily life like pottery, thereby throwing additional light on these same questions. ■

RIGHT: The tomb of Cyrus at Parsagadae. Although Persepolis soon superseded Parsagadae, the latter's association with Cyrus, the founder of the Persian empire, made this place a symbol of the Persian heritage. The remains of palatial buildings and Cyrus' tomb are still evident, and these again became symbols of political legitimacy during the twentieth century when the Shah celebrated the foundation of the Persian empire.

BELOW: A royal tomb at Naksh-i Rustam. Darius and Xerxes, and several later Persian kings had their tombs cut into the cliff face at Naksh-i Rustam, located near Persepolis. The tomb entrances were carved as the façade of a columned building, with relief and inscription overhead that presented the dead king as lord over the subject peoples of the empire. These places kept their connection with imperial power, so that rulers a thousand years later carved their own reliefs at the base of the tombs.

THE FROZEN TOMBS OF PAZYRYK AND UKOK

Until the recent discovery of the Neolithic Ice Man in the Alps (p. 84), the best-known frozen archaeological find was the Iron Age burials from Pazyryk, in the Altai mountains of Siberia. The Pazyryk tombs, excavated between 1929 and 1949, date to the Iron Age, about 400 BC, and contained not only superbly preserved bodies of people and horses, but also lavish textile and leather objects. Recently a similar and equally spectacular tomb was found at Ukok. Such finds provide vital information about the Iron Age societies not only of this remote region but also of the peoples with whom they had contact, notably China and Persia.

The Pazyryk tombs were excavated by the Russian archaeologist Sergei I. Rudenko. They consisted of a group of five large and nine small burial mounds, along with other stone structures such as stone circles and alignments of vertical stones. Rudenko discovered them in 1924 and investigated the first large mound in 1929. He returned to excavate the remaining four large mounds between 1947 and 1949.

The Pazyryk tombs appear on the surface as low earthen mounds, or 'barrows', covered with stones. The large ones excavated by Rudenko are between 36 and 46 m (119 and 152 ft) in

Frozen tombs in the Altai mountains of Siberia have yielded the frozen, mummified remains of tattooed humans and their horses, along with lavish burial offerings, from the Iron Age. These pastoral horse-riding people had contacts with China and Persia which are reflected in the textiles found in the burials. The gold and silver ornaments, the wooden furniture and the garments found in these tombs reflect the wealth of these Iron Age communities.

diameter. Each mound conceals a central tomb shaft between 4 and 5 m (13 and 16 ft 5 in) deep. These shafts must have been dug during the warm season, for otherwise the ground would have been frozen hard. Within the shafts were timber chambers, consisting of two nested log boxes, in which the primary burial and grave goods could be found. Over these were layers of more logs and stones which filled the shaft up to the base of the mound.

Shortly after the Pazyryk tombs were constructed, the residual warm air in the chambers rose. The water vapour it contained condensed on the stones of the fill and the mound and trickled back down. Additional moisture from the outside also seeped through the mound and the shaft-fill into the chamber. All this water impregnated the corpses and the accompanying grave goods and then froze solid during the icy Siberian winter. The mound above insulated the frozen tomb and kept it from thawing, and thus the Pazyryk burials remained refrigerated in ice for over two millennia. The only disturbance came from ancient grave-robbers, who entered each of the tombs and robbed them of many of the objects they contained. What they left behind was so extraordinary that we can only guess at the original richness of these tombs.

Barrow 2 was the least disturbed by the robbers, probably because it was very solidly frozen, and contained the most spectacular finds. Within the burial chamber, which was lined with felt wall-hangings, the embalmed bodies of a man and a woman had been placed in a coffin made from a hollowed-out larch trunk, on which were cut-out leather silhouettes of deer. On the man's body were fantastic tattoos covering the arms and part of a leg. These tattoos depicted imaginary and real animals, including griffins, rams, birds, snakes and deer. The coffin also contained a woollen rug which had been wrapped around the bodies and items of clothing made from linen. Elsewhere in the burial chamber were more clothing and textiles, leather objects, wooden furniture, gold and silver ornaments and mirrors. The other barrows were looted more severely, which caused

A felt wall-hanging from Barrow 5, Pazyryk.

decomposition of many of the objects, but what remained indicates a similar level of richness. The artifacts from Pazyryk can be seen now in the Hermitage museum in St Petersburg.

Relatively undisturbed by the looting in all the tombs were numerous horse burials, between seven and fourteen per tomb, which were off to one side from the main burial chambers. The horse bodies were preserved in some cases, most notably in Barrow 5, along with extraordinary furnishings: bridles, saddles and cloth horse-coats. Among the horses was a large four-wheeled wagon, with a felt canopy ornamented with appliquéd figures of swans.

Tattoo of fabulous beasts from the skin of a chieftain's arm, Pazyryk.

The Pazyryk burials, while spectacular, had nonetheless been damaged by looting and by the relatively crude excavation methods employed. In the summer of 1993, however, an unlooted frozen tomb was discovered by the Russian archaeologist Natalya Polosmak at Ukok, high in the Altai steppes on the Chinese border. Here a barrow was excavated carefully to reveal an intact frozen tomb with the tattooed body of a woman in a log coffin, with textiles and leather items, and wooden salvers bearing cuts of mutton and horsemeat. Just outside the burial chamber were six horses, each killed with a blow to the head, with patches of their chestnut-brown manes and their felt saddle-covers preserved in extraordinary detail.

The Ukok tomb, with the ice-filled coffin, on the eve of the discovery of the mummy.

The people who interred their dead in tombs like the ones of the Pazyryk and Ukok were nomadic horse-riding, sheep-raising folk, sharing many traits in common with central Asian nomads today. In many respects, they had much in common with the Scythians, who lived miles to the west in the steppes north of the Black Sea and who also buried their élite in rich tombs and featured animals prominently in their art. More importantly, similarities in patterns and the use of materials such as silk show that these people had contact with Persia and China at this time. The use of modern scientific techniques in the study of the Ukok tomb, such as DNA analysis, will be able to tell us much more about the day-to-day lives of these people. ■

The mummy of the tattooed woman, revealed after the log coffin had been defrosted, Ukok. In 1995 the 3000-year-old body of a man, with an elk tattoo, was found buried with his horse, also in Siberia.

MASADA

Towering above the surrounding desert on the western coast of the Dead Sea, the rock of Masada is the most dramatic archaeological site in Israel, in both its location and its role in Jewish history.

The natural defences of the rock of Masada had been strengthened by King Herod between 36 and 30 BC as a fortress-palace to which he could retreat in case of disaster. The Herodian fortifications included enormous water-cisterns to sustain the garrison in case of siege, while the administrative palace functions were supplemented by bath houses and a smaller palace, built on three terraces at the northern tip of the rock, whose charms included a spectacular view.

From 1963 to 1965 the Israeli archaeologist Yigael Yadin excavated the site of Masada. His work revealed much about the original Herodian buildings but was more immediately important for two other reasons. Firstly, the nature of the excavation itself: Yadin's military experience was vital in organizing a large excavation in an inhospitable terrain and the success of the work was a triumph of logistics in controlling a large team that was mostly comprised of international volunteers. The Masada excavations were also important for the young state of Israel in providing a focus of national identity through archaeology; Masada was the scene of one of the most remarkable examples in Jewish history of resistance to overwhelming odds, a theme that found echoes in contemporary Israel.

In AD 73 the First Jewish Revolt, which had flared up in AD 66, was all but extinguished by Roman force of arms. The only stronghold remaining under Jewish control was Masada, whose 967 defenders – men, women and children – were able, through the augmented natural defences of the rock, to keep at bay the Tenth Legion. Direct assault was impossible; instead, a policy of containment – by means of an encircling wall (3.2 km/2 miles long) around the base of the rock, plus eight siege camps – was adopted, followed by the construction of an enormous ramp approaching the western side of Masada. Roman activities at Masada are recorded by the historian Josephus in his account of the

View of the rock of Masada, a natural fortress rising from the shore of the Dead Sea.

The Summer Palace of King Herod, rising in three tiers on the northern tip of Masada. Roman activites at Masada were recorded by the historian Josephus in his account of the Jewish War.

Jewish War, but are equally apparent by their visible remains today. Yadin's team were able to recover material from the occupation period – structures such as two ritual baths and a synagogue and small finds that included Old Testament scrolls, two of which were buried beneath the floor of the synagogue before the Roman capture of the fortress. More intriguing still were eleven *ostraka*, fragments of pottery with personal names on them, which might be from vessels identifying their owner, but for which Josephus might suggest an alternative explanation: before Masada was captured by the Romans, Josephus reports, the defenders committed mass suicide – men killing their families, ten men chosen by lot to kill the rest of the garrison, and one man chosen by lot to kill his fellows. It has been suggested that these ostraka may be the very lots used for that terrible death-raffle. ■

Dead Sea scrolls

The most remarkable modern discovery of biblical texts occurred quite by chance in the winter of 1946-7 in some caves among the cliffs overlooking the northwestern shore of the Dead Sea (right).

At that time local Bedouin discovered, in circumstances that still remain obscure, a group of leather and parchment documents that had been stored in pottery jars for safe keeping and seemingly hidden deliberately in these caves. Once reports of this discovery reached the authorities a search for further documents was launched which produced more scrolls and scroll-fragments, including two copper scrolls discovered

in a cave in 1952. These documents were one of two types. Some were biblical, like the large scroll (left) – 7 m (22 ft) long – whose subject is the Book of Isaiah. It is the oldest copy of that text in existence. Non-biblical texts include the so-called 'Manual of Discipline', which some scholars have taken to be a type of rule-book for a monastic community.

The site of Qumran is also on the western shores of the Dead Sea, close to some of the caves which produced scrolls. It may be that Qumran was indeed a type of monastic community occupied by the Essenes, a Jewish sect who had much in common with early Christianity. The Essenes may have occupied Qumran from the late second century BC until the First Jewish Revolt when they, like the defenders of Masada (see p. 158), found it prudent to hide their religious books from the Romans whose ruthlessness in crushing the revolt included the sacking of Jerusalem and the looting of the Temple itself.

THE FAR EAST

PEKING AND JAVA MAN

The earliest finds of *Homo erectus* ('upright man') were made in the Trinil region of central Java by a young Dutch doctor, Eugène Dubois, who was convinced that 'the fossilized precursors of man' would be found in Asia. Working from 1887 onwards in a hospital in the Dutch colony of Indonesia, Dubois spent his spare time searching caves. After making his first 'discovery' – a fossil dug out of a marble quarry by local workers – he opened his own dry-season excavations in the river gravels at Trinil. Here, in 1890–2, he had the good fortune to find what he was seeking: a skull cap, femur and two molars of a true 'missing link', an ape-like man. In 1894 he formally announced the discovery of *Pithecanthropus* (ape-

The immediate ancestors of modern humans, *Homo erectus*, seem to have originated in eastern Africa (see p. 21). Soon after the development of their stone tool technology about two million years ago, they apparently dispersed rapidly throughout the Old World. New dates from both China and Indonesia place the earliest *Homo erectus* fossils yet known at about 1.8 million years ago, though these dates are by no means universally accepted.

man) *erectus*, a transitional form between man and ape, and the ancestor of man.

The largest group of *Homo erectus* fossils comes from the Zhoukoudian cave complex, southwest of Beijing (Peking) in China. Discovered in 1921, they were analysed by Franz Weidenreich, a physical anthropologist whose measurements and characterizations of the species became the standard in the field. Unfortunately, the original fossils he worked on were lost in shipment during the Second World War, and only the plaster casts remain for study. However, more specimens were found at Zhoukoudian in the 1960s and 1970s.

Discoveries in the Zhoukoudian caves of ash, bone and seeds dating to the Middle Pleistocene period provide insights both into the behaviour and lifestyle of early *Homo erectus* and into the changing climate. If our ancestors lived in these caves, they would have been competing for space with hyenas and other den-dwelling animals. Indeed, most of the thousands of animal bones discovered in the caves were probably introduced by such animals. Only a few show clear butchery marks or indications of roasting, and none can be proved definitively to have been tools. The composition of the animal bones from the cave layers shows a shift in climate from cold to warm and back to cold again between 500,000 and 230,000 years ago, as determined by uranium series dating (a radioactive dating method using the half-life of uranium).

The human fossils from Zhoukoudian, dating to between 500,000 and 200,000 years ago, come from several caves in a limestone karst complex. Although they have until now been taken as one population group, researchers are beginning to question the wisdom of lumping together materials from such a long timespan. Nevertheless, they do seem to have more in common with each other than with what are seen as fossils transitional to

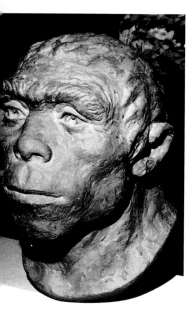

ABOVE: Reconstruction of the head of Peking Man from fossil evidence.

RIGHT: Exterior view of the Zhoukoudian cave complex, where the largest of the *Homo erectus* fossils were found.

LEFT: The fossilized skull of Java man represents one of the earliest finds of *Homo erectus* in the search for 'the missing link'.

modern humans. These transitional fossils – Maba Man and Li-uchang Man from southern China – are considered on the basis of their morphology to represent *Homo sapiens*, the initial form of our own modern species. Some of the features of *Homo erectus* in China are carried forward through these transitional fossils into the modern Asian population, and the presence of these features has been used by East Asian physical anthropologists to argue for the genetic continuity and local evolution of modern humans. This view is challenged by molecular biologists, who assert that our modern species evolved in Africa and southwest Asia between 200,000 and 120,000 years ago, and that this new population then spread out through the Old World replacing the older *Homo erectus* population. Local evolution and continuity from *Homo erectus* in regional populations is not allowed by this view, once termed the 'Eve Hypothesis' (see p. 23). These two contradictory interpretations of the fossil and genetic data have still not been resolved, and debate between specialists continues over the eastern and western material. ■

ROCK ART OF CHINA AND INDIA

Although Chinese rock art has only become known in the twentieth century, even to Chinese researchers, it was actually documented earlier than any other rock art in the world. Li Daoyuan, a geographer of the fifth century AD, wrote a book about places he had seen on his travels, in which he mentions a score of rock art sites in half of China's provinces and describes their techniques (engraving or painting) and their subjects (animals, divinities, and human and animal tracks). Today, rock art is known in many parts of China, but two concentrations are of particular importance. The first is of petro-

Like every other part of the world, Asia is filled with rock art of different types and a wide variety of periods, from prehistory to the Buddhist period. While the local inhabitants have always known of its existence, the world at large has not discovered most of it until recently.

glyphs, thousands of which have been found in the mountains and grasslands of Inner Mongolia – including an extensive series of 'masks' in the Helan Mountains – and the second is of paintings on cliffs along the Zuojiang River in the southwest, near the border with Vietnam. Most of these are 20 to 80 m (66 to 262 ft) above the water, but some are 120 m (394 ft) up, and can only have been done from ladders or scaffolds or, in some cases, by dangling from the cliff top on ropes. The great cliff face known as Huashan, 'Mountain of Flowers', is the biggest rock art panel in the world, over 200 m wide and 40 m high (656 x 131

BELOW LEFT: Detail of the cliff face at Huashan, southwest China, showing some of the human figures, a dog, ring-handled swords and bronze drums.

RIGHT: Two painted animals from Bhopal, India, perhaps a doe and her fawn. Although undated, they are probably prehistoric. Note the characteristic geometric designs inside their outlines.

BELOW RIGHT: Buddha and bodhisattva figures carved into a natural rock face at Pulmunsa Temple, Kyongju, Korea. Historic 'rock art' differs from its prehistoric predecessors in both technology and subject matter.

ft). It has 1819 red figures, from 30 cm to 3 m (12 in to 9 ft 10 in) in height, mostly thought to be chiefs, sorcerers or warriors. What seem to be bronze drums and ring-handled swords suggest that the paintings are about 2000 years old, and this is confirmed by radiocarbon dating of stalactites associated with them.

Rock art is also abundant and widespread in India. The best-known concentration is in the Bhopal region. At Bhimbetka, hundreds of decorated shelters exist in a landscape of towering sandstone rocks. In the last centuries before our era Buddhist hermits used the rockshelters and added Buddhist images to renew the site's sacredness – just as in China there are twelfth-century Buddhist inscriptions among the far older 'mask' images of the Helan Mountains.

Monumental Buddhist sculpture began with Greek influence on Gandharan art in what is now Pakistan. Large sculptures of the Buddha came to replace the noniconic stupa (a monument containing relics) as objects of worship. Across Central Asia, as Buddhism spread with the help of the trade caravans linking the classical Mediterranean world to China, caves and sculptures were hollowed out of suitable rock cliffs by communities of monks. Bamiyan in today's Afghanistan is the westernmost manifestation of this new tradition, with two statues of the Buddha, 35 and 53 m (115 and 174 ft) tall, carved in the half round, towering out of the cliff face. In western China, the cave complex at Dunhuang has numerous sculptures more modest in size and of different construction – many are built of wood frames packed with clay as if they were emerging from the cave walls. Further east, the abundant rock-cut sculptures of Yungang near Datong (p. 168) and Longmen near Luoyang stand as testimony to the investment of fifth- and sixth-century dynastic families in Buddhist patronage. ■

HONGSHAN AND LIANGZHU JADES

Hongshan jades are arguably the first figurative jades (as opposed to discs, bracelets or axe imitations) to have been made in Neolithic China. Birds with spread wings, turtles, and 'pig-dragon' forms were popular among other flared-tube and cloud-shaped pieces. The animal representations have been interpreted as possible totemic markers. The jades were deposited in élite tombs constructed of stone slabs, with clear precincts marked by stone footings and painted pottery cylinders embedded in the ground. At Niuheliang, a ritual landscape encompassing 80 km² (31 square miles) in western Liaoning province in northeast China, thirteen tomb clusters are known on different hill promontories overlooking a valley domi-

Jades from these two Chinese Neolithic cultures have long formed part of worldwide art collections, but it is only within the last decade that sites of these jade cultures have been excavated, and the social context of the manufacture and use of the jade objects brought to light. Niuheliang (p. 168) is part of the regional Hongshan culture (early fourth to early third millennium BC); Sidun and Yaoshan belong to the Liangzhu culture (mid-fourth to late third millennium BC).

nated in the south by Pig Mountain. On a slope of the northern valley is a pit building with plastered walls within which were found fragments of monumental sculpture (see p. 168), indicating its possible function as a temple. The 'pig-dragon' jades are thought by Chinese scholars to resemble the profile of Pig Mountain itself, and the entire complex is treated as a ritually and perhaps cosmologically integrated unit.

Yaoshan, in the Shanghai delta region of southern China, also consists of élite graves, constructed on earthen burial platforms and mounded over with soil. At the nearby Sidun site, one 20 m (65 ft) high mound protected the burial of a young man accompanied by over a hundred jade objects. The Liangzhu jades from these sites are mainly shaped like perforated discs and square tubes with circular bores. Jades of these same shapes, the *bi* and *zhong*, occur in the historic Zhou (1027–221 BC) and Han (206 BC–AD 220) periods as cosmological symbols: the disc or circle representing heaven, the square representing earth. Some speculate that the meanings of these objects developed in Neolithic Liangzhu, while others see only a continuity of form. Most researchers, however, agree that the designs engraved on Liangzhu *zhong* probably served as the source of the 'animal mask' (*taotie*, see p. 173) designs of later Shang period bronzes (1700–1050 BC).

The Liangzhu 'face motif' almost always consists of doubled faces, one above the other. They comprise eyebrows, eyes, noses and/or mouths. The images can be read either as two

A Hongshan jade 'pig dragon' exhibiting technically difficult three-dimensional jade-working in Neolithic China.

A Liangzhu-type *zhong*, unusual in having a cylindrical external profile. The 'face motif' consisting of one 'face' above another is carved out four times around the circumference.

figures or as one wearing a headdress on which is inscribed another 'face'. Such decorated headdresses have been found as independent jade objects. Both the motif and its technique of incising are thought to have been transmitted from the Liangzhu to the Shang cultures, revealing inter-regional influence and exchange among the emerging societies of second-millennium BC China.

Much of the significance of these Neolithic jades resides not only in their depositional context, indicating their role in intricate social systems, but also in their methods of manufacture. Jade is not an easy material to work since it can rarely be broken or flaked by standard stoneworking technology. Its cutting or drilling must be accomplished by abrasion, possibly using high-silicate bamboo with sand. These limitations make it difficult to fashion rounded forms so that the three-dimensionally modelled Hongshan jades are quite outstanding products. The Liangzhu jades exhibit simple relief carving of the essential facial elements and exquisite surface decoration with incised lines, both of which are, again, technically difficult to achieve. ∎

STATUARY OF THE FAR EAST

The three-dimensional depiction of the human figure began in East Asia with the elaborate cult of ceramic figurines during the long Jomon postglacial period (14,000–300 BC). Ranging from solid clay stylizations of the human form to elaborately decorated, hollow-built ceramic figurines up to *c*.45 cm (18 in) in height, the Jomon creations are artistically outstanding, though late within worldwide figurine traditions. Hypotheses abound concerning their function, the most popular interpreting them as ceremonial objects broken during childbirth rituals or the curing of disease and bodily trauma.

Life-size statuary from northeast China now rivals the earliest Egyptian finds in the late fourth millennium BC; a pit building seemingly used as a temple at the site of Niuheliang, Liaoning province, has yielded fragments of at least seven different unbaked clay statues, life-size and three times life-size. Several of the fragments are of breasts, so the statues are thought to be female depictions. The face of one has inset jade eyes and may have been the main object worshipped at the temple. These as-

The depiction of human and animal figures in East Asia varied tremendously through pre- and protohistoric times. The media used might be clay, stone or bronze while the size of the figures ranged from figurines to sculptures several times life-size. Many unrelated traditions have come to light: Jomon figurines, Niuheliang unbaked clay sculptures, the Terracotta Army (see p. 178), monumental Buddhist sculpture (see p. 164), 'spirit path' stone sculptures, *haniwa* funerary sculptures and tomb figurines from the Han to the Tang tomb dynasties.

tounding discoveries occur within a subsistence regime of millet and pig agriculture, yet the Hongshan culture which depended on this simple base succeeded in supporting workers in jade (see p. 166) as well as elaborate stone-built tomb burials for the élite.

In the Early Han period (206 BC–AD 9), large-scale statuary was made not in clay but in stone, while a new tradition of depositing figurines within the tomb also arose. At first, isolated sculptures were placed outside the tombs, in front of the chamber entrances. Later, several such sculptures were arranged in rows leading up to the tomb. These formed the 'spirit path' that was thereafter an integral part of tomb architecture until the fifteenth century. The grand stone bureaucrats, camels, elephants and so on which line the approach to the Imperial Ming Tombs north of Beijing are a sight admired by many tourists today.

Buddhist sculptures carved out of rock at Yungang, near Datong in Shaanxi, China.

BELOW: *Haniwa* noble, a clay sculpture designed to decorate the mounded tomb surface in late Kofun-period Japan.

It is possible that in the fourth century early Japanese embassies to the Chinese court saw these magnificent 'spirit paths' in the royal cemeteries and imitated them on their return to Japan, reverting once more to clay. The early clay *haniwa* statuary of Kofun-period Japan did not represent the human figure, however, but objects that protected and offered refuge for the spirit of the deceased: shields, parasols and houses. In sixth-century Japan, the *haniwa* tradition was broadened to include representations of the many different kinds of nobles, warriors, shamans, farmers, craftsmen and entertainers that populated the emerging state society. Animals also joined in the *haniwa* processions erected on the tomb surfaces: horses with all their trappings, water birds, deer, dogs and, most endearingly, monkeys. As a regional sixth-century aberration within the *haniwa* tradition, stone sculptures were set on tombs in North Kyushu, perhaps echoing the nearby Chinese tradition, which was later taken also into Korea where a few stone statues of grand men adorn mounded tomb precincts.

The Han tradition of depositing small-scale figurines within tombs is a rich source of information about the clothing and cultural traditions of the period, since many different activities are portrayed, such as musical ensembles, dancing, juggling and so on. The baked clay objects were painted in polychrome but left unglazed. By the Three Kingdoms-Six Dynasties period (AD 220–80), glazed figurines were becoming popular, reaching the apex of their sophistication in the three-coloured wares of the Tang period. The elegantly moulded forms of the Tang horse figurines, the dour bureaucrats and the delicately featured court ladies give a view of court society that soon disappeared with the ending of the figurine tradition under the rise of Buddhism (see p. 164). ■

ANYANG

Towards the end of the nineteenth century, bones inscribed with Chinese characters were appearing in druggists' shops in order to be ground into Chinese medicine. By tracing their source, the site of Yinxu was identified in 1899. These 'bones', both cattle shoulder-blades and turtle plastrons (the front 'chest' of their shell) were used by the Shang kings for divination. Holes were scraped out on the backs and red-hot pokers inserted to make the bone crack. These cracks were interpreted as answers to the questions posed by the diviners

Northeast of the modern Chinese city of Anyang lies the Late Shang capital of Yinxu, dating to between 1300 and 1050 BC. Spread over about 3 km² (1.2 square miles), it consists of the remains of a royal cemetery (at Xibeigang village), a palace complex (at Xiaotun village), the tomb of the consort Fu Hao (at Hougang village), several other residential sites of both nobility and commoners, industrial workshops, chariot burials and oracle bone caches.

and those which proved to be auspicious were inscribed with the text of the divination and stored in underground archives. Dug up by Anyang farmers in the late nineteenth century, they eventually came to public attention. These ancient texts give clear documentation of kingly activities in one of the first highly civilized societies in human history.

Excavations were conducted between 1928 and 1937 by the Institute of History and Philology, Academia Sinica, under the direction of Li Chi, doyen of historical archaeology in China.

At the end of the Pacific War, the Academy and its materials were moved to Taipei in Taiwan, where they now reside. Many works on Anyang have since appeared, but the main site report remains unpublished.

In the palace complex at Yinxu are the remains of stamped earthen platforms that held several wooden buildings probably thatched or roofed with organic materials. Nothing remains of them but their postholes. The plans have been reconstructed as a series of open courtyards orientated south to north, with separate altars and attached towers flanking the southern entrance. The ceremonial halls were in the southern half of the complex, while residences were located to the north. Hundreds of human sacrificial burials, ostensibly deposited at the time of hall construction, were found in the earthen foundations, at pillar bases and beside doors. Many contained only heads sprinkled with red ochre.

The royal cemetery consisted of hundreds more sacrifical burials arranged in rows around seven large shaft tombs containing deceased Shang kings. The central shafts held the wooden chamber and coffin, with retainers and sometimes horses and chariots buried on the ledges formed by packing earth around the chamber. Long sloping ramps led down into them either from two or from all four directions, giving a cruciform shape to some tombs. Most of the central burials had been looted by the time of excava-

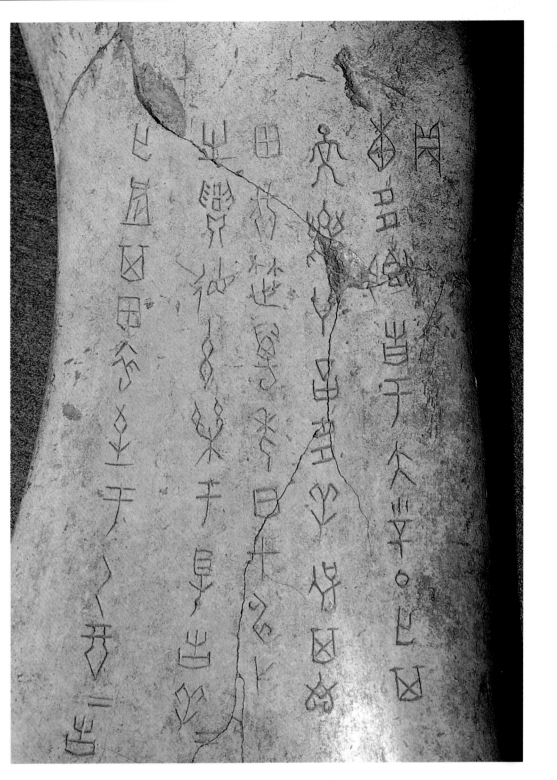

tion, and few bronze and jade objects were recovered.

One tomb that was not looted was that of Fu Hao, a consort of the famous Shang king, Wu Ding. It was neither a shaft tomb nor located in the royal cemetery, which perhaps accounts for its intact preservation. Excavated in 1976 by the Beijing Institute of Archaeology, this pit grave yielded over 1600 objects, including 440 bronzes, 590 jades, 560 bone artifacts, and 7000 cowrie shells.

The objects that were made in the industrial workshops around the site were all for élite consumption. Workshops producing bone objects such as hairpins and arrowheads yielded bone-working tools, unfinished artifacts and caches of raw materials. Many jades and some stone sculptures were found both in workshop contexts and in tombs. These jades differ from those of the Neolithic in portraying a greater range of animals: elephants, serpents, fish, water birds, tigers, horses and some human figures.

Bronzes comprised vessels for wine consumption and for cooking meat in ancestral rituals; crucible fragments, clay models and moulds indicate their production on site. The vessels were cast with *taotie* in the foreground and spiral designs in the background. The *taotie* is a mythical composite of various animal parts, most notable for its splayed depiction to the left and right of two bosses serving as eyes. Horns, claws, feathers and tails are also visible in the design. The *taotie* is thought by some to derive from the Liangzhu 'face motif' (p. 166) and to symbolize the process of transformation from death to afterlife.

Most bronze weapons were found in the chariot burials, which consisted of horse skeletons with all their trappings, and casts left in the loess soil by now-disintegrated wooden chariots. Bow, arrows, halberd, shield, knife and whetstone formed a set. The bladed implements were sometimes inlaid with turquoise, and the animal-head pommels of knives indicate a derivation from the Siberian north. The chariot itself was an import from western Asia, being of exactly the same construction as those distant types, and it is assumed that they were driven across the steppes before being incorporated into Shang material culture. ■

EAST ASIAN BRONZES

The Shang emphasis on vessels probably derived from Late Neolithic élite drinking rituals. Excavations of Neolithic burials show that the cultures on the east coast of the mainland produced a great variety of jugs, pitchers, stemmed goblets and beakers. These vessels are thought to have been employed in exclusive rituals by élites, who used the dramatic occasions and cryptic coding of information to create and enhance their status within society. It is not known whether these rituals were for the ancestors, such as became the bedrock of Chinese society in the first millennium BC. However, the early Shang added the element of feasting to the Neolithic focus on drinking, and the ritual vessels produced in the late second millennium BC included *ding* (legged tripods),

The bronze industry of China, which began in the early second millennium BC, used a completely novel casting method: rather than the lost wax process, the Chinese developed piece moulds based on clay models of the objects to be cast. The first objects to be cast by this method were bronze vessels, which came to typify the Shang bronze culture. Regional bronze traditions also emerged, often using two-piece moulds of stone and comprising very different repertoires of objects.

probably used for cooking meat.

The casting method developed in the Shang period (*c.* 2000–1050 BC) involved piece moulds based on clay models. The inner models were removed before casting, and the pieces of the moulds were held away from the mould core with placers, while the interstices were filled with molten metal. The production of bronze vessels was a huge industry requiring division of labour between the extraction of resources (copper and tin), the making of moulds, the smelting and casting of vessels on a large scale, and the distribution to élite customers. 'Large scale' refers to both number and size: the Tomb of Fu Hao (p. 173), consort of a Shang king, contained over 400 bronze vessels of various shapes and dates of manufacture. One of the largest quadrapods ever to have been cast in the protohistoric period is a Zhou-period (1071–221 BC) vessel that stands almost a metre (3 ft) high. The Zhou political ideal was for a legitimate ruler to own nine *ding*.

Shang culture also produced a considerable number of bronze weapons: early halberd types with turquoise-inlaid hilts were among the more exceptional products. Executioners' axes were sometimes embellished with the open jaws of a beast, and stamps of pictographic insignia on the weapons displayed a beheading as the emblem of the executioners' clan. Thus bronze was used for élite products that were integrated into status and ritual – no mere bronze tools were the focus here.

In contrast, several regional cultures on the periphery of mainland China developed quite different bronze traditions from the late second to early first millennium BC. The southeastern mountains of China supported the bronze production of musical instruments – particularly several types of bells. Some of these were made in graduated tones for fixing on racks to form an ensemble instrument. Bronze was also used in the production of agricultural implements – a secular use that would have been unthinkable in the Shang region.

In the southwest, in the red basin of Sichuan, hollow bronze sculptures of

Shang bronze weapons elaborately decorated with turquoise inlay. Left: a socketed spearhead. Centre and right: *ge* halberds which were fixed at right angles to the haft.

A ding quadrapod, used for cooking meat in ancestor rituals, is uniquely decorated with a realistic human face. Late Shang period, China.

human or animal form with elaborate surface designs are known from the Sanxingdui culture. The largest human sculpture is an extremely stylized figure that stands almost a metre (3 ft) tall. The sources of this tradition are as yet unknown, but the Sanxingdui material challenges the earliest Shang dates at 1500 BC.

Across the north, the steppe regions hosted a bronze culture that is characterized by tools, personal ornaments and mirrors. The decoration of the first two is almost exclusively in animal art, with knife-hilts formed as the heads of sheep or rams, for exam-

ple, or plaques that display animals fighting. This animal art style came to maturity in the last centuries of the first millennium BC, at the same time as the development of the northern-style mirror production in the Korean peninsula. Interestingly, the mirrors of the Korean Bronze Age utilize geometric designs in coarse-line and fine-line versions. The mirror is thought to be a sun symbol, thus referring to a ritual system completely different from the central Chinese tradition of ritual vessels. Contact and interplay between these two systems in the early period can be seen at Anyang (p. 170), the Late Shang capital, where animal-head knives were found; initial coarse-line mirrors were also integrated into the Shang material system very briefly. ■

ROYAL TOMBS OF THE EAST

Traditional Confucian political philosophy promoted the idea that good music ensured good government. In one of the first physical manifestations of this precept, a wooden rack from which were suspended sixty-five bronze bells was excavated in 1978 from the fifth-century BC Leigudun Tomb 1 in Hubei province, China. Belonging to the Marquis of Li, this magnificent collection of bells was part of a 7000-piece burial deposit, including another thirty-two stone chimes on a bronze stand. Three shapes of bells were represented, the largest being 1.54 m (5 ft) tall and weighing 203.6 kg (449 lb). They bore inscriptions describing the musical scales and melodies of several of the early Chinese warring states in the Late Zhou period (475–221 BC).

Prince Liu Sheng of the Early Han Dynasty (206 BC–AD 9), who died in 113 BC, was buried with his wife at Mancheng, Hebei province, China. When unearthed in 1968, they were found to be dressed in jade suits, made of small jade plaques sewn together through edge perforations with gold thread. Each suit comprising about 2500 of these jade plaques, and ten years of skilled craftsmanship are thought to have gone into their making. The prince's tomb itself was lavish in the extreme: 2700 m³ (3534 yd³) of a hillside were hollowed out to make this royal burial, in which 2800 objects were deposited, including at least six carriages with horses.

Throughout East Asia, discoveries in royal burials rival those known from early Mesopotamia and Egypt. Bronzes and jades from the Fu Hao tomb of thirteenth-century BC China (p. 173) were preserved intact, as were the gold girdle and crown of the Heavenly Horse tomb of sixth-century AD Korea. Between these chronological extremes, many fine treasures, and even preserved bodies, have been unearthed from the highest ranking tombs of early Chinese and Korean societies.

The Marquis of Dai, Li Cang, died in 186 BC and was buried with his wife and son in three shaft tombs on the outskirts of modern Changsha City, China, at Mawangdui. These tombs, on being opened from 1974 onwards, have revealed a wealth of waterlogged and therefore well-preserved organic remains, including much red- and black-painted lacquerware, basketry and food, as well as quantities of wooden figurines, musical instruments, textiles and manuscripts. Three pieces of silk bore painted maps – the earliest examples of Chinese cartography known, while the manuscripts, inked on wooden or bamboo slips or silk, provide rare early versions of the *Book of Changes* (*Yijing*), the *Laozi*, the *Zhanguoce*, and treatises on medicine, astronomy and horse physiognomy!

The 'Heavenly Horse' tomb in Kyongju City, Korea, is perhaps the resting place of the Silla king Chijung, who died in AD 513. Excavated in the mid-1970s, it was found to contain intact the royal personage dressed in crown, multi-pendant belt, ear-rings, bracelet and finger-rings – all made of gold. The crown, with tree-shaped spires 32 cm (12.5 in) high, was hung with sparkles of gold foil and curved jade beads. In addition to this sumptuous dress, archaeologists also recovered birch-bark paintings – one depicting a white horse (hence the tomb's name) – two rare glass cups, covered silver and gilt-bronze bowls, and gilt-bronze horse trappings. ∎

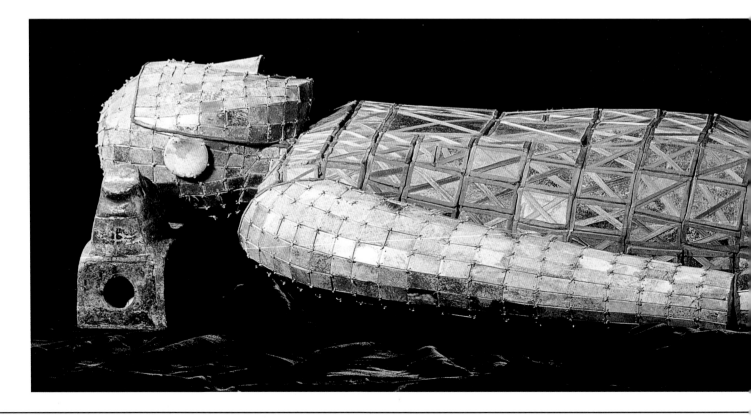

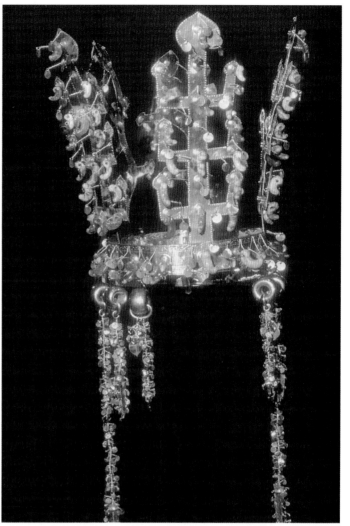

ABOVE: One of the shaft tombs at Mawangdui, Changsha, China, under excavation. Preserved inside were many artifacts of organic materials – wood, basketry, lacquer – dating to the Early Han period.

BELOW: A suit devised of jade plaques sewn together with gold thread. In Zhou-period China, such jade suits were thought to preserve the body of the deceased.

RIGHT: A gold crown of the Silla royalty, Three Kingdoms-period Korea, decorated with jade curved beads. Silla was renowned throughout East Asia for its goldwork.

THE TERRACOTTA ARMY

Large collections of small clay human figures are common in early Chinese aristocratic graves, but the life-size Terracotta Army is unique and spectacular. Each warrior's head is different and individual, fitted to a standard-ized body, and with a wide range of facial expressions. Every racial group in China seems to be represented. More than half have round ear lobes, but nearly 20% have square ones, a proportion similar to modern Chinese. There are twenty-five styles of beard, corresponding to the age, character, facial shape and post of the figure represented. Much has also been learned from the figures about hairstyles, clothing and armour, weaponry, horse trappings and the positioning of categories of soldier. There are generals, officers, infantrymen, kneeling archers, and cavalry-men; more than 600 clay horses and over a hundred war chariots have also been uncovered. Most warriors are muscular, nearly 90% are tall, and every general is depicted as stalwart with thickset bones and well-developed muscles. This is clearly a combat-ready army of strong, healthy soldiers, arranged in ancient Chinese battle formation.

The full names of eighty-five different sculptors have been found discreetly engraved and sealed under the armpits or be-neath the long coats of the warriors. These craftsmen used local clay, fired at a very high temperature (*c*.800°C, 1472°F), which gave the pottery a greyish surface colour. The figures were subse-

Often referred to as the Eighth Wonder of the World, the 'Terracotta Army' was discovered in 1974 near the ancient capital of Xi'an, in China's Shaanxi province, by peasants digging a well. It comprises more than 7000 life-size figures in fired clay, which represent the troops who were to guard China's first emperor, Qin Shihuangdi, after his death in 210 BC.

quently painted with different colours to reproduce the details of the uniforms. The fact that the figures remain hard as rock, despite burial for two millennia, testifies to the skill of the an-cient potters in achieving an ac-curate firing temperature.

It is reckoned that the complex of pits has a floor-space of 25,388 m² (30,364 yd²), and required the removal of 100,000 m³ (130,800 yd³) of earth. They were roofed with 8000 m³ (10,464 yd³) of wood, mostly huge pines and cypresses. The floors were paved with 250,000 fired clay bricks. Together with the Terraco-tta Army itself, this project must have cost a tremendous amount of money and manpower – probably involving hundreds of thou-sands of people over a period of ten years.

The enormous Pit 1, which contains most of the figures, had been destroyed by fire; it is now enclosed within a hangar and forms one of China's – indeed, the world's – major tourist attrac-tions. Pit 2, although smaller than Pit 1, contains a better range and quality of warriors. Now contained within a building, it has a burnt and collapsed roof of pine and cypress logs, and was entered by five sloping ramps. There are thought to be about 1300 figures of men and horses in Pit 2, with eighty wooden chariots. Chinese archaeologists found that Pit 3, discovered in 1976, had collapsed naturally, damaging contents badly. Pit 3 is 21.4 m (70 ft 2 in) long and 17.6 m (57 ft 9 in) wide, and more than 5 m (16 ft 5 in) deep. It contains sixty-eight warriors, four horses and a war char-

iot, as well as thirty-four weapons. This pit seems to represent the headquarters, the army's commanders, together with their personal guard – these warriors are at least 12.7 cm (5 in) taller than average soldiers, and they are drawn up in battle formation.

The emperor himself lies undisturbed in a huge burial mound about 1.6 km (1 mile) away from his terracotta troops – according to contemporary accounts the mound contains booby traps, as well as a three-dimensional map of China with rivers of mercury.

Such has been the success of the Terracotta Army in drawing foreign tourists and their currency to Xi'an that a new airport was built 19 km (12 miles) from the city. In constructing a motorway to link it to Xi'an, a new find was made in 1990: just south of the tombs of the emperor Liu Qi (188–144 BC) and his wife, a site covering 96,000 m² (115,000 yd²), the size of twelve soccer pitches, was encountered. It contains another army of terracotta figures, associated with the two tombs, and housed in twenty-four vaults about 20 m (66 ft) apart, and in fourteen rows aligned north-south. The vaults are 4 to 10 m (13 to 33 ft) wide and 25 to 290 m (82 to 952 ft) long. They are therefore smaller than the Qin dynasty pits, but cover an area about five times as large, and their different sizes may correspond to those of the army units they contain.

All the human statues are of naked men with no arms. They are about 50 cm (19.7 in) high, and the whole body is painted an orange-red colour, with hair, eyebrows, beard and eyes coloured black. Their clothes, probably of linen or silk, have disintegrated. Some researchers believe the now-vanished arms were held on with rods of precious metal which were subsequently stolen, while others suppose they had movable wooden arms that have disintegrated.

The figures have graceful forms and delicate sculptured faces, each one different in age and facial expression, which may range from severe to smiling. In their remarkable realism they resemble the life-size figures which are about a century older, but the Qin figures are hollow, whereas the later army is solid. They are accompanied by weapons of copper and iron, arrowheads and spears, swords, chisels and agricultural tools, carts, jewellery and coins, all of them, like the men and horses, one-third life-size. Hundreds of figures have been uncovered so far, and as excavation continues, estimates of the total vary from 10,000 to a million. ■

TOP AND ABOVE: Details of some of the warriors and a charioteer. Every racial group in China seems to be represented in the figures and there are 25 styles of beard, corresponding to age, character, facial shape and post.

LEFT: General view of Pit 1. Most recently buildings covering 4600 m² (50,000 ft²) have been found around the tomb; these are thought to be sacrificial temples where offerings of ritual food were made daily.

MURAL TOMBS
OF THE ORIENT

Mural tombs of the Han period are best known from Helingeer in Inner Mongolia, Wangdu and Luoyang, which became the Late Han capital in AD 25. The murals, done with paint and ink directly onto hollow bricks, could occur on any surface of the main burial chamber: walls, lintels and partition pediments. Most focused on the protection of the deceased and on his or her ascent to the 'World of the Immortals'. In Tomb 61 at Luoyang, one scene depicts a shaman with a bear-shaped head, accompanied by assistants, while others show courtiers in frozen poses speaking to each other. The pen-and-ink style paintings show little modelling, and facial portraits tend to be stylized into personality types. The Helingeer paintings, on the other hand, are much more lively, with activities

The practice of painting murals in chamber tombs began in China during the Early Han dynasty (206 BC–AD 9) and was also popular during the Tang dynasty (618–907). It was copied by the Koguryo élite in the Three Kingdoms period of Korea (300–668), and may have influenced the sixth-century ornamented tombs of the Kyushu élite associated with the Yamato state in Kofun-period (AD 300–710) Japan.

involving people, objects and architecture – all depicted without spatial depth or perspective.

In Korea, the Koguryo tomb murals began with the formal portrait style of China, and later developed into genre paintings of élite activities, much like the Helingeer paintings. Many of these tombs were discovered and excavated by the Japanese during their colonial period in Korea (1910–45). The paintings, executed on plastered stone walls, depict military processions, aristocratic hunts and active warfare while the unplastered lintels of the corbelled ceilings often bear decorative designs also – such as the Buddhist motif of the lotus,

Interior of the 14th-century tomb of King Kongmin of Korea (r. 1351–74), near Kaesong, North Korea, one of the latest tomb murals in East Asia.

Mural painting in the tomb of Princess Yungtai, Tang Dynasty, China. Such portraiture served as models for mural paintings in Korea and Japan.

which grew in popularity as the new religion took hold.

Many of the mural tombs of Tang China occupy the southern foothills overlooking the Wei River and the Tang capital of Chang'an near modern Xi'an. The tomb of Crown Prince Zhanghuai illustrates the vast differences in construction between these and the earlier Han tombs. Two subterranean chambers in a line, surmounted by a huge mounded pyramid, are entered by a long sloping ramp leading down into the earth. The first portion of the ramp has murals along its length, depicting courtiers in processions. Popular motifs in Tang tombs were the 'spirits of the four quarters': White Tiger of the West, Green Dragon of the East, Red Phoenix of the South, and Black Warrior (snake and turtle) of the North. These also decorate the seventh-century Takamatsuzuka tomb in central Yamato, Japan – a sensational find made in 1972 that resulted in one of the first meetings of North and South Korean scholars in Nara to discuss the murals' origins. The tomb is thought to have been painted by continental artists, perhaps from the Tang court, for a Japanese prince.

Compared to the splendid court tradition of the Tang tombs, the tombs of Kyushu are small, impoverished and crudely painted, mainly with geometric designs. They are outstanding, however, as a regional tradition, with a coherent grammar of symbols and motifs connected with the burial ritual. Concentric circles, triangles, and shattered spiral designs (*chokkomon*) are painted directly onto the rock walls. The Takahara tomb is the exception; it depicts a man leading a horse from a boat, with two ceremonial fans at either side and waves underneath while above is a horse-like figure interpreted as a dragon, with red claws, red feathery sweat, and breathing fire. Overall, mural tombs comprise a small proportion of élite tombs in East Asia (see p. 176), but their contents are spectacular and set them apart from other lavishly furnished burial chambers. ∎

THE SINAN SHIPWRECK

Nine summer excavations salvaged half the wooden hull together with 20,661 pieces of pottery, 729 metal objects – including silver and iron ingots, 43 stone objects, 28 tons of Chinese coins, 1017 pieces of red sandalwood, and 1346 everyday objects. The Chinese vessel – later dubbed the Sinan shipwreck for the town closest to the discovery – was built for the medieval maritime trade from the 'porcelain triangle' of southeastern China to Japan, where Chinese celadons and porcelains were in great demand. Ningbo was the port nearest to both the large kiln complexes at Longquan, producing green-glazed celadon stonewares, and to Jingdezhen, where Qingbai white-glazed porcelains were made. More than a third of the Sinan cargo consisted of Qingbai wares, presumably from Jingdezhen. Flower vases with opposing handles had moulded plum branches or symmetrical designs imitating cast-bronze. Water droppers in the shape of a phoenix or of a boy sitting on an ox contrast with the simplicity of a black-rimmed bowl adorned only with a peony design in relief. The celadons, too, came in a variety of shapes: stemmed cups, simple bowls, or moulded vessels in the shape of bronze incense burners. Most of the ceramics date to the Sung and Yuan dynasties (AD 960–1279 and 1279–1368).

It was perhaps in the year 1323 that the 200-ton keeled sailing ship set off from Ningbo, just south of present-day Shanghai, heading across the Yellow Sea to the coast of the Korean peninsula and then southeast to Japan – only to sink off the southwest coast of Korea. Ceramics brought up in fishing nets in 1975 alerted Korean archaeologists and today the ship and its cargo are the focus of the purpose-built National Maritime Museum in Mokp'o, South Cholla province, Korea.

Together with these Chinese trade objects, archaeologists recovered Korean celadons of the Koryo period (AD 918-1392) and Japanese lacquerwares and wooden sandals. The presence of the former raise the question of whether the ship had already called into a Korean port to take on additional cargo in the form of Koryo celadons bound for Japan. The latter may well have been utilitarian, used for shipboard life, along with basketry, buckets, iron and bronze cooking utensils, tools and food – cinnamon bark, peppercorns, peaches, and so on. Among the metal wares, bronze ritual vessels of archaic shape – such as the *jue* and the tripod incense burner – reflect the antiquarian bent of the Sung dynasty court and may be evidence of the spread of Neo-Confucianism into Korea and Japan. The tons of coins, dating no later than 1310, are an enigma. Each packing box of ceramics contained a few coins for good luck, but many were wrapped (and fused) in bundles. Were they being used partly as ballast on the journey, to be utilized later for their purchasing power in order to bring back many more goods than the ceramics alone could be traded for? Would this mean that this was a short load of ceramics? Or did the captain expect heavy weather which even a full load of ceramics could not overcome?

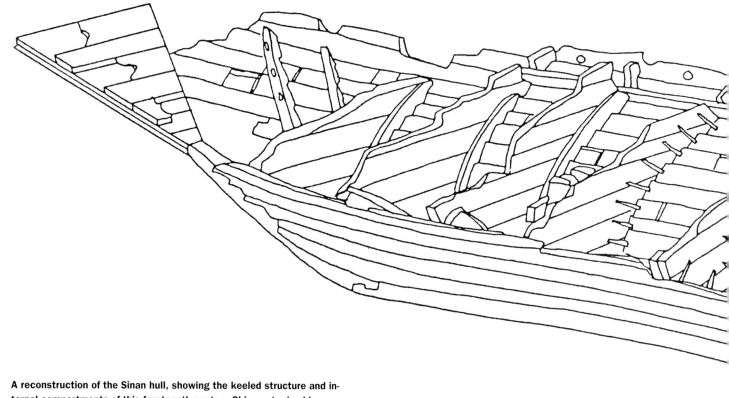

A reconstruction of the Sinan hull, showing the keeled structure and internal compartments of this fourteenth-century Chinese trade ship wrecked off the southwestern Korean coast.

Celadons recovered from the Sinan shipwreck. Such green-glazed stoneware was a popular export item from Sung and Yuan-period China and was distributed all through East and Southeast Asia via maritime trade.

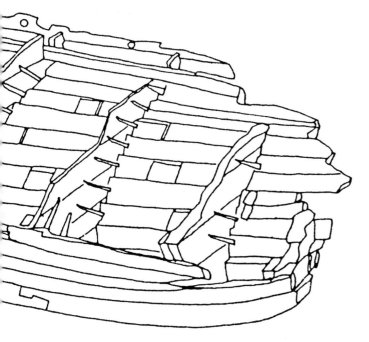

Though the Sinan ship itself succumbed to natural forces, its excavation was a triumph over them, particularly a 2.5 knot current and zero visibility. Only one hour of diving could be accomplished every day, while the tide stood still. The diving team was composed of members of the Korean Navy with advice from the Institute of Nautical Archaeology, Texas A&M University, and the Department of Maritime Archaeology, Western Australia Maritime Museum. A grid was laid out over the remains, the hull was cut into sections for lifting, and the ship's remains have been fully pegged and reconstructed: it was flat-hulled, with a keel shaped from three long timbers, and the body was divided into seven or eight compartments by internal bulwarks. Only the portion below the waterline survives, with no upper floors intact. The cargo is known to have been in a lower hold, however, because some of the lighter objects, which might otherwise have floated away, were in fact held in place by an upper deck until they became waterlogged and silted over. ∎

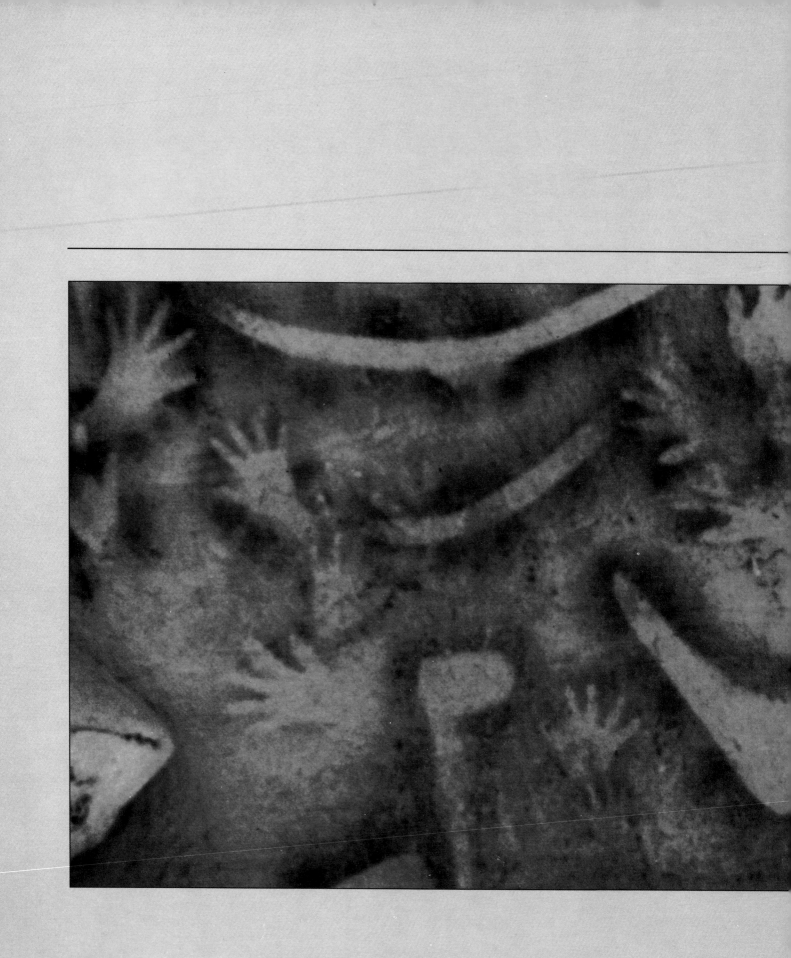

AUSTRALASIA

LAKE MUNGO

Lake Mungo in New South Wales, the site of the world's oldest known ritual cremation, was discovered in 1969, and the remains of more than a hundred individuals have now been found. Many are fragmentary, but they include a virtually complete skeleton. Stone tools, freshwater mussel shells and bones of fish and land animals mark the camping places of people who hunted, fished and gathered on the shores of the Willandra Lakes from about 40,000 to about 15,000 years ago.

The Willandra Lakes are a series of interconnected lake basins in the arid far west of New South Wales. They have been dry now for about 15,000 years, but at various earlier periods they were full of fresh water. In 1968, Jim Bowler, a geomorphologist studying the climatic history of the Willandra Lakes, noticed some burnt bones encrusted with carbonate. They were eroding out of the large crescent-shaped dune on the eastern shore of Lake Mungo. A team of archaeologists removed the remains in a large block, and physical anthropologist Alan Thorne excavated it in the laboratory. It turned out to be the remains of a young woman who had been buried about 25,000 years ago. Her body had been burnt and the bones smashed into tiny fragments. These were then collected and buried in a small depression. In 1974, an even older, more complete skeleton was discovered. This was an inhumation rather than a cremation and dated back about 30,000 years. An adult male had been buried lying on his side and sprinkled with red ochre.

Other sites around the lakes provide a vivid picture of the lives of the people who camped there when the lakes were full. They ate fish and frogs, freshwater mussels and crayfish from the lakes. Study of the fish bones has shown that most are from one species (golden perch) and all of similar size. This uniformity suggests that nets were probably the main method of fishing. The people also hunted animals such as wallaby, wombat and native cat, as well as a wide range of small animals like rat kangaroos and lizards. Meals were cooked on campfires or in ground ovens – one oven at Lake Mungo is 30,000 years old. These ovens were shallow pits and contained ash or charcoal and cooking stones or lumps of baked clay. Ovens such as these are still used by Aborigines today. Stone tools used mainly for chopping, cutting and scraping are common in the area. Recently, Tom Loy has analyzed microscopic traces on the edges of some of them and found that they were used for scraping meat from bone and for cleaning plant tubers.

These were startling finds. The first definite evidence that Aborigines had lived in Australia during the last Ice Age had come from Kenniff Cave in Queensland only in 1962, but the Mungo finds pushed the occupation of Australia back to 30,000 years ago, and provided a picture of a complex lifestyle – including a glimpse of the rich ceremonial life that is such an important feature of Aboriginal culture. Since then, several sites have been found which are up to 40,000 years old. In the 1990s, dates of as much as 60,000 years ago have been claimed for some Northern Territory rockshelters.

The date of the first Aboriginal occupation is of crucial importance to our knowledge of early human abilities, since Australia was never joined to Southeast Asia even at times of low sea-level, so that people moving into the country faced a sea voyage of at least 50 km (31 miles). It is remarkable to recognize this ability at 40,000 years ago, and perhaps even earlier, and to add it to the Aborigines' other achievements during the last Ice Age. ∎

LEFT AND RIGHT: The eroding dune along the eastern shore of Lake Mungo in the Willandra Lakes area, western New South Wales. The spectacular dune formations are known as the 'Walls of China'.

Mungo, Kow Swamp and the origins of the Australians

One of the burials at Lake Mungo during the excavation (right). The human remains found at Mungo raised many questions because the people seemed to have more delicate features than living Aborigines. But in 1967, on the eastern shore of Kow Swamp in Victoria, Alan Thorne found at least forty individuals, including men, women and children, whose characteristics were more robust and rugged. As at Lake Mungo, there were several different styles of burial; in some burials there were grave goods, such as stone tools, animal teeth and mussel shells. One person wore a headband of kangaroo teeth.

The Kow Swamp people were buried between about 13,000 and 9500 years ago and therefore were actually younger than the Mungo finds. This was unusual because normally the more robust forms of fossil humans are older than more gracile forms like those from Lake Mungo. In explanation, Thorne proposed a theory: that there had been at least two separate migrations to Australia from different parts of Southeast Asia. The robust Kow Swamp people were similar to more ancient fossils from Java, while the more gracile Mungo people more closely resembled Chinese finds. Thorne's ideas remain controversial. Other scholars stress the diversity of Aboriginal remains and feel that the differences have been exaggerated. Peter Brown has suggested that some of the features of the Kow Swamp skulls can be explained as the result of the practice of head-binding of infants.

AUSTRALIA'S ROCK ART

Dating rock art is often extremely difficult. There are some sites in Australia, such as Early Man Shelter in Queensland, where engravings are covered by occupation deposits dating to 13,000 years ago. The art must therefore be older than these deposits. Pieces of ochre, some with signs of use as crayons, have been found in the lowest levels of some of the oldest sites in Australia, dating to 50,000 years ago or more. New developments in scientific dating methods are beginning to confirm this picture. It is now possible, for example, to date very tiny samples of organic material. Archaeologists have dated a small sample of pigment with human blood mixed in as a binder at about 10,700 years old, while possible red paint in the rock shelter of Sandy Creek 2,

Rock art is found in most parts of Australia and varies widely in technique and style. It is difficult to date art on rock surfaces, but the few sites that have been dated suggest that both painting and engraving go back more than 20,000 years and are probably much older. Studying Australian rock art provides an insight into rock art elsewhere in the world because it is part of a living cultural tradition.

Queensland, dates from 24,600 years ago.

A different method of dating has been used at sites in South Australia to date desert varnish that has formed over Panaramitee-style rock engravings that specialists believe very ancient. Desert varnish appears as a dark shiny veneer on exposed rock surfaces. It is a chemical crust of bacterial origin, and microscopic organic inclusions trapped within it can be dated by accelerator mass spectrometry (an advanced

Some of the 646 stencils made on the soft sandstone cliffs at the 62 m (203 ft) long 'Art Gallery' site, Carnarvon Gorge, Queensland. Among the hands and forearms can be seen different kinds of boomerang and a stone axe.

RIGHT: Some of the many 'x-ray' style fish painted in the rockshelters of western Arnhem Land; they combine a naturalistic profile and visible external features with a complex infill including bones and intestines. The last known x-ray art was made in 1964 by Najombolmi, a prolific Arnhem Land artist who died in 1967.

BELOW RIGHT: The mythical 'Lightning brothers', painted at the Ingaladdi waterhole in the Victoria River District. On the left is Yagjagbula, the older brother, who is 292 cm (9 ft 7 in) tall with a 66 cm (26 in) penis; Yabiringl, his younger brother, is 317 cm (10 ft 5 in) tall and has a 56 cm (22 in) penis. Both have a rayed headdress with a central plume, and both carry a stone axe in the right hand.

type of radiocarbon dating), providing a possible minumum age for the motif under them. The oldest dates from the varnish on South Australian engravings go back more than 40,000 years, making this the earliest dated rock art anywhere in the world.

Early rock art in Australia seems to take a variety of forms. Sites like Koonalda Cave and caves in the Mount Gambier area contain meandering lines and geometric figures incised in their soft limestone walls. In the open air, engraved designs of geometric motifs and animal tracks belong to a style known as Panaramitee which is very widespread.

More recent art reflects the diversity of Aboriginal culture. Many thousands of sites are known from all over the continent. Some regions are particularly rich in rock art. Arnhem Land with its complex and spectacular x-ray figures is perhaps the best known rock art province. There is also an older tradition of Mimi figures which shows detailed scenes of prehistoric life. Hand stencils are common all over Australia, but in some regions many items of material culture were also stencilled: the most spectacular examples are in southern Queensland where stencils of artifacts include axes, boomerangs and dishes as well as hands, feet and even animals.

For many years there was little interest in Aboriginal art. The European invasion meant the destruction of Aboriginal society in many areas and the abandonment of rock art. Many sites were vandalized and some scholars even attributed the art to other cultures. We now realize that Aboriginal art is an integral part of a rich and complex ceremonial life. Australia is one of the few places where rock art continues to be produced, and therefore has the world's longest-lasting art tradition. ∎

ICE AGE HUNTERS
OF TASMANIA

Kutikina is a massive limestone cave on the Franklin River in the densely forested southwest region of Tasmania. It has more than a metre (3 ft) of archaeological deposits that are extraordinarily rich in animal bones, as well as in stone and bone tools. The discovery of Kutikina's great abundance of artifacts was a major turning point in Australian archaeology. At that time archaeologists believed that Aborigines had never occupied southwest Tasmania, but the finds from Kutikina proved to be between 19,000 and 15,000 years old, providing strong evidence that this rugged region had indeed been

Until 1981, archaeologists thought that the Tasmanian Aborigines had been mainly coast-dwellers and had not occupied the dense rainforests. The discovery of the Kutikina site in 1981, however, revealed that Aborigines were, in fact, living in southwest Tasmania 20,000 years ago when the environment was very different from the way it is today.

occupied during the height of the last Ice Age.

Since this discovery there has been an enormous amount of archaeological research in the area. More than fifty sites dating back more than 10,000 years to the last Ice Age have been discovered and many have been excavated. The first occupation at the oldest of these sites has been dated to about 35,000 years ago, and several others are more than 30,000 years old. Humans must therefore have moved into Tasmania as soon as falling sea levels exposed the land bridge that connected it to the Australian mainland. The environment was, of course, very different

ABOVE: Small thumbnail scrapers appear first about 24,000 years ago and are common in most of the sites after about 18,000 years ago. They seem to have been used for butchering animals and for working various materials such as bone and wood.

LEFT: Bone points have been found at several sites in southwest Tasmania. They were often made from the leg bones of wallabies. They were used for a variety of purposes, including spear points and awls for making skin clothing.

Hand stencils at Ballawinne Cave and Wargata Mina

In 1986, the first evidence of Ice Age rock art was found in southwest Tasmania at Ballawinne Cave. There were twenty-three red ochre hand stencils in a completely dark chamber about 25 m (83 ft) from the main entrance. A second cave with hand stencils, Wargata Mina, was discovered in 1987. Samples of paint have revealed traces of human blood cells which have been dated to about 10,000 years ago.

from today. Instead of dense rainforest there were open grassy plains and bands of forest along sheltered river valleys. The climate was dry and cold and there were glaciers in the high mountain valleys.

Unlike most other Australian sites over 10,000 years old, the caves of southern Tasmania contain very rich and varied deposits showing that life was far from being a hard struggle for existence. Most of the bones, more than 90% in some sites, are from red-necked wallaby. The hunters must have specialized in catching this medium-size species, as they were relatively easy to hunt and would have been common in the open grasslands. Use-wear on some of the bone points suggests they were probably used as spear points. Other bone points were used for making clothing from animal skins.

The sites also have far more stone artifacts than other Australian sites of similar age. Most of the tools were crafted from stone obtained from local sources, but some were made from a distinctive natural glass, which was the result of a meteorite crashing to earth – when it crashed, the force of the collision melted the rock around the point of impact, thus forming glass. Aborigines collected glass from the Darwin meteorite crater, about 25 km (15.5 miles) northwest of Kutikina, and carried it to sites up to 100 km (62 miles) away.

As the ice sheets retreated, the climate became warmer and wetter, and trees and shrubs colonized the grasslands. From about 11,000 years ago, dense rainforest made the region almost impenetrable and there would have been little food. The cave sites of the southwest were all abandoned by the end of the Ice Age and the focus of Aboriginal activity shifted to other areas of Tasmania. ■

COLONIZING THE PACIFIC

By 40,000 years ago, humans had occupied New Guinea and Australia, which at that time formed a single land mass because of lowered sea levels during the last Ice Age. These first settlers must have come from what is now island Southeast Asia and would probably have been well adapted to a maritime way of life. Recent finds have shown that people rapidly moved out into the islands of the Bismarck Archipelago and reached the Solomon Islands by 30,000 years ago. These island communities of the southwest Pacific seem to have been mobile hunter-fisher-gatherers living on the resources of both land and sea. Over time, they developed trade networks for exchanging obsidian, stone tools, shells and foodstuffs.

Just under 4000 years ago, a new cultural complex appeared in the western Pacific. In 1952, archaeologists found sherds of distinctively decorated pottery at the Lapita site in New Caledonia. and quickly realized that Lapita pottery was found all over Melanesia and as far east as Fiji, Tonga and Samoa. The origins of the Lapita culture are still controversial – some archaeologists believe that its roots lie in island Southeast Asia, while others prefer to see a more local origin in the Bismarck Archipelago. Wherever they came from, the Lapita people spread extremely rapidly and established widely dispersed settlements, probably with a mixed economy based on marine resources, animal husbandry and horticulture. Lapita sites were linked through long-distance trading networks.

The Polynesians are the descendants of these Lapita people.

The Pacific Ocean covers one–third of the world's surface and set in it are thousands of islands, most of them tiny isolated specks of land. Archaeologists have discovered that human expansion into the Pacific began more than 30,000 years ago. By 1000 years ago, the southwest Pacific as far as Tonga and Samoa, as well as Easter Island, the Hawaiian Islands and New Zealand had all been colonized – an achievement involving prodigious voyages with neither charts nor navigation instruments.

About 2000 years ago, Polynesian voyagers began the colonization of the rest of the Pacific, settling first the Marquesas, Tuamotus and the Society Islands. By 1000 years ago, they had reached the Hawaiian Islands, Easter Island (see p. 194) and finally New Zealand – the three corners of the Polynesian Triangle. There is little doubt that colonization of these remote areas was deliberate: the Polynesians had developed the double-hulled canoe, capable of undertaking very long voyages; they used sophisticated systems of navigation based on a detailed knowledge of the stars and the ocean; and they certainly carried with them stocks of animals and plants. Thus they established successful and expanding communities based on the cultivation of crops such as breadfruit, bananas and especially taro, though in some instances the result of Polynesian settlement was land degradation brought about by the intensive cultivation needed to meet the needs of a growing population.

The Maori who colonized New Zealand encountered a rather different environment from the small tropical islands to which they were accustomed. Some of their crops would not grow outside the tropics and so they turned to a new food source: the roots of the local ferns, particularly bracken. To encourage the spread of bracken they cleared large areas of forest, much of it by burning. This, however, caused serious erosion. They hunted many species of birds to extinction, including twelve different kinds of moa. Competition for resources became so intense that the Maori became warlike and built elaborate defended settlements known as *pa*. ■

RIGHT: Lapita pottery from the Arawe Islands, off the coast of New Britain. The stamped decoration is typical of the elaborate and distinctive designs on Lapita pottery, which stopped being made about 2000 years ago.

LEFT: Obsidian is a distinctive volcanic glass that can be easily flaked to make very sharp tools. Flakes of obsidian from sources 350 km (217 miles) away are found at sites on New Ireland as early as 20,000 years ago. At Lapita sites, obsidian has been found more than 300 km (186 miles) from its source. This is the entrance to an obsidian mine at Talasea, New Britain.

EASTER ISLAND

According to radiocarbon dates, Easter Island's structures were already well developed by the seventh century AD, and most researchers believe the colonists arrived from eastern Polynesia in the early centuries AD. The island is so remote – 3747 km (2328 miles) from South America and 3622 km (2250 miles) from Pitcairn to the northwest – that it is unlikely there was more than one major influx of people by canoe, and the archaeological record certainly suggests a single unbroken development of material culture. Once settled on the island, the colonists were trapped there, and it constituted their whole world.

The earliest known contact with the outside world occurred on Easter Sunday 1722, when the Dutch navigator Jacob Roggeveen encountered and christened the island, and described its inhabitants. Subsequent eighteenth-century visitors included such famous explorers as Captain Cook and the Comte de La Pérouse. Archaeological investigation began in the late nineteenth century,

The most isolated piece of permanently inhabited land on the planet, Easter Island is a tiny 171 km² (66-miles²) volcanic speck in the South Pacific. It is famous for its astonishing Stone Age culture which produced hundreds of enormous stone statues, many set up on massive stone platforms. Today, the whole island constitutes a gigantic open-air museum: the Rano Raraku quarry and Rano Kau crater are among the most spectacular sights in world archaeology.

but entered a new phase with the Norwegian expedition of 1955, led by adventurer Thor Heyerdahl. He brought in archaeologists, notably the American William Mulloy, who laid the foundations for the research and restoration that continue today. This expedition carried out the first stratigraphic excavations and obtained the first radiocarbon dates and pollen samples, as well as conducting valuable experiments in carving, moving and erecting statues.

As we now know from analyses of pollen, Easter Island – or Rapa Nui (big Rapa) as it is now called by its inhabitants – once supported a rainforest dominated by a species of great palm tree

Some of the approximately 400 statues that remain in and around the quarry of Rano Raraku, in every stage of manufacture. Those that were completed and stand on the quarry's slopes have become buried up to the neck by sediments, giving rise to the popular misconception of 'Easter Island heads'.

similar to the Chilean wine palm, the largest in the world. This situation was disturbed by the arrival of the Polynesian voyagers: probably a few dozen men, women and children in one or more large double-hulled canoes, bringing with them the domestic animals (chickens, rats, pigs and dogs) and food plants (bananas, sweet potatoes, taro, breadfruit) with which they transformed the environment of so many Pacific islands. Pigs and dogs, though, if they ever arrived, did not survive long on Easter Island, and breadfruit could not grow. The colonists set about clearing the forest to plant their crops. The native birds, unused to humans, fell an easy prey to hunters and the rats stole their eggs, so the few remaining seabirds retreated to offshore islets. During this early phase, the islanders seem to have constructed simple types of *ahu* (platforms), with small and relatively crude statues on or in front of them.

The second phase of Easter Island's history, from *c.* AD 1000 to 1500, was its 'golden age' when tremendous energy was devoted to the construction of more and bigger ceremonial platforms (rubble cores encased in well-cut slabs) and hundreds of large statues. As the human population thrived, numbers gradually increased, perhaps reaching a peak of 10,000 or even 20,000 around AD 1500. This put pressure on the supply of land, and the inevitable decline of the forest can be seen clearly in the record of fossilized pollen from the island's crater swamps.

At least 800 *moai* (statues) were carved, almost all in the soft volcanic tuff of the Rano Raraku crater, with basalt hammerstones. All were variations on a theme: a human figure with prominent angular nose and chin, and often elongated perforated ears containing discs. The bodies, which end at the abdomen, have arms held tightly to the sides, and hands held in front, with elongated fingertips meeting at a stylized loincloth. More than 230 statues were transported considerable distances from the great quarry to platforms around the edge of the island, where they were erected, their backs to the sea, watching over the villages around each *aho*, or platform. They are believed to represent ancestor figures. It was traditionally thought that statues were

The view from the ceremonial village of Orongo to the islets, with a few of the numerous bas-reliefs of birdmen in the foreground. The Birdman competition was highly dangerous, involving not only a perilous descent and ascent of the huge cliff, but also a long swim through currents and shark-infested waters.

dragged horizontally to their destinations, but experiments suggest that another efficient mode of transportation was upright, on a sledge and rollers.

At the most prestigious platforms, statues were given eyes of white coral, and a separate *pukao* (top-knot) of red scoria was raised and placed on the head.

The statues placed on platforms vary from 2 to 10 m (6 ft 7 in to 33 ft) in height, and weigh up to 83,000 kg (82 tons). There might be as many as fifteen in a row on a single platform. The quarry still contains almost 400 statues at every stage of man-

The *ahu* Akivi, with its seven *moai*, is unusual in that it lies inland and the statues face the sea. They never had eyes or top-knots. The platform was restored and its statues re-erected by William Mulloy.

ufacture; one of them, 'El Gigante', is over 20 m (66 ft) long and, when completed, would have weighed up to 274,000 kg (270 tons).

The final phase of the island's prehistory saw the collapse of the earlier way of life: statues ceased to be carved, cremation gave way to burial, and 1000 years of peaceful coexistence were shattered by the manufacture in huge quantities of *mataa*, spearheads and daggers of obsidian, a sharp black volcanic glass. Conflict led to the toppling of the statues, and was resolved by an apparent abandonment of a religion and social system based on ancestor worship in favour of one featuring a warrior élite.

An annual chief or 'birdman' was chosen each year at the ceremonial village of Orongo, whose drystone corbelled houses were perched high on the cliff between the Rano Kau crater and the ocean. Each of the candidates had a young man to represent him. Every spring, these unfortunate young men had to make their way down the sheer cliff, 300 m (nearly 1000 ft) tall, to the shore, and then swim over a kilometre (0.6 mile) on a bunch of reeds through shark-infested swells and strong currents to the largest and outermost islet, Motu Nui, where they awaited – sometimes for weeks – the arrival of a migratory seabird, the sooty tern. The aim was to find its first egg. The winner would swim back with the egg securely held in a headband, and his master now became the new sacred birdman. Orongo's rich rock art is festooned with carvings of the birdmen, sometimes holding the egg, which symbolized fertility. This was the system that was still developing when the Europeans arrived, and which ended with the arrival of missionaries in the 1860s.

The causes of the island's decline and change were probably complex, but can be traced to one major factor: pollen analysis indicates the most dramatic deforestation known in the archaeological record. From at least 1200 years ago, one can see a massive reduction in forest cover until, by the arrival of Europeans, there were no large trees left. The imported rats fed on the palm fruits and helped prevent regeneration. Without the palm and other timbers, statues could no longer be moved, ocean-going canoes could no longer be built – thus cutting the population off from the crucial protein-supply of deep-sea fish – and deforestation caused massive soil erosion which damaged crop-growing potential. Chickens became the most precious source of protein, guarded like treasure in fortified structures.

It is impossible to know exactly what happened on Easter Island, but the probably steady growth of the population together with the decline in food and increasing importance of economically useless activities (platform building, statue carving and transportation) clearly led to a collapse. Starvation gave rise to raiding and violence, perhaps even to cannibalism.

By 1722, when the first Europeans arrived, it was all over. The population had been reduced to about 2000, living in poverty amid the ruins of their former culture. The palm tree and several other species became extinct, leaving the island with only one small species of tree and two of shrubs. ∎

THE NEW WORLD

MONTE VERDE AND THE FIRST AMERICANS

When did the first people migrate into the New World and settle there? For many years the earliest indisputable remains of the first occupation of the Americas were those of the Clovis culture in North America, and related cultures throughout Central and South America. These people, who first appeared about 12,000 years ago, made distinctive, elegant spear points of chipped stone. But for some time now, archaeologists have been searching for earlier sites, thinking that the Clovis culture must have antecedents whose traditions did not yet include spear or arrow points.

The best-documented candidate for such a site is Monte Verde, in south-central Chile. In late 1975 a Chilean agronomy student brought some large 'cow' bones to his professor. The

The Clovis culture (p. 202) of 12,000 to 10,000 years ago was long regarded as the earliest undisputed occupation in the New World, but the site of Monte Verde in Chile provides strong evidence for an even earlier occupation, occurring around 13,000 years ago. The remarkable preservation of the site has produced a wealth of artifacts, many made of wood. Moreover, deep excavations there suggest an even earlier occupation at 33,000 years ago.

bones had been found in the bank of a creek by a local family. The professor immediately suspected that the bones might actually be those of very large creatures that became extinct at the end of the Ice Age, more than 10,000 years ago. The student returned to the site and collected more bones, together with a large piece of chipped stone that looked as if it might be an artifact.

In 1976, the American archaeologist Tom Dillehay was teaching at the local university and was asked to look at the bones. He noticed odd marks that might have resulted from the animals

Stone tools (12,000–13,000 BC) from Monte Verde are evidence of a culture that predates the Clovis of North America.

being cut up and butchered by humans. He also found that 80% of the bones were ribs – an intriguing proportion suggesting that they may have been intentionally selected by humans. He visited the site, and in 1977 began a series of excavations that would eventually document the first known site in the Americas to pre-date the Clovis culture.

Fortunately for the archaeologists, Monte Verde is exceptionally well preserved. Shortly after its human inhabitants left, it was covered by a layer of peat, which sealed and protected the site. Dillehay found artifacts of types never before seen – many of them made of wood. In addition he found tools made of chipped stone and worked animal bone. The site was apparently located on an open bit of ground next to a stream. The people built huts with log foundations, wooden posts and branches forming the walls, and covered with animal skins for shelter. In the houses were small clay-lined pits for holding hot coals that were used for both cooking and heating. Food remains indicate that the people ate seeds, nuts, fruits, berries and tubers. They may also have hunted mastodons, an extinct

The early inhabitants of Monte Verde may have hunted mastodons, an extinct relative of the elephant. Parts of the animal that were brought back to the settlement include the rib-cage, with meat for the people, and the skins, which were used to cover their houses. Below: Artifacts from Monte Verde: charred mastodon ribs and tusk, and a palaeo-llama shoulder blade.

relative of the elephant, bringing to their settlements only parts of the animals – usually the rib cage – to supply meat for the people. The skins were prepared and used to cover their houses.

Set apart from the houses was a remarkable structure: its foundation was of sand and gravel, vertical wooden posts supported the walls, and an odd rectangular platform extended outward from the construction, giving it a shape reminiscent of a wishbone. Remains of plants with medicinal qualities were found associated with it, suggesting a possible ritual function.

Radiocarbon dating of the materials found at Monte Verde reveals that the site was occupied around 13,000 years ago, a full thousand years before the earliest Clovis hunters. Clearly Dillehay has demonstrated that a pre-Clovis culture did indeed exist in the Americas, but there remains one enigma at the site – perhaps the most intriguing discovery to date at Monte Verde. Dillehay continued some of his excavations deep below the early village, hoping to find evidence for a slightly earlier development of this local tradition. What he found was far older than he could have imagined: several stones with chips removed from them, stones that look distinctly like artifacts, and three possible fire pits with fragments of charcoal preserved in them. Radiocarbon dating of this charcoal indicates the astonishing date of 33,000 years ago, raising the possibility that people were indeed in the Americas very much earlier than previously suspected. ■

BIG-GAME HUNTING ON THE NORTH AMERICAN PLAINS

The grasslands of North America, which cover about 2.6 km² (1 million square miles), stretch from the Rockies in the west to the middle of the continent, and from Texas in the south to Canada in the north. Until European/American occupation, this vast area was home to nomadic, *tipi*-dwelling tribes like the Sioux, Cheyenne and Blackfoot.

These grasslands supported millions of large animals, including the mammoth (which became extinct here about 11,000 years ago)

The grasslands of North America were once home to millions of large animals like the buffalo. Prehistoric Indians devised highly efficient ways of killing these animals, ways that lasted for thousands of years until the arrival of the Europeans.

and the American buffalo (or more properly the bison), as well as smaller animals such as the pronghorn antelope. Archaeology has recovered a fascinating story of how prehistoric Plains Indians devised ruthlessly efficient methods of killing these animals, both for their meat and for items to make clothing and tools.

The earliest evidence comes from the Palaeo-Indian Clovis culture sites of the western Plains about 11,000 years ago. At sites like Blackwater Draw, in New Mexico, hunters relying primarily

on stone-tipped spears over time killed or at least butchered dozens of mammoth by the side of a swamp, now long since dried. Later, at this same site, Palaeo-Indian Folsom hunters – who used a more delicate stone point – killed extinct forms of bison. Some of the stone points found at this site were made from materials that could be obtained only from quarries up to 240 km (150 miles) away.

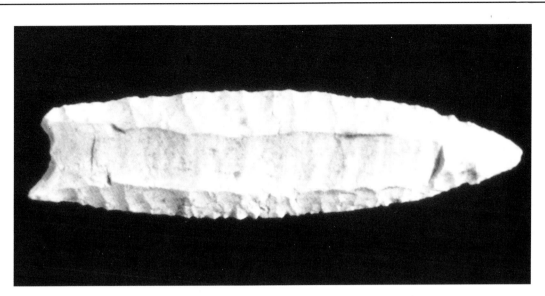

These types of kills may not have been regular events, however, for they required a great deal of management and planning, as well as a fair amount of luck. One archaeologist has quipped that the Palaeo-Indian hunter had perhaps one successful kill per lifetime…and probably never stopped talking about it!

After the mammoth had become extinct, hunters concentrated on the bison, and devised increasingly complex methods of killing them. Although individual animals or small groups were often killed (especially during the historic period when hunters used guns and horses), the herd nature of the bison allowed hunters to organize *communal* kills, in which hundreds of hunters (male and female) would kill hundreds of animals in a single event. These kills took advantage of natural features of the environment. One particularly spectacular method was the cliff jump, in which a herd was stampeded over a cliff. This sort of kill required an incredible amount of planning and patience as small bands of bison were herded into a group large enough for the hunters to start a stampede between drive lines of stones that funnelled to the top of the cliff. Hunters also took advantage of features such as sanddunes and box canyons to pin the animals down so that they could be easily killed. They even built wooden corrals, called pounds, into which the animals could be driven.

TOP: Stone Folsom tip taken from a Palaeo-Indian kill-site is more delicately wrought than the early Clovis points. Both are among the finest examples of the stone-knapper's art.

ABOVE: Beautifully flaked stone tip produced by the Clovis people, who inhabited the western Plains of America about 11,000 years ago.

OPPOSITE: A 19th-century depiction of a bison hunt shows the ancient practice of herding the animals for a communal kill.

Most communal kills were held in the autumn, so that the tribes could get a good store of winter food. Because the kills took so long to plan and because they were so risky (one mistake could scatter the whole herd), they were accompanied by a great deal of religious ritual and taboo (for example, no individual hunting was allowed in the days before a communal kill in case the herd was 'spooked'). These communal kills may in some instances have so depleted the size of bison populations in a particular area that some archaeologists think that the kills were not held annually.

Although the hunting of bison dominated Plains culture, other animals were still important for food and were killed both individually and communally. Several archaeological sites in Wyoming and Montana suggest that herds of other animals could be successfully trapped in ways similar to those used for bison.

Fundamental to the success of a hunt was the projectile point. These stone points were often shaped and flaked well beyond what was necessary to make them fly true, and so archaeologists – backed up by historical evidence – believe that they also had great symbolic power. The reconstruction of Plains prehistory has re-

lied heavily on our study of these tools, for they changed in shape through time and have thus enabled archaeologists to date sites where they were found. The thousands of points recovered from kill-sites have been crucial in understanding the chronology of the area. The earliest ones were used as spear tips. Clovis and Folsom points were beautifully flaked and still stand today as some of the finest examples of the stone-knapper's art. Later on, about 7000 years ago, hunters widely adopted the so-called *atlatl*-dart technique, whereby the projectile was propelled by means of a spear thrower, a thin shaft of wood, perhaps a metre (3 ft) long, that served as an extension of the thrower's arm. About 2500 years ago, the bow and arrow began to make its way across the plains. Both these technical innovations served to increase the killing efficiency of the hunter. ■

ROCK ART IN THE NEW WORLD

Although most American rock art was always known to the indigenous inhabitants – and indeed was still being produced in some areas until the nineteenth century – the first Europeans to notice it were those who came in the wake of the Conquistadors, often clerics, traders and explorers. In 1673, for example, the Jesuit father Jacques Marquette, exploring down the Mississippi River, noted in his journal winged monsters painted high on a cliff in modern Illinois. Garrick Mallery, a US army colonel in command of Fort Rice on Upper Missouri, was the first person to write a major work on North American rock art *Picture-Writing of the American Indians* (1893), after collecting and interpreting a vast amount of material. In it he noted that 'one of the curious facts in connection with petroglyphs is the meager notice taken of them by explorers and even by residents other than the Indians, who are generally reticent concerning them'.

In South America, rock art was noticed even earlier. From the sixteenth century on, 'inscriptions' in Brazil were reported, and sometimes described and illustrated, by Bandeirantes (carriers of

The New World has one of the world's richest collections of rock art, from Patagonia to the northwest coast of Canada, but the vast majority of these images – including some of the most striking ever produced – remain unknown to the public, and even to most archaeologists.

the royal Portuguese banner) who explored the interior of the country. During the sixteenth century, Spanish missionaries realized that some rock art sites had a religious and sacred character for the native population – so they destroyed them, or engraved crosses in high and prominent spots in the rock art sites, either to show the superiority of Christianity or in an attempt to shatter the power of the images.

The first studies of Bolivian rock art also began in the colonial period. Padre Alonso Ramos Gavilán, in his book *Historia de Nuestra Señora de Copacabana* (1621), mentions four rock art sites. In three of them, the Spanish found engraved 'footprints' in the rock and supposed they were the traces of a Christian saint, confirming their theory that there had been a Christian missionary in the Andes in pre-Columbian times. The fourth had 'letters written on a rock' – early explorers often saw rock art as ancient writing.

New World rock art displays a wide variety of techniques: petroglyphs, pictographs or paintings, engravings, geoglyphs (such as at Nasca, see p. 208), cave paintings (see p. 214) and petroforms, that

ABOVE: The 'Holy Ghost Panel' in the Great Gallery, Barrier Canyon, Utah. These ghostly mummylike figures, with no extremities, are probably supernatural beings: the 'Holy Ghost' itself is over 2 m (6 ft 6 in) tall.

RIGHT: These pecked ceremonial figures in the Coso Range, California, are thought to be costumed principals in a sheep cult, or shamans. They appear to have painted bodies, fringed skirts and feathered headdresses, and some are holding bows and arrows or spearthrowers and darts.

Above: 'Tsagaglalal' ('She who watches') is a spectacular, large petroglyph near The Dalles on America's northwest coast. It is thought to represent a mythical being, a guardian spirit who it was hoped – in vain – would ward off the epidemics of new diseases arriving with Europeans in the seventeenth and eighteenth centuries.

Left: Rock art exists throughout the New World. This large painting of a vulture or buzzard is from Roca de Vaca, one of hundreds of decorated sandstone rockshelters in the Piauí region of northeast Brazil.

is, stones arranged into patterns or images on the ground surface. There are major concentrations of petroglyphs in many areas such as the American Southwest, the Northwest, and areas of Peru and Bolivia. Paintings (pictographs) are also widespread, especially in South American rockshelters, but also in Baja California, in Texas, in Utah, and in part of California where the Chumash produced some of the most dazzling polychrome designs anywhere in the world. Naturally, no single explanation can suffice for an art that spans such a huge length of time (organic material in rock varnish – a substance that forms on rocks exposed to desert dust – covering some petroglyphs in California and Arizona has been dated to 18,000 and 14,000 years ago), and displays such a vast range of technique and subject matter. There are hunting scenes, narrative scenes, hand stencils and prints, animals and a wide range of humans and humanoids. Many of the latter are presumably gods or spirits, though some researchers believe that shamanism and trance experiences played a major role in the production of some rock art motifs, notably in the Pecos River area and parts of California. ∎

THE DISCOVERY OF THE OLMEC

It began in 1862 in the Tuxtla Mountains of southern Veracruz when a fieldworker on a sugar-cane plantation encountered an object protruding from the ground which turned out to be a colossal basalt head. Now known as Tres Zapotes Monument A, the head was published in 1869 by José Melgar who saw 'Ethiopic' traits in its thick lips and wide nose. The head eventually became a touchstone for comparison with similar objects turning up in burgeoning art collections at the turn of the century, but such recognition was to take decades.

Indeed archaeologists, less than enthusiastic about exploring a mosquito-infested swamp, paid little heed to Melgar's find until 1925 when Frans Blom and Oliver La Farge pioneered the modern archaeological study of the Olmec. They discovered the site of La Venta, Tabasco, and with it a second colossal head. On San Martín Pajapan volcano in Veracruz, Blom and La Farge also discovered a stunning basalt sculpture of a seated figure with a headdress bearing a strange, snarling visage. Their findings were published in the 1926 classic *Tribes and Temples* which was reviewed in 1927 by the German scholar Hermann Beyer. He compared the style of a carved axe in a private collection to the snarling face on the San Martín sculpture and referred to them as 'olmecan'. In doing so, Beyer christened this still undefined Gulf Coast civilization. The term

The earliest known complex society in Mesoamerica, the Olmec (*c.* 1150–400 BC), inhabited the swampy coastal plain of southern Veracruz and Tabasco on Mexico's Gulf Coast. With their architecture effaced by the tropical forest, the Olmec had long drifted out of historical memory by the time the Spanish reached the shores of Mesoamerica. Their rediscovery is one of the great stories in Mesoamerican archaeology.

'Olmec', meaning 'people from the land of rubber' in Nahuatl, was drawn from sixteenth-century sources mentioning people of that name living on the Gulf Coast.

Unaware of the antiquity of the objects in question, Beyer made the huge mistake of assigning them to a protohistoric group. This fanciful attribution was given further impetus by the American archaeologist Marshall Saville who wrote an influential paper in 1929 describing an 'Olmec style' based on a study of carved votive axes in various collections. This emerging concept of an Olmec culture was further consolidated in a 1932 publication by the American specialist George Vaillant who tentatively defined its regional extent. In the late 1930s these tantalizing hints of a little-known civilization on Mexico's Gulf Coast led Matthew Stirling, director of the Bureau of American Ethnology, to undertake systematic fieldwork at Tres Zapotes, the location of Melgar's original discovery. Stirling quickly made a major find of his own: Tres Zapotes Stela C, an epi-Olmec carving with a readable hieroglyphic date older than the earliest dated Maya material. This raised the spectre of the Olmec as the progenitors of Mesoamerica's high cultures, a position held until then by the Maya. Stirling went on to work at La Venta and San Lorenzo in the 1940s, adding dozens of new Olmec monuments to the known inventory.

Stirling's claim of a pre-Maya antiquity for the Olmec met with considerable resistance, especially from Mayanists, but the evidence continued to pile

ABOVE: The first publication of an Olmec object is this drawing published by the Prussian nobleman Alexander von Humboldt in 1810. As the Olmec awaited discovery for more than a hundred years, von Humboldt called the incised jade celt an 'Aztec axe'. The whereabouts of the Humboldt celt are currently unknown.

LEFT: Ceremonial axes, such as this, were among the first Olmec objects in museum collections that helped define the Olmec style. Note the characteristic Olmec traits: cleft head, flame eyebrows and snarling lips.

Colossal heads, such as La Venta Monument 1, which measures over 2.5 m (8 ft) tall, are among the most distinctive works of art produced by the Olmec, and are believed to be portraits of their rulers.

up in his favour. For instance, in the 1940s ceramics with Olmec traits were found at Monte Albán in Oaxaca and in the Valley of Mexico in conjunction with Preclassic ceramic phases. Finally, the invention of radiocarbon dating in 1948 settled the question once and for all. The first dates run on material from an Olmec site, La Venta, in 1957 confirmed a Preclassic antiquity. Later work at San Lorenzo by Michael Coe and Richard Diehl pushed back the beginnings of the Olmec florescence to 1150 BC. Controversy still surrounds the Olmec, however, for while monuments in the Olmec style are concentrated on the Gulf Coast, they are by no means limited to that area, and some of the finest Olmec portable objects are found in great quantities outside the Gulf Coast. The final chapter of the Olmec discovery has yet to be written. ■

NASCA LINES

The ancient Nasca culture extended over much of the south coast of what is today Peru, including the many branches of the Nasca river valley, as well as valleys to the north and south. It is known for the elaborate and intricate tapestries it produced, as well as vibrantly painted ceramics depicting elements of its world, both natural and supernatural. The Nasca people tamed the barren coastal desert, developing irrigation systems to water their crops and producing an abundance of foods to support the population. Their religious beliefs may be seen in the platform mounds and adobe (mudbrick) pyramids they erected in an elaborate ceremonial centre, and the thousands of people buried in surrounding cemeteries.

On a broad flat plain adjacent to the Nasca valley they also

Etched into the desert plain near Nasca, Peru, are hundreds of lines, some stretching arrow-straight for kilometres, others forming animal figures and geometric shapes. They have been interpreted as many things, from a prehistoric zodiac to landing strips to guide extraterrestrial visitors to earth. While most of the straight lines date to periods between 2000 BC and AD 1500, the animal figures were probably constructed by the Nasca culture of AD 100–500.

made huge drawings of plants and animals. They created their grand artworks, properly termed 'geoglyphs', by moving aside the small stones covering the surface of the ground to expose the lighter coloured soil beneath. The lines so created formed the outlines of a monkey, a spider, a killer whale, several kinds of birds, and other creatures. But the Nasca culture collapsed and fell by the eighth century AD, and with it went the memories of the figures on the desert, until a day in June 1946 when Maria Reiche began her investigations.

Reiche was not the first scientist to know of the Lines of Nasca. The American anthropologist Alfred Kroeber had written about them in the notes from his 1926 visit to the area and the Peruvian archaeologist Toribio Majía Xesspe published an article in 1939, discussing the 'roads' criss-crossing the desert. Reiche was introduced to the lines by an American professor, Paul Kosok, who had seen them from the air while doing a study of ancient irrigation systems in Peru. He took a series of aerial pho-

The Nasca monkey, first recognized by Maria Reiche in 1946.

RIGHT: The wavy design of the Nasca spider was probably completed over a long period of time.

BELOW RIGHT: From 2000 BC to as late as the Spanish Colonial period (AD 1532) the Nasca culture also produced beautifully decorated pottery.

tographs of the lines and visited them on the ground. On midsummer's day in 1941, the June solstice, he was standing on a long straight line that pointed toward the western horizon, when he noticed that the sun seemed to set directly on that point. He was astonished to realize that the lines might have been used for solar or astronomical observations, and sought out someone to undertake a serious investigation. He found Maria Reiche in Lima but unfortunately, as a German national, she was not permitted to leave the city until after the Second World War had ended.

On her very first day of study, Maria began to follow one of the lines that crossed a road, and realized immediately that it formed the shape of a spider. Later, mapping what she thought was a spiral design, she found that the lines continued on to form the outline of the body of a monkey – the spiral was its tail. She was so overcome with the excitement of her discoveries that she sat on the ground and laughed. In the decades that followed she devoted her life to the study of the lines, and to supporting her theory that the figures represented constellations and that many of the lines were used for astronomical purposes.

In addition to the animal figures, there are geometric figures, including enormous triangles and trapezoids, and many kilometres of straight lines. While the figures seem to date to the period of the Nasca culture, other lines were built over a much broader span of time. Many radiate out from single points, called line centres, which are often low hilltops or ends of ridges; broken pottery found at these centres is evidence that religious offerings were made. The pottery dates from as early as around 2000 BC to as late as the Spanish Colonial period, after AD 1532, indicating

that line construction and use took place over a very long time. Some investigators suggest that the lines might point to sacred places such as mountains or that they might be related to water and irrigation. Furthermore, many of the lines appear to have served as pathways, perhaps for religious processions – most of the figures are formed by a single line so that it is possible to walk completely around the design without crossing or retracing one's steps. Indeed, many or all of these theories may be correct. ∎

CHAVÍN

The best-known early civilization in the Andes is Chavín, named after the site of Chavín de Huantar. Its art depicts fierce, fanged humans, along with animals native to the Amazon forests east of the site, suggesting the possibility of a religious cult with origins traceable to the Amazon.

A Spanish missionary travelling through Peru in the early 1600s had this to say about some impressive ruins he saw:

Near this village of Chavin there is a large building of huge stone blocks very well wrought; it was a guaca [shrine], and one of the most famous of the heathen sanctuaries, like Rome or Jerusalem with us; the Indians used to come and make their offerings and sacrifices, for the devil pronounced many oracles for them here, and so they repaired here from all over the kingdom. There are large subterranean halls and apartments, and even accurate information that they extend under the river which flows by the guaca or ancient sanctuary.

Despite its impressive nature, the importance of Chavín in Andean prehistory was not suspected until the 1920s and 1930s when the archaeologist Julio C. Tello realized that it was the centre of a major early civilization. He was a native Peruvian Indian who, despite the prejudices of society, won a fellowship to Harvard University, and eventually became the best-known archaeologist in Peru. Tello excavated at a number of major ceremonial sites on the coast of Peru but, being from the highlands himself, he always looked for a highland origin of Peruvian civilization. In Chavín he found what he had been looking for. He undertook excavations at the site, exposing its great temple structures and elaborate stone carvings with their depictions of snarling fanged humans – perhaps supernatural – and great creatures of the jungle: large birds, crocodiles, jaguars and even parrots. He recognized the similarity between these carvings and some that he had seen at other sites, and concluded that he had discovered the source of a widespread phenomenon. Whether the carvings were the product of a religious cult or the result of pilgrimage, Chavín-style imagery was found throughout the Andes.

BELOW: Chavín was a centre of innovation, and its regional influence can be seen in the appearance of new vessel shapes such as these decorated stirrup-spout bottles.

Part of the head of the 'Smiling' or 'Snarling God', carved in low relief on the Lanzon stone. This slender, knife-shaped stone is 4.5 m (14 ft 7 in) tall, its point embedded in the floor. It may possibly have been an oracle of some kind, with a speaking hole.

Construction of the Chavín temple complex began in about 800 BC; it was a U-shaped building, arranged around a circular sunken court. Excavations by the Peruvian Luis Lumbreras in a tunnel-like gallery near the court revealed that the gallery was filled with of ceramic vessels that had been left there – indeed broken there – as offerings. Most interesting of all, the ceramics were brought from far distant regions, indicating that Chavín served as a pilgrimage centre, much like Mecca or Delphi. At the heart of the temple is a tall carved stone called the Lanzon, on which is depicted a human-like creature with a cat-like fanged mouth, and with snakes for hair. The temple was actually built around the statue, so that it is perhaps the only stone carving at the site still in its original location.

About 400 BC the temple was modified, becoming much larger, but still maintaining the basic U-shaped plan. The most important stone carving at this time was probably of a human figure wearing an elaborate headdress, with arms to his sides, holding a staff in each hand. This 'staff deity', as it is called, reappears in a slightly different form in the cultures of Tiwanaku (p. 230) and Wari. Tello may indeed have been at least partially right when he declared Chavín to be the 'Mother Culture' of the Andes.

On the night of 16 January 1945, a lake at the base of the nearby mountains broke its banks, and a deluge of water, mud and stones rushed down the slope. It carried away the small museum where the artifacts and smaller stone carvings were stored, and deposited a thick layer of mud over the great temples of Chavín. Tello was heartbroken. As he wrote shortly after, 'Thus vanished the dreams of the artist and the archaeologist.' He died two years later. ∎

EL CERÉN

Finding a site like El Cerén buried under 5 m (16 ft) of ash is like looking for a needle in a haystack, so it was with extraordinary luck that in 1976 a bulldozer exposed part of a structure. Radiocarbon tests performed on preserved roof thatching by Payson Sheets of the University of Colorado yielded a date of AD 590 ± 90, the beginning of the Classic period in Maya chronology. The excavation of the site by Sheets has been an ongoing project, interrupted between 1981 and 1988 by El Salvador's brutal civil war.

The volcanic fall-out hit El Cerén sometime on an early evening in August, after farmers had returned from the fields and

A volcanic eruption at the end of the sixth century AD dumped metres of ash on a village, now known as El Cerén, in the Zapotitán Valley of western El Salvador. Like Pompeii, its Old World counterpart, the site offers a unique glimpse at the daily life of an ancient society, in this case preserving a complete inventory of household goods and cultivated plants in the context of peasant architecture.

their families had eaten but not yet rolled out their sleeping mats. Warned by the sound of the explosion, the inhabitants fled. Their household possessions, along with stored grains, garden plants, even the household pests and food residues and paints, were entombed by falling ash.

To date, eleven of El Cerén's structures have been excavated. Archaeologists have identified the 'downtown' area: a large plaza with public buildings, including a sweatbath with an unusual domed ceiling. Household compounds include multiple buildings with specialized functions, such as dwellings, cooking areas, workshops, and storage facilities. The use of specialized buildings, rather than combining all functions in a single large structure (a pattern found in lower Central America), suggests affiliations with El Cerén's Maya neighbours to the northwest. Scholars believe that the inhabitants of El Cerén were culturally, if not ethnically, Maya. The region's ethnicity remains in doubt, though most probably it was Maya or Lenca.

Among the most exciting discoveries at El Cerén is the preservation of artifacts (many of wood) and plant materials in their daily utilitarian context. For instance, grinding stones (*metates*) are ubiquitous at Mesoamerican sites, but only at El Cerén have they been found on forked wooden posts raising them to a more comfortable working level. So-called 'doughnut' stones, generally thought to be weights for digging sticks, contained nut residues, suggesting that they were also used as mortars. Obsidian blades were found in roof thatching, presumably stored there to protect them from damage and delicate feet from injury. Seeds were stored in ceramic pots, and harvested crops in wooden bins.

The unique challenge of excavating a site like El Cerén engaged a multidisciplinary team of experts: archaeologists, geophysicists, biologists, volcanologists, conservationists and even proctologists and dentists! Their combined efforts paint a vivid picture of life at El Cerén. The inhabitants lived well, eating out of polychrome bowls and sleeping on benches at the rear of the house. Their kitchen gardens provided maguey for cordage, as well as cacao and manioc, while maize was planted farther away – rows of maize have been found preserved in the fields. They also consumed tomatoes, beans, squash, chillies and a variety of local fruits, and kept ducks and dogs in the yard. As Sheets has noted, the material existence of the war-torn masses of El Salvador is in most respects less enviable than that of their ancient predecessors. ∎

A cataclysmic eruption of Ilopongo volcano in AD **175**, affecting the greater part of El Salvador, depopulated the Zapotitán Valley until the fifth century, when El Cerén was established. The site, seen at the bottom, thrived for only about a century until it was devastated by an eruption of Laguna Caldera, at top.

ABOVE: Stored in a niche of Structure 2 of Household 2 is a covered ceramic bowl, the bottom of which contains food residue streaked by finger-marks. To the front and left is a nested pile of painted gourds. Their surfaces had collapsed, leaving just the paint fragments. At first this was mistaken for a pre-Columbian screenfold book.

RIGHT: Typically, structures are built on clay and grass mounds fired to harden them. Walls are of adobe (mudbrick) or mud reinforced with vertical and horizontal poles, locally known as *bajareque*. The corners of buildings are reinforced on the interior with square adobe columns. These houses, with their sleeping benches, high thatched roofs and porches, provided a comfortable existence and are sturdier than modern peasant domestic architecture.

Naj Tunich and Maya Cave Art

Recognition of the importance of caves in Maya culture is hardly a recent phenomenon and can be traced back to the travels of John Lloyd Stephens and Frederick Catherwood in 1840. In the late nineteenth century, inspired by Palaeolithic finds in Europe (see p. 58), Edward Thompson, Teobert Maler and Henry Mercer set out to record archaeological data in caves in Yucatán. In spite of its long history, however, Maya cave archaeology was then, and remained for the better part of the twentieth century, the poor stepchild of mainstream archaeology. A few persistent individuals produced a series of site reports in the 1960s and 1970s but, generally speaking, Maya cave archaeology was not taken seriously.

The discovery of the cave now called Naj Tunich changed all that and put cave archaeology on the map, if not at the forefront, of Maya research. The cave preserves the richest collection of archaeological material ever found in a Mesoamerican cave. It con-

In 1980, deep in a cave in the southeastern corner of the department of Peten in Guatemala, in the foothills of the Maya mountains, was found a collection of cave paintings whose calibre and magnitude rocked the archaeological world.

tains stone buildings and walled alcoves that may have served as tombs, as well as thousands of polychrome ceramic sherds, jade, bone and stone implements. Far within, at depths approaching 2 km (1.25 miles), scattered areas of pottery and human bones were found, as well as the unprecedented collection of cave paintings.

These paintings, numbering around a hundred, date to the apogee of Maya calligraphic painting in the eighth century AD, as witnessed by magnificent painted ceramics from this period. In fact, the cave paintings reflect their refined linear style and were probably painted by artists/scribes who also decorated pottery. What is so important about the paintings is that they include dozens of hieroglyphic inscriptions with dates, names, and Emblem Glyphs which specify where individuals came from. This epigraphic evidence suggests that Naj Tunich was enmeshed in a political network that involved numerous local states such as Ixkun, Ixtutz and Sacul, as well as more distant and powerful ones like Caracol.

Naj Tunich, like other Maya caves with archaeological remains, was primarily a sacred shrine with a ritual function. In Amerindian religion the landscape was imbued with supernatural power.

Naj Tunich Drawing 82. This magnificent text, measuring about 1.5 m (5 ft) across, includes several Emblem Glyphs which reveal ritual participation by individuals from different regional sites.

RIGHT: Naj Tunich Drawing 18. This graphic scene of sexual intercourse has puzzled investigators. While the male at left is anatomically accurate, the presumed female has masculine characteristics. This has prompted speculation that Drawing 18 is a homoerotic scene or that the right-hand figure is a female impersonator. The latter suggestion seems more likely, given that the pigtail worn by this figure is an unmistakable sign of female gender.

BELOW: Naj Tunich Drawing 81, detail. Enigmatic profile faces adorn the walls of Naj Tunich. Presumably they are the pilgrims who recorded their presence in the cave for posterity.

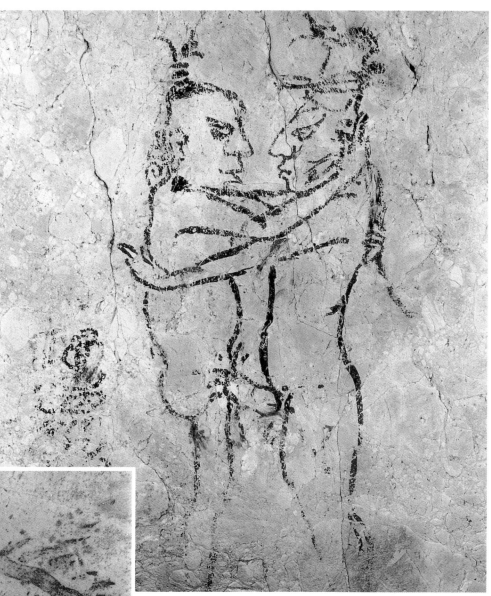

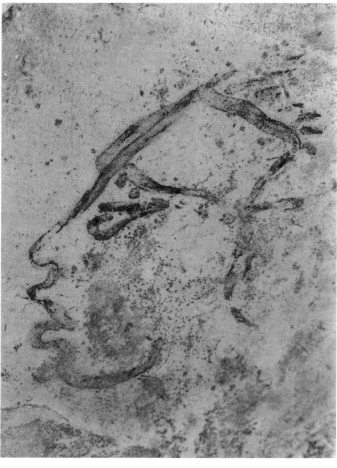

Caves, in common with other dramatic topographic features, were seen as portals to the spirit world. In the Maya area pilgrimages were made to caves to encounter spirits through private acts of blood sacrifice, incense-burning and other rites. Some of the Naj Tunich paintings depict these introspective moments in graphic detail, affording a unique window onto a little-known aspect of Maya culture. Thus it is a tragedy of immeasurable proportions that an act of vandalism in 1989 resulted in the obliteration of twenty-three major paintings.

Naj Tunich stimulated a small revolution in Maya cave archaeology. After its discovery, more painted caves came to light, resulting in an important new synthesis of this material, one of the very few documented traditions of deep cave art in the world. The excavator of Naj Tunich, James Brady, has continued to pursue cave studies, refining survey techniques and, more importantly, a much-needed theoretical framework for the field. Even mainstream Maya archaeologists now acknowledge the importance of caves and many include a local cave survey as a standard part of their site excavations. Cave archaeology has emerged, thanks to Naj Tunich, as one of the most exciting frontiers of Maya research. ∎

PALENQUE: THE TOMB OF PACAL THE GREAT

It is not apparent from the exterior that the Temple of the Inscriptions is anything but an imposing pyramid-temple built against low-lying hills. The 24 m (79 ft) high platform, tiered in nine levels, supports a sanctuary, originally a symphony of painted stucco sculpture with a majestic roof comb. Most of it has not survived, though the piers separating the doorways preserve images of Pacal's son and successor, Chan Bahlum, in the guise of a Maya serpent-footed god. The sanctuary has a portico and inner room: the former bears two large hieroglyphic tablets plastered on the rear wall, and the latter a third tablet. These three tablets, which gave the Temple of the Inscriptions its name, contain over 600 hieroglyphs, comprising the second longest inscription known from the Maya world.

While much of this had been documented in 1840 by John Lloyd Stephens, an American lawyer and traveller, it was the Mexican archaeologist Alberto Ruz Lhuillier who in 1952 penetrated the temple's innermost secrets. He became curious about the sanctuary floor which, unlike others at Palenque, was formed from well-cut large stone slabs. In the rear chamber one slab has a double row of circular depressions filled with stone plugs which Ruz surmised might have been used for its removal. He also no-

Though Maya temples are sometimes referred to as 'pyramids', they are utterly different in one respect from the Egyptian variety, in that they were not planned as royal tombs – that is, with one major exception, the Temple of the Inscriptions at Palenque, Mexico. This temple is unique in Maya architecture in having been conceived from its inception as a funerary monument, to house the sarcophagus of Palenque's most powerful king, Pacal the Great, who reigned between AD 615 and 683.

ticed that the rear wall of the second chamber continued down below the floor level. In 1949 he removed the slab, exposing a vaulted rubble-filled opening quickly revealed as a stairwell. Perhaps his most difficult task was clearing the stairwell – it took nearly a solid year of work over four field seasons.

In 1952 workmen arrived at the base, which was blocked by masonry fill. Here Ruz found a stone box containing ceramic bowls, shells full of red pigment, jade earplugs, beads and a pearl. Beyond that lay another compartment with the skeletons of six sacrificed individuals. Finally, removing a huge triangular slab that blocked the passage, Ruz saw the open doorway to a crypt lying under the temple's central axis, over 25 m (82 ft) below the level of the sanctuary. A short stairway leads down into a 10 x 4 m (33 x 13 ft) chamber with calcite-encrusted walls decorated with nine guardian figures in carved stucco. Filling the chamber is the sarcophagus of Pacal the Great elevated on six stone supports.

The sarcophagus, measuring 3 x 2 m (9 ft 10 in x 6 ft 7 in), has a womb-shaped opening covered in red cinnabar, sealed by a stone plug. Removal of the plug revealed Pacal's skeleton. Controversy surrounds the age at death of the skeleton, as Mexican physical anthropologists assign it an age of forty years, though the glyphic evidence says that Pacal died at the age of eighty. This discrepancy has not yet been resolved.

Pacal was buried with a treasure trove of jade: a jade diadem, ear ornaments, necklaces, pectorals, wristlets and a jade ring on each finger. A jade mosaic mask covered his face, and he clutched a piece of jade in either hand. Two jade statuettes were found near his feet, and on the sarcophagus lid lay the remains of a jade belt with three masquettes. Under the sarcophagus lay ceramic dishes for food and two life-size stucco heads.

The limestone sarcophagus lid, about 4 m (13 ft) long, is carved with one of the most famous scenes in all Maya art. It shows Pacal in a foetal position falling into the underworld, which is depicted as a great U-shaped maw. From his body rises a world tree and a supernatural bird, the whole intersected by a two-headed arching serpent. Pacal is seen, then, at the centre of the cosmos and, though he descends like the setting sun into the underworld, a cycle of renewal is implied in the images carved on the sides of the sarcophagus. Here we see ten Palenque dynasts (hereditary rulers) sprouting from the ground like trees. In addition, a mortar tube leads from the sarcophagus, eventually joining a stone tube on the stairwell which follows all sixty-seven steps and emerges on the sanctuary floor. Pacal was thus connected to the world of the living by a ' psychoduct' and he has been immortalized by the discovery of his magnificent tomb. ■

The Temple of the Inscriptions, seen to the right of the palace complex, is the largest single building at Palenque.

ABOVE: This life-size stucco head, originally painted, forms part of Offering 3 and was found under Pacal's sarcophagus. The delicate facial features closely match other depictions of Pacal.

LEFT: The sarcophagus lid is the most elaborate representation of death left to us by the ancient Maya. In addition to the image of Pacal's descent into the underworld, the Maya depicted ancestors, shown as heads, emerging from caves at the top and bottom. The sides of the lid are inscribed with glyphs that list the death dates of Pacal's royal predecessors.

THE DECIPHERMENT OF MAYA HIEROGLYPHICS

In its earliest stages, the study of the Maya script was held back by a paucity of published texts. The very first appeared in the scientific traveller Baron Alexander von Humboldt's *Vues des cordillères, et monuments des peuples indigènes de l'Amérique* of 1810 which reproduced five pages of the Dresden codex. Unfortunately, early drawings of inscriptions on stone monuments, beginning in 1822 and persisting for decades, were highly inaccurate. Even Frederick Catherwood's sensitive drawings, published by John Lloyd Stephens in the 1840s, could not fill the void. The availability of accurate reproductions improved greatly in the second half of the nineteenth century with the publication in toto of three Maya codices and the superb photographs and drawings of monumental inscriptions from Tikal, Copán, Quirigua, Yaxchilán and other sites, in Alfred Maudslay's *Biologia centrali-Americana* (1889–1902).

From the outset, the lack of accurate texts did not stop would-be Champollions from speculating on the nature of the Maya script. The first decipherment can be credited to Constantine Rafinesque who published on Maya writing as early as 1827 and discovered the value of the bar and dot system (a dot equals one, and a bar five). Progress on the analytical front received a major boost in 1864 with the publication of *Relación de las cosas de Yucatán*, a report on the Maya of Yucatán written shortly after the Conquest by the infamous Bishop Diego de Landa. Known only from a copy discovered in Madrid by the abbé Brasseur de Bourbourg, this manuscript has rightly been called the Rosetta

That the natives of Mexico possessed books with writing was known in Europe even before the fall of Tenochtitlán (see p. 236). Indeed, among the treasures sent back to Spain by Cortés in 1519 were Maya screenfold books, or codices, their pages covered with strange hooks, squiggles and dots. The Europeans who first laid eyes on this curious writing could hardly have suspected that one day, hundreds of years later, it would elucidate a long-lost era of Central American history and religion.

Stone of Maya hieroglyphic decipherment. Landa's informant drew and identified by their Yucatec name the glyphic versions of the twenty days of the 260-day calendar and the eighteen months of the 365-day calendar. This information was a small but important stepping stone to unravelling the calendrical, and ultimately the astronomical, portion of Maya texts, a task which was quite advanced by the end of the century.

Landa's manuscript also included an unusual alphabet. By hav-

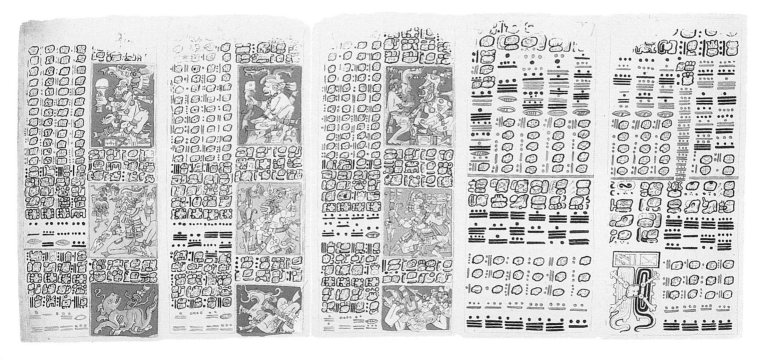

LEFT: Painted text on a cylindrical vase, seen here in a rollout photograph. David Stuart deciphered the word 'to write' and the word for 'scribe' on one vase, revealing that many works of Maya art were signed by their makers.

ABOVE: The first published Maya inscription, five pages of the Dresden Codex, from Alexander von Humboldt, 1810.

ing his informant draw his a, b, c and so on in glyphs, Landa inadvertently recorded equivalences between the spoken form of the Spanish alphabet (ah, bay, say, etc.) and syllabic signs in Maya writing. This key to phonetic decipherment was not successfully exploited, however, until the 1950s with the work of the Russian linguist Yuri Knorosov who showed that Maya writing, like the Egyptian hieroglyphic writing which he had formerly studied, combined word signs (logograms) and phonetic signs representing consonant-vowel syllables. Using Landa's alphabet, he was able to decipher short texts from the codices and also to assign phonetic values to glyphs that did not appear in Landa. This represented an unprecedented breakthrough in the reading of non-calendrical Maya inscriptions. Knorosov's work was, unfortunately, opposed by such influential Mayanists as J. Eric S. Thompson, but his basic assumptions have withstood the test of time.

As the phonetic approach to decipherment was making headway, in the 1960s the Russian born American scholar Tatiana Proskouriakoff worked out the syntax of monumental inscriptions and the first dynastic history of a Maya site, namely that of Piedras Negras. With Heinrich Berlin's decipherment in 1958 of Emblem Glyphs, which name individual sites, a productive era of historical reconstruction was under way. The dynastic histories of many Maya cities are now well understood, and new inroads into the Maya script, by such brilliant epigraphers as David Stuart and Linda Schele, have begun to illuminate their esoteric content. These discoveries have revolutionized Maya archaeology, lending it an historical framework unmatched anywhere else in pre-Columbian America. ■

THE MOUNDBUILDERS

Along the Illinois, Ohio and Mississippi Rivers, which flow through North America's heartland to the southeastern part of the continent, are located the remains of thousands of earthen mounds. These mounds provide clues to one of the most complex prehistoric societies that existed in the continent, and during the nineteenth century played an important role in the development of American archaeology as an objective, intellectual discipline.

The mid-west and southeastern parts of the United States are home to spectacular earthen structures. These mounds – the remains of complex societies – spawned one of the great intellectual debates of the nineteenth century.

Small, conically shaped mounds were constructed as burial mounds during the Adena and Hopewell cultures, approximately 1000 BC to AD 500. The Adena culture may well represent not the remains of an actual 'people' but rather a religious burial complex. At first, Adena mounds were simple affairs, with a small mound covering a single body placed in a shallow pit. By the end of the Adena period, however, the mounds were constructed over elaborate wooden burial chambers, and were in

some instances extremely big, the largest being the Grave Creek mound on the banks of the Ohio River in West Virginia, which is over 18 m (60 feet) high. These burial mounds were clearly built for important people in society, although the smaller ones at least did not require a great deal of communal effort.

The Hopewellian Complex is, like the Adena, now seen not as a culture in the sense of representing a people, but rather as the archaeological remains of a widespread exchange and ceremonial complex that overlay regional 'cultures'. Hopewell almost certainly developed out of Adena. The Hopewell Complex also has burial mounds like those of the Adena, but they are found in larger groups. The Great Serpent Mound, which belongs to the Adena/Hopewell continuum, comprises an earthen snake over 366 m (1200 ft) long, with a burial mound constructed within its open mouth.

The larger, flat-topped mounds, sometimes called temple mounds, belong to the Mississippian Tradition (approximately AD 700–1700), and were the bases for large buildings, such as temples, chiefs' palaces and associated structures. The most spectacular of these sites is the large complex of Cahokia, located just east of St Louis. The heyday of this ancient city was during the eleventh to thirteenth centuries and it covered about 800 hectares (2000 acres), of which the inner 200 were enclosed by a log wall. The complex comprises about a hundred earthen mounds, some of which were burial mounds. The largest is Monk's Mound, a four-terraced flat-topped mound over 33 m (108 ft) in height. As many as 30,000 people may have lived in the area.

The controversy in the nineteenth century over who built the mounds is a case-study in how archaeology cannot escape wider political and social issues. On one side were people, motivated in

ABOVE: This pot with an incised representation of a duck was found with a burial at the Hopewellian site of Mound City, a large necropolis that has provided much information on Hopewellian ceremonial activity.

LEFT: Monk's Mound, the largest pre-Columbian structure north of Mexico, is the centre of the site complex called Cahokia. Monk's Mound is named after a group of Trappist monks who occupied the general site area at the beginning of the 19th century.

large degree by racism, who could not see the ancestors of present-day Indians as being capable of making these mounds. They attributed the mounds to people such as the Toltecs from Mexico, Hindus on their way to Mexico, Welshmen, Vikings and people from the lost island of Atlantis. On the other was a small group of antiquarians who believed that the mounds were indeed constructed by the ancestors of Native Americans and who used the techniques of archaeology to prove their point.

Antiquarians such as Caleb Atwater, Ephraim George Squier and Edwin Hamilton Davis did magnificent work in the early part of the nineteenth century. They made accurate recordings of the earthworks and speculated on their origins, but they balked at unequivocally attributing them to the ancestors of modern Indians. Samuel Morton, the father of American physical anthropology, after studying skulls removed from mounds, decided that the moundbuilders and contemporary Native Americans were the same race, but also proposed that the civilizations of Mexico and the less spectacular cultures of North America were made by two different groups, Toltecan and Barbarous.

During the rest of the century evidence mounted in favour of the mounds having been built by indigenous peoples. Frederic Ward Putnam, for example, one of the great figures in American archaeology, proposed in 1888 that the mounds were not built by a single 'race' but by different groups. This is, of course, the modern position. In 1894, after thirteen years of field research funded by the Bureau of Ethnology, Cyrus Thomas was able to put the matter to rest and concluded that the mounds had indeed been built by ancestors of modern Indians. The myth of the moundbuilders was finally over. ■

RIGHT: The Great Serpent Mound created by the Adena/Hopewell culture is an earthen snake over 366 m (1200 ft) long, 6 m (19 ft) wide and contains a burial mound within its open mouth.

BELOW: Mortuary figures, such as this, were common in burials throughout the Moundbuilder period. Some figures may portray buried individuals.

ANCIENT FARMERS OF THE DESERT

The American South-west is a magnificent landscape of arid deserts and towering buttes. Stretching from Las Vegas, Nevada to Las Vegas, New Mexico, and from Durango, Colorado to Durango, Mexico, this land has captured the imagination of poets, artists and archaeologists since the nineteenth century, for here are found some of the best-preserved archaeological sites of the whole continent. When early European explorers and settlers came across ruins like those of the Mesa Verde in southwestern Colorado, it was as though their ancient inhabitants had left only the day before: beautifully preserved houses made of stone and wood, sandals made from the yucca plant, and magnificently painted pots, some still full of corn.

BELOW: Pueblo Bonito, the largest Anasazi town in Chaco Canyon, dominated much of the prehistoric northern Southwest in the 11th century.

In the deserts of the Southwest, prehistoric farmers were able to develop some of the most remarkable cultures known to North American archaeologists. These cultures still exist today and stand as testimony to humankind's ability to succeed in the harshest of environments.

Although the prehistoric farmers of the Southwest shared much in the way of pottery, architecture and farming techniques, there is enough variation for archaeologists to define different cultural traditions. The Anasazi occupied what is now the Four Corners region (where Arizona, Utah, Colorado and New Mexico meet). The Hohokam lived in present-day southern Arizona and the Mogollon in eastern Arizona and western New Mexico. These archaeological cultures are the ancestral forms of present-day Indian groups like the Hopi and the Pima-Papago (O'odham) who still reside and flourish in the American Southwest.

Inhabitants of the Southwest began growing corn, beans and squash about 2500 years ago, plants that were first domesticated in Central America several thousand years earlier. Later on, the farmers added such plants as cotton and tobacco to their repertoire but, with the exception of the dog and the turkey, they never relied on domesticated animals.

The dryness of the climate created special problems for these farmers, and they responded superbly. Relying on what must have been a detailed knowledge of the environment and the geography of the area, in the space of a few centuries they moved from 'dry-farming' strategies (using only the natural rainfall) to the construction of huge check-dams and irrigation canals to channel the water to their fields. The site of Snaketown in central Arizona has one of the best sets of irrigation ditches yet recovered by archaeologists. This Hohokam town covered over 1 km² (0.4 square miles), and besides numerous houses and refuse mounds also contained a ball court similar to those in Central America.

The success of their farming techniques allowed these people to construct elaborate multi-storey towns and to develop extensive economic systems. Chaco Canyon, located in north-central New Mexico, is an excellent example. Here, farmers first lived in small, single-family pit houses that were semi-subterranean, but by about a thousand years ago, the canyon was home to one of the most remarkable prehistoric societies in North America. Chaco Canyon contains thirteen Anasazi villages, of which the largest is Pueblo Bonito. The villages had as many as 700 rooms and thirty-four *kivas* (semi-subterranean stone-built structures that served as a combination of ceremonial place and social centre). Many of the sites had astronomical significance. For example, the supernova of July 1054, is recorded at one site. Chaco Canyon was the centre of a web of well-made roads that connect the canyon to outliers, locations that probably served specialized functions within the overall economic system.

Despite their success, not even these farmers could withstand forever the droughts that racked the northern part of the Southwest during the thirteenth century and they were ultimately forced to abandon the Four Corners region. The completeness of this abandonment is well exemplified at Mesa Verde. Its Anasazi sites range from early pit houses to large villages built into overhangs on the walls of the canyons that dissect the 'mesa' (or flat-topped mountain). These cliff dwellings, of which the largest is Cliff Palace, must have been teeming centres during their heyday, with fields of corn and other crops scattered along the mesa tops. Specially cut stairs allowed the inhabitants to reach their fields on the mesa tops. The decision seems to have been rapid for when, hundreds of years later, the first Europeans came to sites like Cliff Palace, they recorded that it was as though the town had only just been abandoned. ■

ABOVE: The archaeological treasures at Cliff Palace in Mesa Verde National Park ignited a public outcry against their loss that led to national laws protecting archaeological sites.

BELOW: Pithouses, like this one at Mesa Verde National Park, were used as primary habitation structures and were the architectural precursors of kivas used in religious and social meetings.

SIPÁN: MOCHE CULTURE

Between the first and eighth centuries AD, the Moche civilization stretched along the north coast of Peru. One of the driest deserts in the world, this region was tamed by ancient inhabitants who built irrigation channels to water the desert. The Moche inherited a land rich in agricultural potential, rich also in the bounty of the sea.

The Moche culture has, at least until recent discoveries, been known primarily for its monumental architecture and its ceramic art. In each valley within its realm the Moche built enormous mudbrick pyramids. The largest, called the Pyramid of the Sun, is

Moche civilization flourished on the north coast of Peru between AD 1 and 750. The discovery in 1987 of a series of spectacular tombs at a small mudbrick pyramid has shed new light on this culture and on the power wielded by its rulers. The tomb of the Lord of Sipán is the richest burial ever found in the New World.

found in the valley that gives the culture its name, and it is estimated that more than 125 million mud bricks went into its construction! At the time it was built, it was probably the largest human-made structure in the New World. Moche is perhaps best known for its ceramics, which were sometimes painted with elaborate scenes of religious and political rituals. Other vessels were modelled in the shape of animals or people and depicted many aspects of Moche life. 'Portrait pots' were jars modelled in the form of a human head – facial features were so carefully executed and are so distinctive that they were probably portraits of actual Moche people, perhaps their rulers. Another class of vessels includes the so-called 'erotic' pottery. These detailed, realistically modelled vessels depict various combinations of humans, animals and supernatural creatures engaged in a bewildering variety of sexual acts. It has been suggested that such acts may have served religious rather than procreative purposes, given that few of the acts depicted would have resulted in impregnation.

Because of the richness of Moche archaeological sites – not just the pyramids, but also vast cemeteries – looting of sites has been a major activity in the region since the Spanish Conquest. It was the activities of looters, however, that revealed the most spectacular Moche discovery of all: the tombs of Sipán. On 16 February 1987, a group of looters digging clandestinely at night in a small mudbrick pyramid broke into an intact royal tomb. The exquisite gold artifacts, and their sheer quantity, were unprecedented. But the looters soon began to quarrel over their finds and one of them informed the police of the discovery. The police called in local archaeologist Walter Alva, who, immediately realizing the impor-

ABOVE: One of the finest pieces of pre-Columbian jewellery ever found, this tiny ear ornament of gold and turquoise from the warrior priest's burial contains a minute figure wearing a similar outfit to its owner – a movable nose-piece, a crescent headdress, ear ornaments and a necklace of owl heads.

RIGHT: Some of the huge adobe brick pyramids and platforms of the Moche, now heavily eroded and barely recognizable as man-made structures.

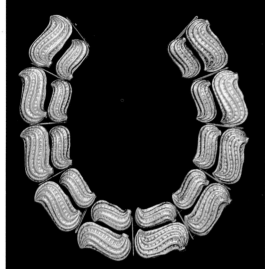

ABOVE: This gold-and-silver necklace of peanut-shaped beads belonged to the warrior priest buried in the first royal tomb. The gold, being on the right side, may have represented masculinity, and the silver on the left side femininity.

RIGHT: Excavated rich burial at Sípan.

tance of the discovery, had the site sealed off and placed an armed guard to protect it and the archaeologists.

The archaeologists cleaned out the tomb, which had been ransacked by the looters, and found that very few objects remained in their original place. Then they noticed another part of the pyramid where mud bricks had been removed to make a large rectangular hole in the structure. They began to dig. First they came upon the remains of a man who was buried with his feet cut off. Was he the guardian of something of value below? Had his feet been cut off to prevent him from leaving his post? Further excavation proved this to be the case: he was guarding a royal tomb. In the space hollowed out inside the pyramid the archaeol-

ogists found a wooden coffin filled with an astonishing array of artifacts: feather headdresses, metal-decorated royal clothing, royal banners, shell bead pectorals, jewellery of gold, silver and precious stones, a gold headdress – and they found the body of the Lord of Sipán, a man of about forty years old. Arranged around his coffin were five others, containing two men (one buried together with a dog) and three women.

Further excavation in the pyramid has revealed several more tombs, and some of them are still unexcavated at the time of writing. It is now apparent that Moche culture was far more complex, and its rulers much more powerful, than archaeologists had ever suspected. ∎

TEMPLE OF THE FEATHERED SERPENT, TEOTIHUACÁN

The Ciudadela (Citadel), an immense plaza measuring some 400 m (1312 ft) per side, which marked the site's southern boundary, was left largely untouched until the Mexican archaeologist Manuel Gamio carried out a major excavation programme between 1917 and 1922. Under Gamio's direction, Ignacio Marquina cleared a grass-covered mound, about 65 m (213 ft) per side, occupying the centre of the Ciudadela. It was found to have seven *talud-tablero* terraces, and the profile of each consisted of a vertical panel (*tablero*) resting on a low outsloping wall (*talud*). These panels bear repeated images of feathered serpents constructed in brightly painted stone. Unfortunately, all the magnificent façades had collapsed except for the principal one on the west, which was sheltered by an enormous stepped platform (*plataforma adosada*) built about a century later. This western façade is one of the most famous buildings in all Mesoamerica and has proved critical in our understanding of Teotihuacán during the early Tlamimilolpa phase (*c.* AD 200). Indeed, its importance was far-reaching in Mesoamerican history.

Gamio christened the building the Temple of Quetzalcoatl, the Aztec name for the Feathered Serpent. However, as we do not know what language was spoken at Teotihuacán, most scholars now opt for the more neutral Temple of the Feathered Serpent. The significance of the building did not fully emerge until the

Teotihuacán, which flourished between AD 100 and 750, was never a lost city – certainly not to the Aztecs, who believed that the world was created there. With its broad avenues and towering pyramids, the largest in Mesoamerica, Teotihuacán attracted archaeologists as early as 1864. Between 1905 and 1910 Leopoldo Batres undertook the first government-sponsored excavations, focusing his efforts on the great Pyramid of the Sun, which he restored (and unfortunately dynamited) to its present condition.

1980s, when excavations carried out by Mexico's Instituto Nacional de Antropología e Historia revealed extensive burial pits under and in front of the building, confirming earlier reports of burials. In total, the pits held 120 individuals who were sacrificed as part of an elaborate dedicatory offering. Most appear to have been warriors. Their bodies, dumped in multiple burials of up to twenty individuals, were found in a flexed position with their hands tied behind their backs. They were all garbed in similar warrior uniforms which included grisly necklaces of carved shell made to resemble human upper jaws, though one individual wore real human upper jaws, and another wore a necklace of canine upper jaws. They also wore shell necklaces resembling strings of human teeth and pyrite-encrusted slate discs in the small of their back. Worn centuries later by Aztec warriors who called them *tezcacuitlapilli*, these back mirrors confirm the martial identity of the slain men. Their bodies were accompanied by rich offerings that include hundreds of projectile points made of obsidian (volcanic glass) and thousands of greenstone and shell ornaments.

These discoveries have radically altered our view of the Temple of the Feathered Serpent. It was long thought to be exclusively a religious edifice but it now appears to have been at the centre of a powerful military cult that dominated Teotihuacán from the early Tlamimilolpa phase. Moreover, its symbols and ideology were highly influential in Mesoamerica. This is especially evident in the façade sculpture which shows a mosaic serpent head riding on the tail of the feathered serpent. This serpent head is now known to represent a type of military headdress worn by Maya élite in conjunction with warfare triggered by the position of Venus. As we know that the Aztecs associated the Feathered Serpent with Venus, this suggests that the Temple of the Feathered Serpent combines all aspects of the Venus war cult, and it is also its earliest manifestation at AD 200. The Temple of the Feathered Serpent can be seen, therefore, as the prototype of the feathered serpent warrior imagery that is pervasive in Postclassic Mesoamerica. ∎

LEFT: Heads of feathered serpents projecting out of the western façade are said to weigh 4064 kg (4 tons) apiece. The serpent's body runs across the façade in low relief while a mosaic serpent head-dress, indicative of a warfare theme, projects forward at the tail.

RIGHT: Discovered in 1975, the Cacaxtla murals (*c.* AD 800) exemplify a type of Mesoamerican military imagery which drew inspiration from Teotihuacán. The feathered serpent upon which an eagle warrior stands can be traced back to the Temple of the Feathered Serpent.

TIWANAKU: PREHISTORIC EMPIRES IN THE ANDES

When the Spanish conquered the Inka Empire in 1532, they had no idea that great civilizations had existed before the Inka. Indeed, the Inka themselves told the Spanish that all that had existed before them were barbarian cultures and that they, the Inka, had brought civilization to the Andes. One early Spanish visitor, Pedro de Cieza de León, travelled the length of the Inka Empire during the first decade after the Spanish Conquest, marvelling at their great achievements. But he also observed grand sites lying in ruins, which caused him to doubt the Inka propaganda, and he wondered if perhaps earlier civilizations had existed. He noted large ruins (Wari) in central Peru that were clearly very ancient and, on the high plateau near Lake Titicaca, he observed another ruin at Tiwanaku, also very ancient. Considering the two sites together, he wrote, 'I venture to say that it could have been that before the Inkas ruled, there must have been another people of wisdom in these realms, who came from some unknown

One of the first archaeological sites known in the Andes, Tiwanaku was described in travellers' accounts but in many ways remained a mystery. Long thought to be the remains of the first – and perhaps only – pre-Inka civilization in the Andes, this enigmatic monumental site on the wind-swept high plateau of Bolivia may have been the capital of one of the first empires.

place, who made these things.'

Later travellers, among them the American Ephraim George Squier, who published an account of his travels in 1877, were impressed by the monumentality of Tiwanaku. Most awe-inspiring was a powerful image carved upon a monumental gateway: a human figure standing on a stepped platform, arms outstretched to his sides with a long staff in each hand, wearing an elaborate head-dress with appendages ending in the heads of animals; he was flanked on either side by three rows of figures, half human, half bird. For the most part, however, the site was in a terrible condition. The Spanish in their zeal to stamp out idolatrous religion had pulled down carved stones and temple walls; local people had taken to collecting stones from the site to build their homes and communities.

A young German archaeologist named Max Uhle was fortunate to have the opportunity to help analyse materials excavated from Tiwanaku by other German archaeologists in the 1890s. He embarked on a research programme in Peru, and in his excavations near Lima he

BELOW: **Ephraim George Squier (1821–88) travelled through the Andes of southern Peru and Bolivia, observing and photographing the remains of Inka and pre-Inka civilizations. Etchings made from his photographs were published with his written account in 1877.**

discovered ceramics with designs similar to those of the stone carvings of Tiwanaku. From this he deduced that the Tiwanaku culture was much more extensive than anyone had thought, perhaps extending far into Peru. As years went by and more research was done, however, it came to be realized that there were actually two separate realms that shared a similar art style: Wari in Peru and Tiwanaku in Bolivia – the very two sites about which Cieza de León had speculated more than four centuries before.

While Wari was certainly a conquest empire that lasted only from the eighth to the eleventh centuries AD, Tiwanaku probably began as an important religious centre, perhaps as early as the third century AD. It has large open plaza areas designed to bring people into the site and monumental stone carvings that can be seen only by going to Tiwanaku – it is likely that people made long pilgrimages to visit the site. Only at the end of its history does it appear that Tiwanaku extended its power outside the high plateau, perhaps as an empire like Wari.

Recent work at Tiwanaku by the American archaeologist Alan Kolata has allowed the reconstruction of some of the monumental architecture, especially the large pyramid called Akapana. This, which was apparently designed to facilitate the flow of water over, around and through the structure, probably served as a water shrine of some sort. Kolata's evidence indicates that Tiwanaku society collapsed in the eleventh century AD after an extended drought caused its agricultural base to fail. ∎

ABOVE: Classic Wari-style polychrome vessel.

BELOW: The famous Gate of the Sun at Tiwanaku, carved from a single block of stone. Perhaps to encourage sales of book, or to give his readers more of what they were expecting, some of Squier's etchings exaggerated the size and magnificence of some of the ruins.

MONTE ALBÁN: TOMB 7

It was a discovery made by the greatest student of ancient Oaxacan culture, the Mexican archaeologist Alfonso Caso, that brought to light the full genius of Mixtec craftsmanship. Caso directed excavations at Monte Albán, Oaxaca's largest pre-Columbian city, over seventeen field seasons (1931–48), and in the process explored a hundred of the 170 tombs known. In his first field season, he had the great good fortune to discover Tomb 7, which at the time it was excavated in 1932, was the most spectacular pre-Columbian tomb known from the Americas. It yielded over 500 objects made from an astonishing variety of materials, including gold, silver, copper, jade, turquoise, jet, amber, coral, shell and pearls. It also housed fine polychrome ceramics, onyx urns, paper-thin obsidian ear flares, dozens of intricately carved bones, rare examples of carved rock crystal and a unique necklace of crocodile and wolf's teeth.

Tomb 7 preserved the finest collection of Mesoamerican metalwork ever found. Its 121 gold objects quadrupled the number of pre-Columbian gold objects known from Meso-america, and the twenty-four silver objects were, with a few exceptions, the only ones known in that material. The gold was fashioned into containers and items of personal adornment, such as pectorals, rings, ear ornaments, bracelets and pendants. The most impressive are multicomponent cast objects decorated with false filigree (cast wax threads made to look like hand-fashioned filigree). Mixtec craftsmen were able to draw calendar dates and complex symbols, comparable to those painted in Mixtec screenfold books, in the delicate medium of false filigree.

All this splendour was housed in a rather simple, double-chambered tomb constructed from rough-hewn stone slabs. The construction style and associated pottery date the tomb to a period of Zapotec occupation during Monte Albán IIIB (AD 500–750). Mixtecs, residing in the Mixteca Alta, expanded into the Valley of Oaxaca sometime after AD 1000 and displaced local Zapotec rulers. During Monte Albán V (1000–1520) some Mixtec interlopers broke into Tomb 7, cleared out the Zapotec contents, ex-

During the Late Postclassic period (c. AD 1200–1521) the skill of the Mixtec, inhabitants of the Mexican state of Oaxaca, in metalsmithing and small-scale working of stones was unsurpassed. In the fifteenth century they were subjugated by the Aztecs to whom they paid tribute payments in the form of cast gold trinkets, turquoise mosaic masks, carved rock crystal and other fine crafts. Indeed, in many museum collections such items are usually attributed to the Aztecs, but they are most probably Mixtec creations.

cept a few odd ceramics, and placed nine individuals and the grave goods in the tomb. They filled the entrance with rubble and exited through the roof. Recently it has been suggested that the tomb's best-preserved skeleton is a high-ranking Mixtec woman. She was found near dozens of weaving tools, including combs, picks, spindle whorls, spinning bowls, thimbles, and a remarkable collection of thirty-four miniature weaving battens carved from deer and eagle bones. The lavish treatment of this woman's grave accords with Mixtec history recorded in screenfold books where women play prominent roles. If the treasures of Tomb 7 were her possessions, then she may actually be one of the important historical figures known in Mixtec pictorial manuscripts. ∎

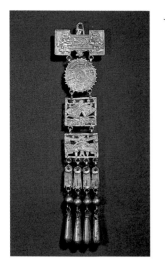

This complex gold pendant cast by the lost-wax technique depicts, from top to bottom, two figures in an I-shaped ball-court, a sun disk, a butterfly-dagger, and an earth monster. The sections are joined by rings and the imitation feathers dangle from the bottom.

The Zapotec occupation of Monte Albán began around 500 BC. Their earliest sculptured monuments are conquest slabs, commonly called _danzantes_ (dancers), depicting nude, slain captives. The slabs were displayed on façades, such as that of Building L. They bear some of the earliest hieroglyphs known in Mesoamerica.

Monte Albán sits majestically on a hill outside Oaxaca City, the state capital. Tomb 7 is found on a lower terrace northeast of the main plaza.

VIKING SETTLEMENTS OF NORTH AMERICA

During the ninth and tenth centuries, thousands of Norwegians emigrated to the newly discovered lands of Iceland. From here more venturesome souls went even further west. The Sagas tell of Erik the Red's voyage in AD 986 to what is now Greenland (so named in a period when the climate was much warmer than it is today, and Greenland less icy). The Greenland settlement could support only a few thousand settlers, however, and so his son, Leif Erikson, continued the westward push, finally reaching the coasts of Baffin Island and Labrador, where they encountered Eskimo peoples, to whom they gave the name 'Skraelings'.

The Vikings sailed south along the coast, naming a section of coast Markland, where the forests came down to the ocean and reminded them of their Norwegian homes, and finally settled in a land they called Vinland. It is unclear precisely where Vinland is but they probably got no further than southern Maine.

One good candidate is the vicinity of a remarkable site called L'Anse aux Meadows, a Norse village on the Newfoundland

Norse expansion westward across the Atlantic in the tenth century ultimately led to the New World. Although the Icelandic Sagas give us the basic elements of this story, archaeology is increasingly enlarging our knowledge of the first European settlement of the New World.

coast, excavated by Helge and Anne Ingstad in the 1970s. It has the remains of eight sod structures, Norse fireplaces, a smithy, smelted iron and pins and other objects that date it to the late tenth or early eleventh century. Unfortunately this area does not support the wild grapes of which the Sagas spoke (hence the name Vinland), and so some archaeologists have questioned the Vinland connection. Despite later colonizing voyages, Vinland itself was in fact abandoned soon after its discovery, probably because of the harshness of the environment and because of the hostility of the local inhabitants, with whom the Vikings had less than cordial relations.

Evidence of a Viking presence is found elsewhere in northern North America, although it is still unclear whether Norse artifacts reached these more distant places through the actual physical presence of Vikings themselves or simply through trade. It does seem likely that even after Vinland had been abandoned, contact be-

BELOW: Today's bleak environment at l'Anse aux Meadows indicates the difficulties faced by the first European colonists to the New World.

tween the Norse and North America continued until as late as the fourteenth century.

One of the best-documented pieces of evidence has been produced by the Canadian archaeologist, Peter Schledermann. On Ellesmere Island in the Canadian High Arctic, Schledermann and his colleagues have excavated Viking artifacts, such as parts of a wooden box and barrels, iron and copper pieces, boat rivets and even a piece of chain mail. Moreover, an eleventh-century Norse coin has been found on the Maine coast, probably as a result of later trade.

The allure of the Vikings has, however, produced some rather questionable claims, too. For example, in the town of Newport, Rhode Island, a stone windmill built in the Colonial Period has been interpreted by some as a Viking church. The Kensington Stone, from the town of that name in Minnesota, is a nineteenth-century forgery of runic inscriptions. However, many amateur archaeologists still consider it to be authentic. ■

LEFT: A reconstruction of the turf house shows the wooden framework. Most dwellings contained stone hearths – smoke escaped through holes in the roof – and beds were on raised platforms along the walls.

BELOW: The cluster of low mounds at L'Anse aux Meadows turned out to be huts with walls of piled turf and roofs of turf supported by a wood frame (now reconstructed on site). Three were multi-roomed dwellings similar to those built by the Norse in Iceland and Greenland; the rest are smaller outbuildings. The largest structure contained five rooms with an attached work-shed; it probably housed several families. Excavation produced only 130 artifacts. This, along with the lack of evidence for rebuilding, indicates that the site was a short-lived settlement.

THE TEMPLO MAYOR OF TENOCHTITLÁN

Excavations under Mexico City have periodically turned up remains from Tenochtitlán's ritual precinct. Among the earliest finds was the famous Calendar Stone discovered in 1790. A few sections of the Templo Mayor had also been discovered in the first half of the twentieth century, but in 1978 the chance find, by city electrical workers, of a circular relief was a catalyst for systematic excavations of the temple. Eduardo Matos Moctezuma of the Instituto Nacional de Antropología e Historia and a multidisciplinary team of experts undertook this mammoth project that required first the tearing down of blocks of existing buildings just a stone's throw away from the Metropolitan Cathedral in Mexico City's main plaza.

Colonial descriptions of the Templo Mayor agree that it had twin sanctuaries resting on a tiered pyramidal platform. One shrine was dedicated to Tlaloc, a god of rain and agriculture, and the other to Huitzilopochtli, a solar war god and patron of the Aztecs. A key myth in which Huitzilopochtli kills his sister Coyolxauhqui explains the presence of the circular relief: lying at the foot of a staircase, it depicts Coyolxauhqui's dismembered body, cast down the temple like a hapless sacrificial victim. Recent excavations have shown that an image of the vanquished Coyolxauhqui, a thinly veiled reference to Aztec imperial might, accompanied every construction phase of the Templo Mayor.

The political and spiritual centre of the Aztec empire was a walled precinct in the heart of their island capital, Tenochtitlán. Naturally the Spanish conquerors targeted this area for immediate destruction in 1521 and built upon its smouldering ruins the seat of government of New Spain – but memory of the ritual precinct and, above all, of the principal temple, which the Aztecs called the *huey teocalli*, meaning 'great temple' or '*templo mayor*' in Spanish, lived on in colonial writings.

founding of Tenochtitlán in 1325). With an associated date of 1390, Stage II has the best-preserved sanctuaries. The walls of the Tlaloc shrine have brightly painted stripes and circles, and in front of the doorway archaeologists found a Chac Mool, a type of reclining figure best known from Tula and Chichén Itzá. In front of Huitzilopochtli's shrine, a wedge-shaped stone used to arch the chests of sacrificial victims is a grim reminder of the temple's ritual function. In Stage III, with an associated date of 1431, eight life-size stone statues were found on the staircase leading to Huitzilopochtli's sanctuary. Stage IV represents the level of the Coyolxauhqui relief and

Excavations of the Templo Mayor uncovered six superimposed stages with twin temples oriented to the west: Tlaloc's shrine occupied the north side, and Huitzilopochtli's the south, all in agreement with colonial sources. The earliest remains come from Stage II (Stage I is hypothetical and is placed at the

ABOVE: Measuring over 3 m (10 ft) in diameter and carved from basalt, the Coyolxauhqui Stone shows the nude body of the goddess. Her severed limbs and head issue blood, while down-balls on her hair mark her as one to be sacrificed. The bells on her cheek allude to her name, which roughly translates as 'face decorated with bells'.

LEFT: This skull-rack or *tzompantli* was used to display human bones as grisly war trophies. It was found north of the Great Temple at the level of Stage VI.

Head detail of one of two life-size ceramic statues of an eagle warrior, dated to Stage V, found in the Temple of the Eagles north of the Templo Mayor.

carved plaques suggest dates of 1454 and 1469. This stage was decorated with monumental stone serpents and huge braziers. Little of Stage V remained, and Stage VI includes flanking temples and halls, some with marble floors. Nothing was left of the version of the Templo Mayor that faced the Spanish onslaught, Stage VII, except traces of the foundation.

Over a hundred caches found in sub-floor chambers in and around the Templo Mayor have greatly expanded our understanding of the Aztec political economy. The vast majority of offerings are of foreign origin and came from tribute-paying regions of the Aztec empire. They include not just the expected luxury goods, but also exotic faunal remains, some never before seen in Mesoamerican archaeological contexts. Excavations of the Templo Mayor have laid bare its multidimensional character as the most important religious edifice in the Aztec world, in addition to being a political symbol of the highest order steeped in the ideology of a conquest state. ■

MACHU PICCHU

The Inka site of Machu Picchu sits atop a high ridge between two mountain peaks, and commands a spectacular view of the Urubamba valley below. It was built by the first great Inka emperor, Pachacuti, to serve as one of his royal retreats in this so-called 'Sacred Valley' of the Inkas. The Inka capital was at Cuzco, in the Andes mountains of what is today southern Peru, a four- or five-day walk from Machu Picchu. In the mid-fifteenth century AD the Inka began a series of conquests that was to culminate in the largest empire known in the New World, before European contact. The Inka realm stretched from southwestern Colombia, through highland Ecuador, Peru, Bolivia, northwest Argentina, and the northern half of Chile, and they commanded a population of perhaps ten million souls. The empire lasted barely a century, however, and its control ended in 1532 when the Spaniard Francisco Pizarro and his small band of Conquistadors invaded Peru and took prisoner the fifth Inka emperor, Atahuallpa. Despite the payment of a fabulous ransom of gold and silver, the Spanish put the emperor to death and took control of the empire.

Machu Picchu was probably abandoned shortly after the Spanish Conquest, as there was no need for the descendants of the emperors to continue to maintain the royal estates. It came again to the attention of the world in the early twentieth century when it was rediscovered by the Yale historian Hiram Bingham. In July 1911 Bingham, director of an expedition to explore and study

Machu Picchu, sometimes called the 'Lost City of the Inkas', was discovered in 1911 by the American, Hiram Bingham. The site was built at the time of the Inka empire, which controlled most of western South America at the time of the Spanish Conquest in 1532. Hailed variously as the place of origin of the Inka dynasty, or as their last refuge site while the empire was falling, Machu Picchu actually served as a royal country estate of one of the great emperors.

parts of southern Peru, set off in search of the lost Inka city of Vilcabamba: after the Spanish had wrested control of Cuzco and the empire from the Inkas, the last remaining Inka ruler had escaped toward the jungles northeast of Cuzco and established a last refuge at Vilcabamba from which he vainly tried to keep the empire together.

On the morning of 11 July 1911, Bingham climbed to the top of a ridge that connected the two mountain peaks, Huayna Picchu and Machu Picchu, to investigate reports of an Inka ruin there. Farmers living on the site had burned off some of the dense vegetation to clear small agricultural plots, so Bingham was able to see that the site was very impressive indeed. However, beyond making a few notes and sketches of the site that day, Bingham does not seem to have taken much interest in Machu Picchu, and he continued down the valley the next day in his quest for Vilcabamba (he came very close to discovering that site, but was

ABOVE: **Hiram Bingham (1878–1956) found fame with the discovery of Machu Picchu. After his Peruvian exploits he went on to become a United States senator.**

LEFT: **After removing the families living in the abandoned buildings, Bingham began clearing the site – a dangerous task given the poisonous snakes.**

RIGHT: **General view, with the peak of Huayna Picchu in the background. The topography of the ridge dictated the long, narrow site and series of open plazas.**

ultimately unsuccessful). However, he did send a survey team to Machu Picchu several weeks later to map the visible ruins.

In 1912 Bingham launched the expedition that would bring Machu Picchu to the attention of the world. The National Geographic Society devoted the entire April 1913 issue of their magazine to the photographs and accounts of the discovery and clearing of the site. They called Bingham's exploits 'one of the most remarkable stories of exploration in South America in the past fifty years'. Once the site was cleared of vegetation one could see that it included some of the finest Inka architecture known, including religious shrines and temples, watercourses and baths, living quarters for royalty and their retainers. In sum, the site had all the comforts of home: everything an emperor could want on a royal estate.

A prominent temple with three windows gave Bingham his first ideas about the nature of the site. According to Inka legend, their original ancestors had emerged from a cave with three windows at a place called Tampu Tocco. Bingham speculated that perhaps Machu Picchu was this actual place of Inka origins. As the years went by, he also became convinced that Machu Picchu was the lost city, Vilcabamba, for which he had been searching since 1911. If so, then Machu Picchu represented both the cradle and the deathbed of the Inka empire. Research in recent decades, however, has located the true site of Tampu Tocco and the lost city of Vilcabamba, and Machu Picchu is now known to have been just a royal estate belonging to one of the emperors and his descendants. Its spectacular location, its exquisite examples of Inka architecture, and its breathtaking views of the mountains and valleys have made it perhaps the most popular place to visit in Peru today. ■

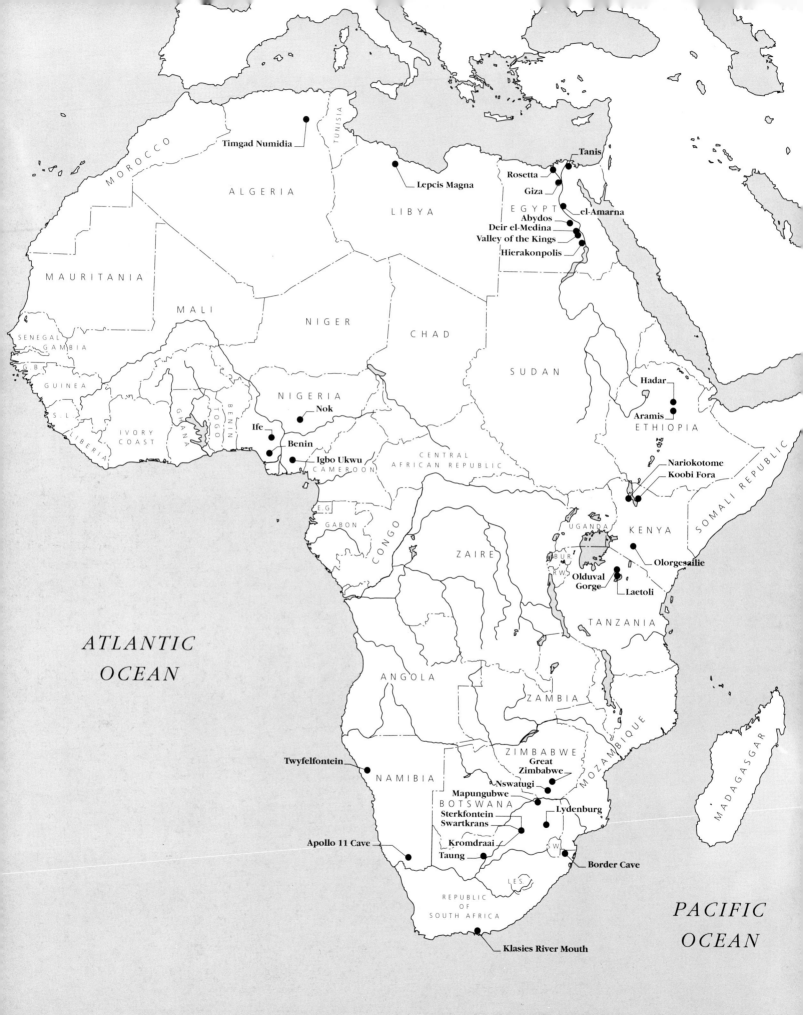

ATLANTIC
OCEAN

PACIFIC
OCEAN

MOROCCO
TUNISIA
ALGERIA
LIBYA
MAURITANIA
MALI
NIGER
CHAD
SUDAN
EGYPT
SENEGAL
GAMBIA
G.B.
GUINEA
S.L.
LIBERIA
IVORY COAST
GHANA
TOGO
BENIN
NIGERIA
CAMEROON
E.G.
GABON
CONGO
CENTRAL AFRICAN REPUBLIC
ZAIRE
UGANDA
KENYA
SOMALI REPUBLIC
ETHIOPIA
BUR.
RW.
TANZANIA
ANGOLA
ZAMBIA
ZIMBABWE
MOZAMBIQUE
NAMIBIA
BOTSWANA
MADAGASCAR
S.W.
LES.
REPUBLIC OF SOUTH AFRICA

Timgad Numidia
Lepcis Magna
Tanis
Rosetta
Giza
el-Amarna
Abydos
Deir el-Medina
Valley of the Kings
Hierakonpolis
Hadar
Aramis
Nariokotome
Koobi Fora
Olorgesailie
Olduvai Gorge
Laetoli
Nok
Ife
Benin
Igbo Ukwu
Twyfelfontein
Great Zimbabwe
Nswatugi
Mapungubwe
Lydenburg
Sterkfontein
Swartkrans
Kromdraai
Taung
Apollo 11 Cave
Border Cave
Klasies River Mouth

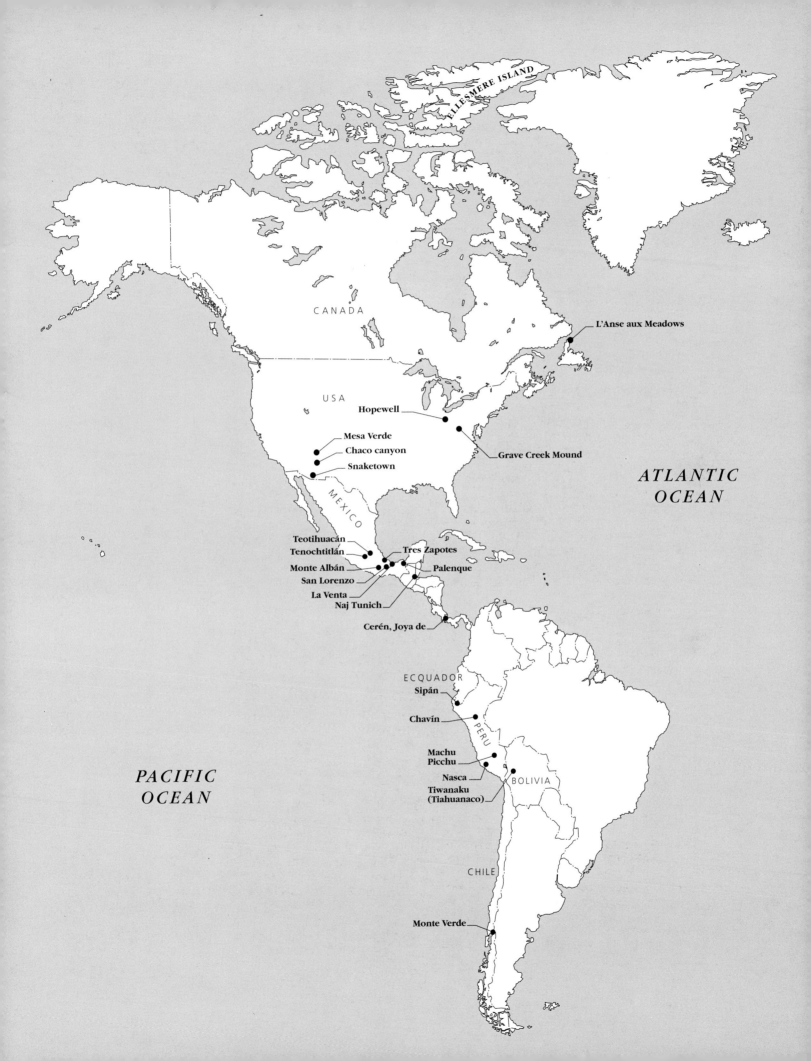

ELLESMERE ISLAND

CANADA

L'Anse aux Meadows

USA

Hopewell

Mesa Verde

Chaco canyon

Snaketown

MEXICO

Grave Creek Mound

ATLANTIC
OCEAN

Teotihuacán

Tenochtitlán

Tres Zapotes

Monte Albán

San Lorenzo

La Venta

Naj Tunich

Palenque

Cerén, Joya de

ECQUADOR

Sipán

Chavín

PERU

Machu
Picchu

Nasca

Tiwanaku
(Tiahuanaco)

BOLIVIA

PACIFIC
OCEAN

CHILE

Monte Verde

ICELAND

ARCTIC O

IRELAND

Newgrange

Skara Brae

Sweet Track
UNITED
KINGDOM

NORWAY

Piltdown
Vindolanda

SWEDEN

Zambujal

Flag Fen
Grimes Graves

Gokstad Sling

FINLAND

PORTUGAL
Côa

Altamira

Sutton Hoo

Gundestrup
Tollund Fen

Gavrinis

SPAIN

Grand Pressigny

Grauballe

Lascaux
La Mouthe

Spiennes
FRANCE

Neander Valley
Köln-Lindenthal
Cologne

ESTONIA

Bruniquel
Domme

Hochdorf

LATVIA

Los Millares

Chauvet Cave

Vogelherd Cave

Mauer

Biskupin

RUS. FED.

MOROCCO

Veyrier

Hohlenstein-Stadel

LITHUANIA

Zürich-Utoquai

SWITZ.

Prezletice

Novgor

CZECH

Vallonet

Dolní Vestonice

REPUBLIC

Predmostí

Oslonki

Iceman

ITALY

Willendorf

POLAND

BELORUSSIA

Hallstatt

ALGERIA

Tarquinia

SLOVENIA

SLOVAKIA

Krakow-Spadzista

Dobranichevka

CROATIA

Cerveteri

HUNGARY

Mezhirich

Herculaneum

BOSNIA-

Kostenki

Pompeii

HERZEGOVINA

TUNISIA

Altamura

YUGOLSLAVIA

ROMANIA

UKRAINE

Lepenski Vir

MOLDAVIA

Maltese Temples

ALBANIA

Vergina

MACEDONIA

BULGARIA

GREECE

Varna

MEDITERRANEAN SEA

Mycenae

BLACK SEA

Pylos

Troy

LIBYA

Athens

Knossos

Thera

Aphrodisias

TURKEY

Çatal Hüyük

GEORGIA

Dmanisi

EGYPT

CYPRUS

ARMENIA

AZ

Berelekh

RUSSIAN FEDERATION

Buret

Mal'ta

Pazyryk

Ukok

MONGOLIA

KAZAKHSTAN

CHINA

SPIAN SEA

ARAL SEA

RUSSIAN FEDERATION

KAZAKSTAN

UZBEKISTAN

TURKMENISTAN

KYRGYZSTAN

TAJIKISTAN

IRAN

AFGHANISTAN

PAKISTAN

MONGOLIA

CHINA

NEPAL

INDIA

BANGLADESH

BURMA

Bhimbetka

LAOS

THAILAND

VIETNAM

CAMBODIA

Hongshan

Imperial Ming Tombs

Yungang

Zhoukoudian

Anyang

Helan Mts

Qin

Xi'an

Longmen

Luoyang

NORTH KOREA

SOUTH KOREA

Yaoshan

Kyongju City

Sinan Shipwreck

TAIWAN

Changsha

Huashan 'Mt of Flowers'

PHILIPPINES

Bismark Archipelag

New Brit

MALAYSIA

SABAH

BRUNEI

SARAWAK

PAPUA NEW GUINEA

SUMATRA

INDONESIA

Trinil Region

JAVA

INDIAN OCEAN

AUSTRALIA

Mandu Mandu Creek

Lake Mungo

Koonalda Cave

Kow Swamp

Devil's Lair

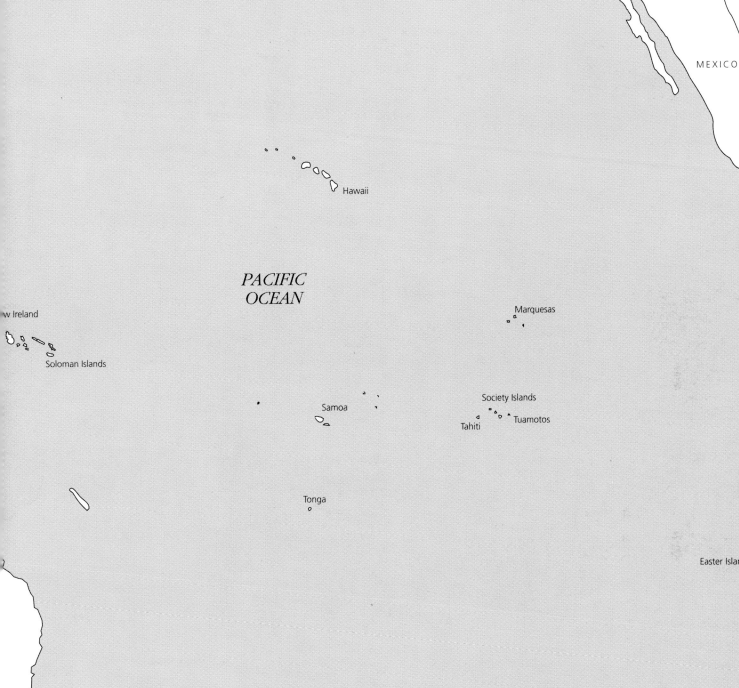

PACIFIC
OCEAN

USA

MEXICO

Hawaii

Marquesas

w Ireland

Soloman Islands

Society Islands

Samoa

Tahiti   Tuamotos

Tonga

Easter Island

NEW ZEALAND

BLACK SEA

RUSSIA

KAZAKHSTAN

GEORGIA

TURKEY

ARMENIA AZERBAIJAN

CASPIAN SEA

UZBEKISTAN

TURKMENISTAN

Ebla

Khorsabad
Nineveh
Nimrud

SYRIA

LEBANON

Mount Carmel

Babylon

Bamiyan

ISRAEL

Jericho
Qumran

IRAQ

IRAN

AFGHANISTAN

Masada
JORDAN

Ur

Persepolis

Harappa

PAKISTAN

PERSIAN GULF

Mohenjo-daro

SAUDI ARABIA

RED SEA

OMAN

ARABIAN SEA

YEMEN

SOUTHERN YEMEN

GULF OF ADEN

ETHIOPIA

INDIAN
OCEAN

BIBLIOGRAPHY

Preface
Bahn, P. G. 1989. *The Bluffer's Guide to Archaeology.* Horsham: Ravette.

Bahn, P. G. (ed.) 1992. *The Collins Dictionary of Archaeology.* Glasgow: HarperCollins/Denver: ABC Clio.

Bahn, P. G. (ed.) 1996. *The Cambridge Illustrated History of Archaeology.* Cambridge: Cambridge University Press.

Fagan, B. M. 1985. *The Adventure of Archaeology.* Washington D.C.: National Geographic Society.

Renfrew, C. and P. Bahn. 1991. *Archaeology: Theories, Methods and Practice.* London and New York: Thames & Hudson; 2nd edition 1996.

Scarre, C. (ed.) 1988. *Past Worlds, The Times Atlas of Archaeology.* London: Times Books.

AFRICA

1. THE DISCOVERY OF HUMAN ANTIQUITY
Bahn, P. G. (ed.) 1996. *The Cambridge Illustrated History of Archaeology.* Cambridge: Cambridge University Press.

2. THE TAUNG CHILD: THE DISCOVERY OF THE FIRST AUSTRALOPITHECINE
Brain, C. K. 1981. *The Hunters or the Hunted? An Introduction to African Cave Taphonomy.* Chicago: University of Chicago Press.

Brain, C. K. (ed.) 1993. *Swartkrans: A Cave's Chronicle of Early Man.* Pretoria: Transvaal Museum Monograph No. 8.

Dart, R. A. 1959. *Adventures with the Missing Link.* New York: Harper and Brothers.

Jones, S., R. Martin, D. Pilbeam (eds) 1992. *The Cambridge Encyclopaedia of Human Evolution.* Cambridge: Cambridge University Press.

Tattersall, I. 1993. *The Human Odyssey: Four Million Years of Human Evolution.* New York: Prentice-Hall.

3. AUSTRALOPITHECINES FROM EAST AFRICA
Johanson, D. and M. Edey 1981. *Lucy: The Beginnings of Humankind.* New York: Simon and Schuster.

Jones, S., R. Martin, and D. Pilbeam (eds). 1992. *The Cambridge Encyclopaedia of Human Evolution.* Cambridge: Cambridge University Press.

Leakey, M. 1984. *Disclosing the Past.* London: Weidenfeld and Nicolson.

Tattersall, I. 1993. *The Human Odyssey: Four Million Years of Human Evolution.* New York: Prentice-Hall.

4. OLDUVAI GORGE: GRAND CANYON OF PREHISTORY
Cole, S. 1975. *Leakey's Luck: The Life of Louis Seymour Bazett Leakey, 1902–72.* London: Collins.

Jones, S., R. Martin, and D. Pilbeam (eds) 1992. *The Cambridge Encyclopaedia of Human Evolution.* Cambridge: Cambridge University Press.

Leakey, M. 1979. *Olduvai Gorge: My Search for Early Man.* London: Collins; 1984. *Disclosing the Past: An Autobiography.* London: Weidenfeld and Nicolson.

Tattersall, I. 1993. *The Human Odyssey: Four Million Years of Human Evolution.* New York: Prentice-Hall.

5. OUT OF AFRICA, ALWAYS SOMETHING NEW
Jones, S., R. Martin, and D. Pilbeam (eds) 1992. *The Cambridge Encyclopaedia of Human Evolution.* Cambridge: Cambridge University Press.

Klein, R. G. 1992. "The archeology of modern human origins", *Evolutionary Anthropology*, 1(1): pp 5–14.

Nitecki, M. H. and D. V. Nitecki (eds) 1994. *Origins of Anatomically Modern Humans.* New York and London: Plenum Press.

Tattersall, I. 1993. *The Human Odyssey: Four Million Years of Human Evolution.* New York: Prentice-Hall.

6. SOUTHERN AFRICAN ROCK ART: IMAGES OF POWER
Castiglioni, A., Castiglioni, A. and G. Negro 1986. *Fiumi di Pietra: Archivio della Preistoria Sahariana.* Varese: Edizioni Lativa.

Dowson, T. A. 1992. *Rock Engravings of Southern Africa.* Johannesburg: Witwatersrand University Press.

Lewis-Williams, J. D. 1983. *The Rock Art of Southern Africa.* Cambridge: Cambridge University Press.

Lewis-Williams, J. D. and T. Dowson 1989. *Images of Power: Understanding Bushman Rock Art.* Johannesburg: Southern Book Publishers.

Muzzolini, A. 1995. *Les Images Rupestres du Sahara.* Toulouse: Muzzolini.

Willcox, A. R. 1984. *The Rock Art of Africa.* New York: Holmes & Meier.

7. ABYDOS
Petrie, W. M. F. 1900–01. *The Royal Tombs of the First Dynasty.* London.

Adams, B. 1974. *Ancient Hierakonpolis.* Warminster.

Quibell, J.E. 1900–02. *Hierakonpolis: i–ii.* London.

8. THE PYRAMIDS AT GIZA
Edwards, I. E. S. *The Pyramids of Egypt.* London: Penguin.

El-Baz, F. 1988. "Finding a pharaoh's funeral bark", *National Geographic* 173 (4): pp. 512–33.

9. AMARNA
Aldred, C. 1973. *Akhenaten & Nefertiti.* London.

Peet, T. E., C. L.Woolley, J. D. S. Pendlebury, et al 1923–51. *The City of Akhenaten i–iii.* London.

10. TUTANKHAMEN
Carter, H. 1923–33. *The Tomb of Tut.ankh.Amen i–iii.* London.

Reeves, N. 1990. *The Complete Tutankhamun.* London.

11. DEIR EL–MEDINA
Bierbrier, M. 1982. *The Tomb–Builders of Pharaoh.* London.

Bruyère, B. 1927–53. *Rapport sur les fouilles de Deir el–Medineh,* 17 vols. Cairo.

12. TANIS
Coutts, H. (ed.) 1988. *Gold of the Pharaohs.* Edinburgh.

Montet, P. 1947–60. *La Necropole royale de Tanis i–iii.* Paris.

13. THE ROSETTA STONE
Quirke, S. 1988. *The Rosetta Stone.* London.

14 ROMANS IN NORTH AFRICA
Mattingly, D. J. 1995. *Tripolitania.* London: Batsford.

Ward-Perkins, J. B. 1981. *Roman Imperial Architecture.* Harmondsworth: Pelican History of Art.

15. NIGERIAN ART: A 'FABERGÉ-LIKE VIRTUOSITY'
Hall, M. 1987. *The Changing Past: Farmers, Kings and Traders in Southern Africa, 200–1860.* Cape Town: David Philip.

Shaw, T. 1970. *Igbo Ukwu.* London: Faber; 1978. *Nigeria. Its Archaeology and Early History.* London: Thames and Hudson; 1981. "The Nok sculptures of Nigeria", *Scientific American*, 244 (2): pp.154–66.

16. THE GREATEST ZIMBABWE OF THEM ALL
Garlake, P. S. 1973. *Great Zimbabwe.* London: Thames and Hudson.

Hall, M. 1987. *The Changing Past: Farmers, Kings and Traders in Southern Africa, 200–1860.* Cape Town: David Philip.

Huffman, T. N. 1987. *Symbols in Stone: Unravelling the Mystery of Great Zimbabwe.* Johannesburg: Witwatersrand University Press.

EUROPE

17. EARLY HUMANS IN WESTERN EUROPE
Bahn, P. G. (ed.) 1996. *The Cambridge Illustrated History of Archaeology.* Cambridge: Cambridge University Press.

18. ICE AGE SETTLEMENT OF THE NORTH
Dennell, Robin 1983. *European Economic Prehistory: A New Approach.* London: Academic Press.

Gamble, Clive 1994. *Timewalkers: The Prehistory of Global Colonization.* Cambridge: Harvard University Press.

Klein, Richard G. 1989. *The Human Career: Human Biological and Cultural Origins.* Chicago: University of Chicago Press.

19. MAMMOTH-BONE HOUSES OF EASTERN EUROPE
Gladkih, M. I., N. L. Kornietz, and O. Soffer 1984. "Mammoth-bone dwellings on the Russian Plain", *Scientific American*, 251(1): pp. 164–175.

Lister, Adrian and Paul Bahn 1994. *Mammoths.* New York: Macmillan/London: Boxtree.

Soffer, Olga 1985. *The Upper Paleolithic of the Central Russian Plain.* San Diego: Academic Press.

20. PALAEOLITHIC PORTABLE ART
Bahn, P. G. and J. Vertut. 1988. *Images of the Ice Age.* Leicester: Windward/ New York: Facts on File.

21. PALAEOLITHIC CAVE ART
Bahn, P. G. and J. Vertut 1988. *Images of the Ice Age.* Leicester: Windward/New York: Facts on File.

22. ICE AGE ART AND BURIALS OF CENTRAL EUROPE
Bhattacharya, D. K. 1977. *Palaeolithic Europe: A Summary of Some Important Finds with Special Reference to Central Europe.* Atlantic Highlands: Humanities Press.

Kozlowski, Janusz K. 1992. *L'Art de la Préhistoire en Europe Orientale.* Paris: CNRS.

23. ICE AGE ART AND BURIALS OF EASTERN EUROPE

Abramova, Z. A. 1967. "Paleolithic art in the USSR.", *Arctic Anthropology*, 4(2): pp. 1–179.

Klein, Richard G. 1973. *Ice-Age Hunters of the Ukraine*. Chicago: University of Chicago Press.

Soffer, Olga. 1985. *The Upper Paleolithic of the Central Russian Plain*. Orlando: Academic Press.

24. THE FISHERS OF LEPENKSKI VIR

Srejovic, Dragoslav 1969. *Lepenski Vir*. London: Thames and Hudson; 1988. "Neolithic of Serbia: a review of research", *Neolithic of Serbia: Archaeological Research 1948–1988*, pp. 5–19. Belgrade: Center for Archaeological Research, University of Belgrade.

25. ÇATAL HÜYÜK

Mellaart, James 1967. *Çatal Hüyük*. New York: McGraw-Hill.

26. THE LAKE DWELLINGS OF THE ALPINE FORELAND

Barker, Graeme 1985. *Prehistoric Farming in Europe*. Cambridge: Cambridge University Press.

Höneisen, Marcus 1990. *Die ersten Bauern*. Zürich: Schweizerisches Landesmuseum.

Whittle, Alasdair 1988. *Problems in Neolithic Archaeology*. Cambridge: Cambridge University Press; 1995. *Neolithic Europe* (2nd ed.). Cambridge: Cambridge University Press.

27. EARLY NEOLITHIC LONGHOUSES IN EUROPE

Bogucki, Peter 1988. *Forest Farmers and Stockherders: Early Agriculture and its Consequences in North-Central Europe*. Cambridge: Cambridge University Press; 1995. "The largest buildings in the world (in 5,000 B.C.)", *Archaeology* vol. 48 (6): pp. 57-59.

Milisauskas, Sarunas 1986. *Early Neolithic Settlement and Society at Olszanica*. Ann Arbor: Museum of Anthropology.

Modderman, P. J. R. 1988. "The Linear Pottery culture: diversity in uniformity", *Berichten van de Rijksdienst voor het Oudheidkundig Bodemonderzoek*, 38: pp. 63–139.

28. NEOLITHIC FLINT MINES

Holgate, Robin 1991. *Prehistoric Flint Mines*. Princes Risborough: Shire Publications.

29. HOUSES FOR THE LIVING AND THE DEAD

Ritchie, Anna and Graham 1978. *The Ancient Monuments of Orkney*. Edinburgh: Her Majesty's Stationery Office.

Renfrew, Colin (ed.) 1985. *The Prehistory of Orkney*. Edinburgh: Edinburgh University Press.

30. FLAG FEN AND THE SWEET TRACK

Coles, Bryony and John 1986. *Sweet Track to Glastonbury: the Somerset Levels in prehistory*. London: Thames and Hudson.

Pryor, Francis 1991. *Flag Fen: prehistoric Fenland centre*. London: Batsford/ English Heritage.

31. MALTESE TEMPLES

Evans, J. D. 1959. *Malta*. London: Thames and Hudson; 1971. *The Prehistoric Antiquities of the Maltese Islands*. London: Athlone press.

32. LIKE A CIRCLE IN A SPIRAL: THE MYSTERIES OF MEGALITHIC ART

Mohen, Jean-Pierre 1989. *The World of the Megaliths*. London: Cassell.

O'Kelly, Michael J. 1982. *Newgrange: archaeology, art and legend*. London: Thames and Hudson.

33. THE ICEMAN

Bahn, P. G. 1995. "Last days of the Iceman", *Archaeology*, 48 (3): pp. 66–70.

Spindler, K. 1994. *The Man in the Ice*. London: Weidenfeld and Nicolson.

34. VARNA: A COPPER AGE CEMETERY

Fol, Alexander and Jan Lichardus (eds) 1988. *Macht, Herrschaft und Gold. Das Gräberfeld von Varna (Bulgarien) und die Anfänge einer neuen europäischen Zivilisation*. Saarbrücken: Moderne Galerie des Saarland-Museums.

Renfrew, Colin 1978. "Varna and the social context of early metallurgy", *Antiquity*, 52: pp. 199–203; 1980. "Ancient Bulgaria's golden treasures", *National Geographic*, 158 (1): pp. 112–29.

35. LOS MILLARES AND ZAMBUJAL

Chapman, Robert 1990. *Emerging complexity: the later prehistory of south-east Spain, Iberia and the West Mediterranean*. Cambridge: Cambridge University Press.

36. BRONZE AGE BARROWS

Clarke, D.V., T.G. Cowie and A. Foxon 1985. *Symbols of power at the time of Stonehenge*. Edinburgh: National Museum of Antiquities of Scotland.

37. EVANS AT KNOSSOS

Evans, Joan 1943. *Time and Chance: The Story of Arthur Evans and his Forebears*. London.

38. THE DECIPHERMENT OF LINEAR B

Chadwick, John 1958. *The Decipherment of Linear B*. Cambridge: Cambridge University Press.

39. THE COLLAPSE OF THE MINOAN CIVILIZATION

Doumas, Christos 1983. *Thera, Pompeii of the Ancient Aegean*. London.

40. SCHLIEMANN AT TROY AND MYCENAE

Deuel, Leo 1978. *Memoirs of Heinrich Schliemann: A Documentary Portrait Drawn from his Autobiographical Writings*. London.

41. BLEGEN AT PYLOS

Blegen, Carl W. and Marion Rawson 1967. *A Guide to the Palace of Nestor*. Cincinnati: University of Cincinnati.

42. THE ULU BURUN SHIPWRECK

Bass, George F. 1987. "Oldest known shipwreck reveals splendors of the Bronze Age", *National Geographic*, 172: pp. 693–734.

43. HALLSTATT: AN EARLY IRON AGE MINING CENTRE

Kromer, Karl 1959. *Das Gräberfeld von Hallstatt*. Florence: Sansoni.

Wells, Peter S. 1980. "Iron Age central Europe", *Archaeology*, 33 (5): pp. 7–11; 1986. "Europe's first towns and entrepreneurs", *Archaeology*, 39(6): pp. 26–31.

44. HOCHDORF: A 'TUT'S TOMB' OF THE IRON AGE

Biel, Jörg 1980. "Treasure from a Celtic tomb", *National Geographic*, 157: pp. 428–438; 1986. *Der Keltenfürst von Hochdorf*. Stuttgart: Konrad Theiss.

Wells, Peter S. 1980. "Iron Age Central Europe", *Archaeology*, 33(5): pp. 6–11; 1984. *Farms, Villages, and Cities: Commerce and Urban Origins in Late Prehistoric Europe*. Ithaca: Cornell University Press.

45. BISKUPIN: A WATERLOGGED IRON AGE SETTLEMENT

Bogucki, Peter 1990. "A glimpse of Iron Age Poland", *Archaeology*, 43(5): p. 745.

Rajewski, Zbigniew 1970. *Biskupin*. Warsaw: Arkady.

Wells, Peter S. 1984. *Farms, Villages, and Cities: Commerce and Urban Origins in Late Prehistoric Europe*. Ithaca: Cornell University Press.

46. ETRUSCAN TOMBS

Brendel, O. J. 1978. *Etruscan Art*. Harmondsworth: Pelican History of Art. 1992. *Les Etrusques et l'Europe*. Paris: Musées Nationaux.

Macnamara, E. 1990. *The Etruscans*. London: British Museum Publications.

47. VERGINA

Andronikos, M. 1978. "Regal treasures from a Macedonian tomb", *National Geographic*, 154 (1): pp. 54–77.

Andronikos, M. 1984. *Vergina: The Royal Tombs and the Ancient City*. Athens: Ekdotike Athenon.

Ginouves, R. 1994. *Macedonia: from Philip Ii to the Roman Conquest*. Athens: Ekdotike Athenon.

48. BOG BODIES: FACES FROM THE PAST

Brothwell, Don 1986. *The Bog Man and the archaeology of people*. London: British Museum Publications.

Glob, P. V. 1969. *The Bog People: Iron Age man preserved*. London: Faber and Faber.

49. THE ATHENIAN AGORA: THE HEART OF DEMOCRACY

Camp, J. M. 1986. *The Athenian Agora: excavations in the heart of Classical Athens*. London and New York: Thames and Hudson.

Camp, J. M. 1990. *The Athenian Agora: a guide to the excavation and museum*. Athens: The American School of Classical Studies at Athens (4th ed. revised).

50. APHRODISIAS

Erim, K. T. 1992. *Aphrodisias: City of the Venus Aphrodite*. Muller, Blond and White.

Roueche, C. and K. Erim, 1990. *Aphrodisias Papers 1*. Ann Arbor: University of Michigan.

Smith, R. R. R. and K. Erim. 1991. *Aphrodisias Papers 2*. Ann Arbor: University of Michigan.

51. MEDITERRANEAN SHIPWRECKS

Musée des Docks Romains. n.d. Marseilles: Musée des Docks Romains. See also a 'Special maritime section' of *Antiquity*, 64, June 1990.

52. POMPEII AND HERCULANEUM

Ling, R. 1991. *Roman Painting*. Cambridge: Cambridge University Press.

Richardson, L. 1988. *Pompeii: an architectural history*. Baltimore: Johns Hopkins University Press.

Ward-Perkins, J. and A. Claridge 1977. *Pompeii AD 79*. London: Royal Academy of Arts.

53. VINDOLANDA

Birley, R. 1977. *Vindolanda: a Roman frontier post on Hadrian's Wall*. London and New York: Thames and Hudson.

Bowman, A. K. 1994. *Life and Letters on the Roman Frontier: Vindolanda and its people*. London: British Museum Publications.

54. SUTTON HOO

Bruce-Mitford, R. L. S. 1968. *The Sutton Hoo Ship Burial: a handbook*. London: British Museum Publications.

55. VIKING SHIPS

Binns, Alan 1980. *Viking Voyagers: then and now*. London: Heinemann.

Brogger, A.W. and Haakon Shetelig 1951. *The Viking Ships: their ancestry and evolution*. London: C. Hurst and Co.

Graham-Campbell, James and Dafydd Kidd 1980. *The Vikings*. London: British Museum Publications.

56. NOVGOROD: A MEDIEVAL CITY IN RUSSIA

Kolchin, Boris Aleksandrovich 1989. *Wooden Artefacts from Medieval Novgorod*. Oxford: British Archaeological Reports, International Series.

Medyntseva, A. A. 1984. "Novgorodskie nakhodki i dokristianskaia pis'mennost' na Rusi" (Novgorod finds and pre-Christian Russian writing), *Sovetskaya arkheologiia*, 1984 (4): pp. 49–61.

Yanin, Valentin I. 1990. "The archaeology of Novgorod", *Scientific American*, 262 92: pp. 84–91.

WESTERN AND CENTRAL ASIA

58. JERICHO

Kenyon, Kathleen 1957. *Digging Up Jericho*. New York: Praeger.

Mellaart, James 1975. *The Neolithic of the Near East*. New York: Charles Scribner's.

59. UR

Woolley, L. and P .R. S. Moorey 1982. *Ur of the Chaldees*. London: Herbert Press.

60. BABYLON

Oates, Joan 1986. *Babylon* (rev. ed.). London and New York: Thames and Hudson.

61. EBLA AND CUNEIFORM WRITING

Matthiae, Paolo 1981. *Ebla: An Empire Rediscovered*. New York: Doubleday.

Pettinato, Giovanni 1981. *The Archives of Ebla: An Empire Inscribed in Clay*. New York: Doubleday.

62. NINEVEH AND ASSYRIAN PALACES

Gadd, C. J. 1936. *The Stones of Assyria*. London: Chatto and Windus.

Saggs, H. W. F. 1984. *The Might That was Assyria*. London: Sigdwick and Jackson.

63. MOHENJO-DARO AND THE INDUS CIVILIZATION

Allchin, Bridget, and Raymond Allchin 1982. *The Rise of Civilization in India*. Cambridge: Cambridge University Press.

64. PERSEPOLIS

Cook, J. M. 1983.*The Persian Empire*. New York: Schocken Books.

Frye, Richard 1963.*The Heritage of Persia*. Cleveland: The World Publishing Company.

65. THE FROZEN TOMBS OF PAZYRYK AND UKOK

Polosmak, Natalya 1994. "A mummy unearthed from the Pastures of Heaven", *National Geographic*, 186(4): pp. 80–103.

Rudenko, Sergei 1970. *Frozen Tombs of Siberia: the Pazyryk Burials of Iron Age Horsemen*. Berkeley and Los Angeles: University of California Press.

66. MASADA

Yadin, Y. 1966. *Masada: Herod's Fortress and the Zealots' Last Stand*. London.

Burrows, M. 1956. *The Dead Sea Scrolls*. London.

FAR EAST

67. PEKING AND JAVA MAN

Shapiro, H. L. 1974. *Peking Man: the discovery, disappearance and mystery of a priceless scientific treasure*. London: Allen and Unwin.

Weidenreich, F. 1946. *Apes, giants and early man*. Chicago: University of Chicago Press.

Wu, Rukang and John W. Olsen (eds) 1985. *Palaeoanthropology and Palaeolithic archaeology in the People's Republic of China*. Orlando: Academic Press.

68. ROCK ART OF CHINA AND INDIA

Dunhuang Institute for Cultural Relics 1981. *The Art Teasures of Dunhuang*. Hong Kong and New York: Joint Publishing Co. and Lee Publishers Group, Inc.

Jiang Zhenming 1991. *Timeless History. The Rock Art of China*. Beijing: New World Press.

Juliano, A. 1980. "Buddhism in China", *Archaeology*, 33 (3): pp. 23–30.

Neumayer, E. 1993. *Lines on Stone. The Prehistoric Rock Art of India*. New Delhi: Manohar.

69. HONGSHAN AND LIANGZHU JADES

Huang, Tsui-mei 1992. "Liangzhu – a late Neolithic jade-yielding culture in southeastern coastal China", *Antiquity*, 66: pp. 75–83.

Liaoning Provincial Cultural Relics Protection Bureau, et al 1990. *The valuable cultural and historic sites of Liaoning province*. Shenyang: Liaoning Artistic Publishing House.

Rawson, Jessica. 1980. *Ancient China: art and archaeology*. London: British Museum.

70. STATUARY OF THE FAR EAST

Cottrell, A. 1981. *The first emperor of China*. London: Macmillan.

Kidder, J. Edward, Jr 1965. *The birth of Japanese art*. London: George Allen and Unwin.

Kuhn, Dieter (ed.) 1993. *Chinas Goldenes Zeitalter*. Heidelberg: Edition Braus.

Pirazzoli-t'Serstevens, Michèle 1982. *The Han civilization of China*. Oxford: Phaidon.

71. ANYANG

Chang, K. C. 1980. *Shang civilization*. New Haven and London: Yale University Press.

Chang, K.C. (ed.) 1986. *Studies of Shang archaeology*. New Haven and London: Yale University Press.

Li Chi 1977. *Anyang*. Washington: University of Washington Press.

72. EAST ASIAN BRONZES

Franklin, U. M. 1983. "On bronze and other metals in early China", *The Origins of Chinese Civilization* (D. N. Keightley, ed.). Berkeley: University of California Press.

Rawson, J. and E. Bunker 1990. *Ancient Chinese and Ordos Bronzes*. Hong Kong: Oriental Ceramic Society.

Wen, Fong (ed.) 1980. *The Great Bronze Age of China*. London: Thames and Hudson.

73. ROYAL TOMBS OF THE EAST

Kim, Won-yong 1983. "Tomb 155 (The tomb of the Heavenly Horse)", *Recent archaeological discoveries in the Republic of Korea*, W. Y. Kim. Paris and Tokyo: UNESCO and The Centre for East Asian Cultural Studies.

Leigudun No. 1 Tomb Archaeological Excavation Team 1984. "Valuable relics unearthed in a tomb at Leigudun", *Recent discoveries in Chinese archaeology*. Beijing: Foreign Languages Press.

Pirazzoli-t'Serstevens, Michèle 1982. *The Han civilization of China*. Oxford: Phaidon.

74. THE TERRACOTTA ARMY

Cotterell, A. 1981. *The First Emperor of China*. London: Macmillan.

The Coloured Figurines in Yang Ling Mausoleum of Han in China. 1992. China Shaanxi Travel & Tourism Press.

75. MURAL TOMBS OF THE ORIENT

Kidder, J. Edward, Jr 1964. *Early Japanese art: the great tombs and treasures*. London: Thames & Hudson.

Kim, Won-yong 1986. "Wall paintings of Koguryo tombs", *Art and archaeology of ancient Korea*, W. Y. Kim. Seoul: Taekwang.

Kuhn, Dieter (ed.) 1993. *Chinas Goldenes Zeitalter*. Heidelberg: Edition Braus.

Pirazzoli-t'Serstevens, Michèle 1982. *The Han civilization of China*. Oxford: Phaidon.

76. THE SINAN SHIPWRECK

Green, Jeremy 1983. "The Sinan excavation, Korea: an interim report on the hull structure", *The International Journal of Nautical Archaeology and Underwater Exploration*, 12 (4): pp. 293–301.

Keith, D. 1979. "A 14th century cargo makes port at last", *National Geographic*, 156 (92): pp. 230–43; 1980. "A fourteenth-century shipwreck at Sinan-gun", *Archaeology*, 33 (2): pp. 33–43.

AUSTRALASIA

77. LAKE MUNGO

Flood, Josephine 1995. *Archaeology of the Dreamtime* (3rd edn). Sydney/London: Collins.

78. AUSTRALIA'S ROCK ART

Layton, Robert 1992. *Australian Rock Art*. Cambridge: Cambridge University Press.

Walsh, Grahame L. 1988. *Australia's Greatest Rock*

Cambridge: Cambridge University Press.
Walsh, Grahame L. 1988. *Australia's Greatest Rock Art*. Bathurst: E. J. Brill-Robert Brown and Associates.

79. ICE AGE HUNTERS OF TASMANIA
Flood, Josephine 1995. *Archaeology of the Dreamtime* (3rd edn). Sydney/London: Collins.

80. COLONIZING THE PACIFIC
Bellwood, Peter 1987. *The Polynesians* (rev. ed.). London and New York: Thames and Hudson.
Irwin, Geoffrey 1992. *The Prehistoric Exploration and Colonisation of the Pacific*. Cambridge: Cambridge University Press.

81. EASTER ISLAND
Bahn, P. and J. Flenley 1992. *Easter Island, Earth Island*. London and New York: Thames and Hudson.
Orliac, C. and M. Orliac 1995. *The Silent Gods: Mysteries of Easter Island* (translated by Paul G. Bahn). London: Thames and Hudson/New York: Abrams.

NEW WORLD

82. MONTE VERDE AND THE FIRST AMERICANS
Dillehay, Tom D. 1989. *Monte Verde: A Late Pleistocene Settlement in Chile*. Volume 1, Palaeoenvironment and Site Context. Washington DC and London: Smithsonian Institution Press.

83. BIG-GAME HUNTING ON THE NORTH AMERICAN PLAINS
Fagan, Brian 1995. *Ancient North America*. London and New York: Thames and Hudson.
Frison, George 1991. *Prehistoric Hunters of the High Plains* (2nd ed.). New York: Academic Press.

84. ROCK ART IN THE NEW WORLD
Wellmann, K. F. 1979. *A Survey of North American Rock Art*. Graz: Akademische Druck- und Verlagsanstalt.

85. THE DISCOVERY OF THE OLMEC
Coe, Michael D. 1968. *America's First Civilization: Discovering the Olmec*. New York: American Heritage.
Stirling, Matthew 1939. "Discovering the New World's oldest dated work of man", *National Geographic*, 76: pp. 183–218.
Wicke, Charles R. 1971. *Olmec: An Early Art Style of Pre-Columbian Mexico*. Tucson: University of Arizona Press.

86. NASCA LINES
Aveni, Anthony F. (ed.) 1990. *The Lines of Nasca*. Philadelphia: The American Philosophical Society
Reiche, Maria 1968. *Mystery on the Desert*. Heinrich Fink GmbH and Co.

87. CHAVÍN
Burger, Richard L. 1992. *Chavín and the Origins of Andean Civilization*. London and New York: Thames and Hudson.
Rowe, John H. 1967. "Form and meaning in Chavín art", *Peruvian Archaeology, Selected Readings* (John H. Rowe and Dorothy Menzel, eds), pp.

72–103. Palo Alto: Peek Publications.
Vasquez de Espinosa, Antonio 1942. *Description of the Indies* (c. 1620). Translated by Charles Upson Clark. Smithsonian Miscellaneous Collections, Volume 102. Washington DC: Smithsonian Institution Press.

88. EL CERÉN
Sheets, Payson (ed.) 1983. *Archaeology and Volcanism in Central America*. Austin: University of Texas Press.
Sheets, Payson 1992. *The Cerén Site: a Prehistoric Village Buried by Volcanic Ash in Central America*. Case Studies in Archaeology series (Jeffrey Quilter, ed.). New York: Harcourt, Brace, Jovanovich.
Sheets, Payson 1994. "Tropical time capsule", *Archaeology*, 47 (4): pp. 30–33.

89. NAJ TUNICH AND MAYA CAVE ART
Brady, James E. and Andrea Stone. 1986. "Naj Tunich: entrance to the Maya Underworld", *Archaeology*, 39 (6): pp. 18–25.
Stone, Andrea 1995. *Images from the Underworld: Naj Tunich and the Tradition of Maya Cave Painting*. Austin: University of Texas Press.
Stuart, George E. 1981. "Maya art treasures discovered in cave", *National Geographic*, 160 (2): pp. 220–35.

90. PALENQUE: THE TOMB OF PACAL THE GREAT
Robertson, Merle Greene 1983. *The Sculpture of Palenque: vol. 1, the Temple of the Inscriptions*. Princeton: Princeton University Press.
Ruz Lhuillier, Alberto 1954. "Exploraciones en Palenque: 1952", *Anales del Instituto Nacional de Antropología e Historia*, 6: pp. 107–110; 1973. *El Templo de las Inscripciones, Palenque* (ed.), Colección Científica 7. Mexico City: INAH.

91. THE DECIPHERMENT OF MAYA HIEROGLYPHICS
Coe, Michael D. 1992. *Breaking the Maya Code*. London & New York: Thames and Hudson.
Stuart, George E. 1989. "The beginning of Maya hieroglyphic study: Contributions of Constantine S. Rafinesque And James H. McCulloh, Jr.", *Research Reports on Ancient Maya Writing* 29. Washington DC: Center for Maya Research.

92. THE MOUNDBUILDERS
Fagan, Brian 1995. *Ancient North America*. London and New York: Thames and Hudson.
Silverberg, Robert 1970. *The Mound Builders*. Ballantine Books.

93. ANCIENT FARMERS OF THE DESERT
Cordell, Linda 1984. *Prehistory of the Southwest*. New York: Academic Press.
Fagan, Brian 1995. *Ancient North America*. London and New York: Thames and Hudson.

94. SIPÁN: MOCHE CULTURE
Alva, Walter 1988. "Discovering the world's richest unlooted tomb", *National Geographic*, 174 (4): pp. 510–49; 1990. "New tomb of royal splendor", *National Geographic*, 177 (6): pp. 2–15.
Alva, Walter and Christopher Donnan, 1993. *Royal Tombs of Sipán*. Los Angeles: Fowler Museum of

Cultural History, UCLA.

95. TEMPLE OF THE FEATHERED SERPENT, TEOTIHAUCÁN
Cabrera Castro, Rubén Saburo Sugiyama and George Cowgill. 1991. "The Templo de Quetzalcoatl Project at Teotihuacán", *Ancient Mesoamerica*, 2: pp. 77–92.
Cabrera Castro, Rubén 1993. "Human sacrifice at the Temple of the Feathered Serpent", *Teotihuacán: Art from the City of the Gods* (Kathleen Berrin and Esther Pasztory, eds), pp. 100–107. London and New York: Thames and Hudson.
Carlson, John 1993. "Rise and fall of the City of the Gods", *Archaeology*, 46 (6): pp. 58–69.
Taube, Karl. A. 1992. "The Temple of Quetzalcoatl and the cult of sacred war at Teotihuacán", *Res: Anthropology and Aesthetics*, 21: pp. 53–87.

96. TIWANAKU: PREHISTORIC EMPIRES IN THE ANDES
Kolata, Alan 1993. *Tiwanaku: Portrait of an Andean Civilization*. Oxford: Blackwell.
Schreiber, Katharina J. 1992. *Wari Imperialism in Middle Horizon Peru*, Anthropological Papers 87. Ann Arbor: Museum of Anthropology, University of Michigan.
Squier, E. George 1877. *Peru: Travel and Exploration in the Land of the Incas*. New York: Henry Holt and Co.

97. MONTE ALBÁN: TOMB
Caso, Alfonso 1932. "Monte Albán: richest archaeological find in America", *National Geographic*, 62: pp. 487–512; 1965. "Lapidary work, goldwork and copperwork from Oaxaca", *Handbook of Middle American Indians*, vol. 3, pp. 896–930. Austin: University of Texas Press; 1969. *El Tesoro de Monte Albán*. Memorias del Instituto Nacional de Antropología e Historia, Mexico.
McCafferty, Sharisse D. and Geoffrey G. 1994. "Engendering Tomb 7 at Monte Albán: respinning an old yarn", *Current Anthropology*, 35 (2): pp. 143–66.

98. VIKING SETTLEMENTS OF NORTH AMERICA
Ingstad, Anne 1985. *The Norse Discovery of America*. Norwegian University Press.

99. THE TEMPLO MAYOR OF TENOCHTITLÁN
Boone, Elizabeth H. (ed.) 1987. *The Aztec Templo Mayor*. Washington DC: Dumbarton Oaks.
Matos Moctezuma, Eduardo. 1984. "The Great Temple of Tenochtitlán", *Scientific American*, August, pp. 80–88; 1988. *The Great Temple of the Aztecs: Treasures of Tenochtitlán*. London and New York: Thames and Hudson.

100. MACHU PICCHU
Bingham, Alfred M. 1989. *Portrait of an Explorer: Hiram Bingham, Discoverer of Machu Picchu*. Ames: Iowa State University Press.
Bingham, Hiram 1913. "In the wonderland of Peru". *National Geographic Magazine* 24(4).

ACKNOWLEDGEMENTS

We would like to thank Coralie Hepburn at Weidenfeld & Nicolson for her editing skills, and also Joanne King, picture researcher extraordinaire. For providing pictures we would like to thank:

Page 10 Society of Antiquaries of London; **p11** (tl) Mick Sharp, (br) Muséum National d'Histoire Naturelle; **pp12-13** British Museum; **p14** R. J. Clarke/University of Witwatersrand; **p15** (bl) & (tr) Dr Gerald Newlands/Transvaal Museum; **p16** Science Photo Library; **p17** Natural History Museum, London; **p18** l & r John Reader/Science Photo Library; **p19** Alan Walker/National Museums of Kenya; **pp20 & 21** (tl) Ancient Art & Architecture Collection, (br) NHM; **p22** Institute of Human Origins/Don Johanson; **p23**(tl) South African Museum/L. W. T. Lawrence, (br) P. M. Faugust/University of Witwatersrand; **p24** Werner Forman Archive; **p25** (bl) Sonia Halliday Photography, (tr) & (cr) AAAC; **p26** (l) & (r) Dr Stephen Snape; **p27** (bl) BM, **p27** (r) & **p28** WF; **p29** (t) & (b) WF; **p30** (l) & (r) BM; **p31** (l) WF, (br) BM; **p32** (tr), (bl) & **p33** AAAC; **p34** (tl) WF, (br) AAAC; **p35** Robert Harding Picture Library; **p36** (l) & (r) BM; **p37** Werner Forman Archive; **p38** (l) & (r) Henri Stierlin; **p39** AAAC; **p40** Henri Stierlin; **p41** (t) BM, (b) Dr Stephen Snape; **pp42 & 43** (t) & (b) Professor Nancy Ramage; **pp44 & 45** (l) & (br) WF, **p45** (tr) South African Museum; **pp46 & 47** WF; **pp48-9** Jean Vertut; **p50** Rheinisches Landesmuseum, Bonn; **p51** (tl) AAAC, (r) Dr Paul Bahn; **p52** Dr John Hoffecker; **p53** (t) Museum für die Archäologie des Eiszeitalters, (b) Mochanov 1988: 43, fig.6; **p54** (l) Novosti, **pp54-55** C.M. Dixon; **pp56 & 57** (l) Jean Vertut, (r) Museum für die Archäologie des Eiszeitalters; **pp58 & 59** Jean Vertut; **pp60-61** (tr) Jean Clottes - Ministère de la Culture et de la Francophonie - Direction du Patrimoine - Sous-Direction de l'archéologie; **p61** (r) Dr Paul Bahn; **p62** (l) NHM; **pp62** (r) & **63** (l) Moravské Zemské Muzeum, **p63** (r) AAAC; **pp64 & 65** (t) & (b) Novosti; **pp66 & 67** (t) & (b) Scala/Archaeological Museum, Belgrade; **pp68 & 69** (tl) & (bl) M. A. Mellaart, (tr) CMD; **pp70 & 71** (tl) & (br) National Museum of Switzerland; **p72** Konrad Theiss Verlag; **p73** Dr Peter Bogucki; **p74-5** English Heritage; **p75** (t) Mick Sharp Photography; **pp76-7 & 77** (t) & (b) Charles Tait Photography; **p78** Fenland Archaeological Trust; **p79** Somerset Levels Project; **pp80-81** Robert Harding Picture Library; **p 81** (t) Dr David Trump, (b) Michael Jenner; **p82** Mick Sharp Photography; **p83** RHPL; **pp84 & 85** (t) & (b) Frank Spooner Pictures; **pp86 & 87** AAAC; **pp88-9** Dr Colin Shell; **p89** Haddon Library, Faculty of Archaeology and anthropology, Cambridge; **pp90** (bl), **90-1, 91** (tr) E. T. Archive/Devizes Museum, (tl) BM; **pp92-3** ET; **p93** (tl) CMD; **p94** Hulton Deutsch Collection; **p95** (t) AAAC; **pp95** (b) & **96** Henri Stierlin; **p97** CMD; **p98** (c) Hulton Deutsch Collection, (b) Henri Stierlin; **p99** CMD; **pp100 & 101** (t) & (b) Piet de Jong; **pp102 & 103** Bill Curtsinger; **pp104 & 105** (t) & (b) CMD; **pp106-7, 107** (tl) & (cr) Konrad Theiss Verlag; **p108** Dr Peter Bogucki; **p109** (tr) & (br) State Archaeological Museum, Warsaw; **pp110-11** ET; **p111** (r) Museoe di Villa Giulia, Rome; **pp112 & 113** (tr) Agence Dagli Orti, (l) Manchester Museum; **pp114 & 115** (t) Silkeborg Museum, Denmark, (b) Nationalmuseet, Copenhagen; **p116** Sonia Halliday; **p117** Sonia Halliday; **p118** Sonia Halliday Photography; **p119** (t) Henri Stierlin, (b) RHPL; **pp120 & 121** (l) & (r) AAAC; **p122** CMD; **p123** ET; **p124** (bl) WF; **pp124-5** AAAC; **p126 & 127** (b) Vindolanda Trust, (t) English Heritage; **pp128-131** BM; **p132** (bl) ET; **pp132-3** Aalborg Historiske Museum; **p133** (t) University Museum of National Antiquities, Oslo, Norway; **pp134 & 135** (t) & (b) Novosti; **pp136-7** BM; **pp138-140** Zev Radovan; **p141** (t) CMD, (b) Palestine Exporation Fund; **p142** BM; **p143** Scala; **p144 & 145** BM; **p146** Staatliche Museen zu Berlin/Bildarchiv Preussischer Kulturbesitz; **p147** Henri Stierlin; **p148** AAAC; **p149** National Geographic Society/James L Stanfield; **p150** Oriental Institute, University of Chicago; **p151** (t) AAAC, (b) BM; **pp152 & 153** (br) RHPL, (tl) CMD; **pp154 & 155** (tr) & (b) Henri Stierlin; **p156** Novosti; **pp156-7** (t) CMD (b) 157 (tr) RHPL; **pp158 & 159** (tr) Sonia Halliday Photography, (cr), (bl) AAAC; **pp160-1** Dr Paul Bahn; **p162** NHM; **p162-3** (t) CMD; **p163** Sonia Halliday; **pp164 & 165** (t) & (b) Dr Paul Bahn; **pp166 & 167** Sir Joseph Hotung; **p168** RHPL; **p169** (l) Kyoryokukai/Tokyo National Museum, (r) Dr Gina Barnes; **pp170-1** MacQuitty International Photographic Collection; **p171** (t) RHPL; **p172** Agence Dagli Orti; **p173** MacQ; **p174** BM; **pp175 & 176-7** (t) RHPL; **p176-7** (b) MacQ; **p177** (tr) AAAC; **p178** ET; **p178-9** (t) Robert Harding; **p179** (bl) AAAC, (bc) MacQ; **p180** Artephot/Percheron; **p181** RHPL; **pp182 & 183** National Maritime Museum of Korea; **pp184-5** Dr Paul Bahn; **p186** NHPA/ANT/Otto Rogge; **p187** (t) & (b) Jim Bowler; **pp188 & 189** (br) Dr Paul Bahn, (tr) NHPA/Patrick Fagot; **p190** (l) & (r) R. Frank; **p191** Richard Cosgrove; **pp192 & 193** Dr Chris Gosden; **pp194 & 195** Paul Bahn, **pp196-7** RHPL; **pp198-9** Paul Bahn; **pp200 & 201** RHPL; **p202** Range/Bettmann; **p203** (tr) & (cr) Pictures of Record; **pp204** (bl) & (br) & **205** (t) & (b) Dr Paul Bahn; **pp206** (r) American Geographic Society Collection, University of Wisconsin-Milwaukee Library, (l) & **207** ET; **pp208 & 209** (t) & (b) Dr Katharina Schreiber; **p210** (l) Henri Stierlin, (r) ET; **p211** Dr Katharina Schreiber; **pp212 & 213** (t) Professor Payson Sheets, (b) Karen Kievit; **pp214 & 215** (t) & (b) Chip & Jennifer Clark; **p216** Henri Stierlin; **p217** (t) & (b) Merle Greene Robertson; **pp218-9** Justin Kerr; **p219** (t) American Geographic Society Collection, University of Wisconsin-Milwaukee Library; **pp220-1** Cahokia Mounds Museum Society; **pp221** (r), **222** (l) Pictures of Record; **p222-3** Museum of the American Indian; **pp224 & 225** (t) Mick Sharp (b) William Ferguson; **pp226** (br) Dr Katharina Schreiber, (cl), **227** (tl) & (r) Fowler Museum of Cultural History, UCLA; **p228** Richard Atkinson; **p229** Henri Stierlin; **pp230** (bl), **230-1** from: Squier, Ephraim George: *Peru: Travel and Explorations in the Land of the Incas*, 1877; **p231** RHPL; **p232** (l) Henri Stierlin, (r) Henri Stierlin; **p233** Richard Atkinson; **pp234 & 235** (tl) & (b) Canadian Heritage, Parks Canada; **p236** (bl) & (cr) Dr Paul Bahn; **p237** ET; **p238** (bl), (cr) National Geographic Magazine Vol XXIV, No.4, April 1913; **p239** Dr Katharina Schreiber.

Front Jacket: Charles O'Rear/Robert Harding Picture Library

Back Jacket: Silkeborg Museum, Denmark

Endpapers: AAAC

Title Page: Richard Atkinson

Abbreviations

AAAC = Ancient Art & Architecture Collection BM = British Museum
CMD = C. M. Dixon ET = E. T. Archive
MacQ = MacQitty International Photographic Collection NHM = Natural History Museum
RHPL = Robert Harding Picture Library
WF = Werner Forman Archive